Idioms and Idiomaticity

DESCRIBING ENGLISH LANGUAGE

SERIES EDITORS
John Sinclair · Ronald Carter

Idioms and Idiomaticity

Chitra Fernando

Oxford University Press 1996

Oxford University Press, Walton Street, Oxford OX2 6DP

Oxford New York
Athens Auckland Bangkok Bogotá Bombay
Buenos Aires Calcutta Cape Town Dar es Salaam
Delhi Florence Hong Kong Istanbul Karachi
Kuala Lumpur Madras Madrid Melbourne
Mexico City Nairobi Paris Singapore
Taipei Tokyo Toronto

and associated companies in Berlin and Ibadan

Oxford and *Oxford English* are trade marks of Oxford University Press.

ISBN 0 19 437199 9

© Chitra Fernando 1996

Typeset by Wyvern Typesetting Ltd, Bristol
Printed in Hong Kong

To my students

Contents

3 Ideational idiomatic expressions: images of the world

Contents

Contents

Acknowledgements

Every scholarly topic has its own special set of problems. Few more so than idioms and idiomaticity. The following pages will show, I hope, that idioms and idiomaticity are pervasive features of a language. As such, they demand from the analyst who wishes to do justice to this pervasiveness a sense of the amplitude of language both in general and particular terms. What this means in practice is that in talking about idioms and idiomaticity the idiomatologist must also talk about the vocabulary, syntax, semantics, and sociolinguistics of a language, and adopt, preferably, a theoretical 'consensus' orientation for this purpose. This is another way of saying that general linguistics provides the best background and training for an idiomatologist.

For the opportunity to acquire such a background and training I am indebted to the linguistics discipline of Macquarie University, as established and developed by Arthur Delbridge and developed further by his successor, Christopher Candlin. The eclectic philosophy adopted by the linguistics discipline there, permitting as it does different linguistic persuasions as well as a range of courses in theoretical and applied linguistics to be taught, makes life congenial for the general linguist. In such an environment a linguist is free to teach in several areas, adopting different orientations, as I did, in syntax, semantics, contrastive linguistics, sociolinguistics, and language learning at various periods in the many years I spent at Macquarie University. Also helpful in enlarging and shaping my understanding of how language works, more specifically how English works, was the experience I gained in the English Unit of the Sri Lankan Education Department, where I was involved in the mid 1960s in preparing language learning materials for use in local schools. Periods spent overseas as a visiting scholar at the universities of Edinburgh, Exeter, London, Reading, Birmingham, and Pennsylvania have contributed to my understanding not only of language but also to my understanding of linguistic scholarship. All these experiences have in one way or another shaped this book.

The immediate inspiration for this work, however, was a thesis completed in 1981, though this book adopts a theme and a focus very different from its progenitor. These changes, which have considerably enlarged the scope of my earlier research on idioms and idiomaticity, I owe to John Sinclair and Ronald Carter, the editors of this series, who offered several valuable suggestions and comments. I found their comments on the importance of focussing on collocations—a focus which allowed the inclusion of many areas of investigation and their associated language forms which might otherwise have been ignored—especially valuable. Several others, known and unknown, have also helped shape this book, either by commenting on drafts of this book or on my earlier work on idioms. Among those known are Arthur Delbridge, Roger Flavell, Michael Halliday, Reinhard Hartmann, Marlena Norst, and Euan Reid. Needless to say, any shortcomings that may still exist are entirely my own.

Nic Witton (Modern Languages, Macquarie University) gave me much needed and generous help in understanding how adverb particles work in German, and Pearl Adisheshan (Institute of Languages, New South Wales) provided me with useful material on teaching multiword expressions of various sorts.

My bibliography is another testimony of the debt I owe to numerous scholars working in the same or related fields. I should, however, like to make special mention of three idiom dictionaries: *The Longman Dictionary of English Idioms* (1979) and *The Oxford Dictionary of Current Idiomatic English, Volume 1* (1975) and *Volume 2* (1983). I have drawn on all three in framing slightly modified definitions for particular idioms, but these make no significant difference to their meanings.

Last but by no means least, are my students. They have greatly enhanced my intellectual life by their interest, enthusiasm, and appreciation. Their contribution to this work is evident in several of the examples cited. Their questions, observations, and disagreements on a variety of topics, some of which have been dealt with here, have made me revise my thinking on specific points, and have contributed to greater precision in my analysis of data.

Many people have contributed to getting the nuts and bolts of this book into place. Christopher Candlin first drew my attention to this topic in the flyer announcing the Describing English Language series in 1987, one of those chance happenings with fruitful results.

Thanks are due to Ron Carter for permitting me to air various issues and anxieties in a six-year correspondence.

I would also like to thank David Wilson, formerly of Oxford University Press and now of the Université de Neuchâtel, who contributed to the clarification of the overall theme of the book over a pleasant lunch, and, with Antoinette Meehan of Oxford University Press, provided sympathetic support and editorial expertise. Their careful and microscopic scrutiny of the manuscript resulted in the elimination of many inconsistencies and in the development of several of my observations throughout the text.

Finally, I am very grateful to Corinne Cheung, Barbara Albertini, and Mary Feely for the dedication they brought to putting my typescript on disk, a service which has helped significantly in the materialisation of this book.

Acknowledgements

The author and publishers would also like to thank the following for permission to reproduce material that falls within their copyright:

Collins Dictionaries, HarperCollins, London, for extracts from The Birmingham Collection of English Text.

New South Wales University Press, Australia, for an extract from *Engendered Fictions* by A. Cranny-Francis (1992).

The author
and series editors

Chitra Fernando lectured in the School of English, Linguistics, and Media at Macquarie University, Sydney from 1968 to 1994. Before that she worked in the English Language Unit of the Education Department in Colombo, Sri Lanka and in the English Department of the Government Teacher Training College, Colombo District. While at Macquarie University, she taught courses in syntax, semantics, language and culture contact, the language component in migration studies, and teaching English to migrants. Her research has been in the areas of idiomatology, bilingualism, and language policy.

John Sinclair has been Professor of Modern English Language at the University of Birmingham since 1965. His main areas of research are discourse (both spoken and written) and computational linguistics—with particular emphasis on the study of very long texts. He has been consultant/adviser to a number of groups, including, among others, the Bullock Commitee, The British Council, and the National Congress for Languages in Education. He holds the title of Adjunct Professor in Jiao Tong University, Shanghai. Professor Sinclair has published extensively, and is currently Editor-in-Chief of the Cobuild project at Birmingham University.

Ronald Carter is Professor of Modern English Language in the Department of English Studies at the University of Nottingham, where he has taught since 1979. He has been Chairman of the Poetics and Linguistics Association of Great Britain, a member of CNAA panels for Humanities, and a member of the Literature Advisory Committee of The British Council. Professor Carter has published widely in the areas of language and education, applied linguistics, and literary linguistics. He has been Director of the Centre for English Language Education at the University of Nottingham, and from 1989 to 1992 was National Co-ordinator for Language in the National Curriculum.

Foreword

Describing English Language

The Describing English Language series provides much-needed descriptions of modern English. Analysis of extended naturally-occurring texts, spoken and written, and, in particular, computer processing of texts have revealed quite unsuspected patterns of language. Traditional descriptive frameworks are normally not able to account for or accommodate such phenomena, and new approaches are required. This series aims to meet the challenge of describing linguistic features as they are encountered in real contexts of use in extended stretches of discourse. Accordingly, and taking the revelations of recent research into account, each book in the series will make appropriate reference to corpora of naturally-occurring data.

The series will cover most areas of the continuum between theoretical and applied linguistics, converging around the mid-point suggested by the term 'descriptive'. In this way, we believe the series can be of maximum potential usefulness.

One principal aim of the series is to exploit the relevance to teaching of an increased emphasis on the description of naturally-occurring stretches of language. To this end, the books are illustrated with frequent references to examples of language use. Contributors to the series will consider both the substantial changes taking place in our understanding of the English language and the inevitable effect of such changes upon syllabus specifications, design of materials, and choice of method.

John Sinclair, *University of Birmingham*
Ronald Carter, *University of Nottingham*

Idioms and Idiomaticity

It has become something of a commonplace recently to read that vocabulary has become the neglected area of language study; however, even after ten years or so of sustained attempts to address this neglect, it is still not unusual to read such statements about vocabulary. One reason for the recurrence of such commonplaces is that they remain true.

In this series issues in the description and study of lexis have received explicit treatment in books by John Sinclair and by Michael Hoey. Chitra Fernando's book continues the line by focusing on idioms and idomaticity, an area which is, paradoxically, one in which a lot of knowledge is felt to have been accumulated but which Chitra Fernando demonstrates to be a continuingly complex and demanding topic.

One main reason for the fascination of Fernando's book is that she moves the study of idiom firmly out of the domain of the phrase and the sentence into a consideration of the function of idioms in contexts of communication. This enables an exploration of the role and function of idioms in texts and discourses, both spoken and written, and in this process Fernando makes valuable contributions to our understanding of the role of idiomatic expressions in the construction of interpersonal meanings, in the formation of coherent text, and in the creation of stylistic effects. By taking a more discoursal view she also convincingly demonstrates the bipolar nature of idiomaticity in the balance between routinized expression and linguistic creativity. She does this without sacrificing the rigorous and systematic analysis of idiom structure which has characterized many previous studies.

Chitra Fernando's book has had a long gestation and in her painstaking approach to evidence she has followed meticulously the series principle of seeking out corpora of naturally-occurring data in support of statements. In recent years she has suffered a long and painful illness and has undertaken this task with particular fortitude. She is committed to an innovative approach and to saying new things. In the view of both John Sinclair and myself she has achieved this goal with this book.

Ronald Carter

Text data, its sources, and presentation

Data labelled [A] describes the author's data, which consists of conversations taken down verbatim after occurrence, and texts taken from real-life communication such as letters, advertisements, notices, etc. In some places it was necessary to invent examples, and these are labelled [I]. Data was also used from The Birmingham Collection of English Text, and this is labelled [BCET]. Elsewhere information about the source of the data is given in parentheses.

1
Review and setting

Idiomaticity is important for this reason, if for no other, that there
is so much of it in every language.
(Weinreich 1969: 23)

1.1 Introduction

Idioms, or conventionalized multiword expressions, often but not
always non-literal, are hardly marginal in English, though they have
been relatively neglected in lexical studies of the language. This
neglect is especially evident in respect of the functions of idioms. One
of the aims of this book, accordingly, is to account for the ubiquity
of idioms by analysing what they do in different discourse types,
both spoken and written. *Bread and butter*, *red herring*, *spill the
beans*, *bless you*, *go to hell*, *on the contrary*, and *in sum* are idioms
put to different functional uses. *Bread and butter* 'livelihood' constitutes a package of information, a specific experiential representation,
working together with the other packages of information carried by
its co-text to convey a message, for example, *It was a simple bread
and butter issue*, part of the text fragment cited below. *Bless you*
signalling conviviality and *go to hell* signalling conflict, on the other
hand, are expressions indicating a speaker and addressee, usually
physically present, in an interpersonal exchange. *In sum* and *on the
contrary* are different again, performing as they do a relational role
between the parts of a discourse, the conclusion to a text in the first
instance and a denial of the preceding statement in the second.

The three language functions identified by Halliday (1973, 1985)
can also be usefully applied to part of a language, in this case a
component of the vocabulary, namely idioms. I have retained
Halliday's terms *ideational* and *interpersonal* to describe two of
the functions idioms perform, but I have replaced the third term
textual, signifying cohesive relationships within a text, with *relational*, a term which captures more precisely the connective functions
carried out by this idiom type in achieving both cohesion and
coherence.

1

One of the aims of this book, as stated above, is to explore the functions of idioms—*what* purposes they fulfil. A second and complementary aim is to show *how* they are used, for how they are used enhances what they are meant to do, a claim which brings me to the thesis of this study:

When language-users produce discourse, they usually combine the novel and the conventional in varying degrees.

The conventional and novel use of *bread and butter* in:

It was a simple *bread and butter* issue. I examined *my bread* very closely to see where it was *buttered*. (*The Australian*, 29 June 1991: 3, Review Section)

is a good example of this practice: both uses convey the idiomatic meaning but the second, a variation of the idiom, is also a play on the literal meaning of this expression. Ideational idioms attract word play, as Chapters 2 and 3 show, whereas interpersonal and relational ones tend to be conventionally used (see Chapters 4 and 5).

I began this chapter by referring to the relative neglect of idioms in lexical studies. Such a claim does not mean that no substantial work has been done on the topic. What it means is that the treatment of idioms in comparison with similarly ubiquitous phenomena such as metaphor is less rounded: much past work on idioms focuses on their form and, to a lesser extent, on their semantics to the neglect of their discoursal functions. However, the ubiquity of idioms is fully explainable only in terms of these functions. Detailed analyses of the nature of idiomaticity and the functions of different types of idioms are presented in later chapters in an effort to fill this gap. This chapter presents readers with a review of other work on idioms and idiomaticity as a setting for the study that follows.

Though little has been done on idioms and idiomaticity in comparison with other areas of English vocabulary, there is enough to warrant selectivity. The works I have chosen for comment identify those linguistic features seen as characteristic of idioms and so are useable as defining criteria. Additionally, by exploring the structural and semantic properties of idioms, these works provide insights useful in explaining why and how idioms perform the functions they do.

As the scholars discussed below work from different theoretical standpoints, differences of opinion exist; yet differences among some scholars are balanced by agreements among others. Both differences and agreements will be clear from the review making up the rest of this chapter. It is, however, useful to preface this discussion with the most frequently mentioned features of idioms:

1   *Compositeness*: idioms are commonly accepted as a type of multiword expression (*red herring, make up, smell a rat, the coast is clear*, etc.) though a few scholars (Hockett 1958; Katz and Postal 1963) accept even single words as idioms.

2   *Institutionalization*: idioms are conventionalized expressions, conventionalization being the end result of initially *ad hoc*, and in this sense novel, expressions.

3   *Semantic opacity*: the meaning of an idiom is not the sum of its constituents. In other words, an idiom is often non-literal.

The widespread occurrence of these three features in common word combinations has resulted in many types of multiword expressions identified by some other term such as *slang, proverbs, allusions, similes, dead metaphors, social formulae*, and *collocations* also being identified as idioms, a practice evident in the works discussed below.

This review of works on idioms and idiomaticity covers two over-lapping but slightly different aspects of the field: Makkai (1972); Weinreich (1969); Fraser (1970); and Strassler (1982) focus on lexically and grammatically regular idioms; Roberts (1944); Smith (1925); Jespersen (1924); and Fillmore *et al.* (1988) focus on the idiosyncrasies of English, many of which are lexically and grammatically irregular. Cowie *et al.* (1975, 1983) include both types in their two idiom dictionaries.

1.2 Lexically and grammatically regular idioms

1.2.1 A. Makkai (1972)

Makkai's *Idiom Structure in English*, an extended version of his doctoral thesis (1965), identifies two major types of idioms: those of encoding and decoding. Makkai finds a rationale for this division in sense 3a of *idiom*, the headword listed in the *Oxford English Dictionary* (*OED*) (1970). Sense 3a also appears in an identical form in the *OED* (1989):

A form of expression, grammatical construction, phrase etc., peculiar to a language; a peculiarity of phraseology approved by the
usage of a language, and often having a significance other than its
grammatical or logical one.

Idioms of decoding such as the non-literal *red herring*, *take the bull
by the horns*, etc. are the focus of Makkai's attention in his book, not
those of encoding as exemplified by the English *drive at 70 m.p.h.*
instead of *with* as in French, both constructions peculiar to their
respective languages.

Following the tradition of Soviet phraseology as developed by
Vinogradov, Amosova, Babkin, Sanskij, Mel'cuk, and others, as well
as the Anglo tradition established by Weinrich (1969), Healey
(1968), and others, Makkai reserves the term *idiom* for units realized
by at least two words. These units are glossed as 'any polylexonic
lexeme made up of more than one minimal free form or word (as
defined by morphotactic criteria)' (Makkai 1972: 122). Such a decision is also in line with the *OED* definition. Requiring an idiom to
have at least two independent lexical items excludes expressions
consisting of one free form and one or more bound forms added by
affixation as the grammar provides adequate decoding rules for such
types. Thus, as Makkai argues, the suffix *-wards* has the meaning 'in
the direction of' in *forwards*, *backwards*, etc., as well as in the more
unusual *Chicagowards*, **treewards*, and **pigwards*, the last from
Lord Emsworth ambled pigwards, stated by Makkai to be from one
of the works of P.G. Wodehouse. Noun + *wards* has a predictable
meaning, hence all new forms created on this pattern are similarly
interpretable. By contrast, the meaning of an idiom is not predictable
from its component parts, which are empty of their usual senses
(ibid.: 118).

However, though the constituents of an idiom are empty of their
usual senses when the expression is interpreted idiomatically as in *hot
potato* 'embarrassing issue', the individual constituents of *hot potato*
should be capable of occurring with their customary or literal meanings 'food item at a high temperature' (ibid.: 25). The potential ambiguity of idioms of decoding, what Makkai calls their 'disinformation
potential', arises from this capacity. Accordingly, expressions with
unique elements like *kith* in *kith and kin* (Makkai's example) inca-
pable of appearing in other discoursal environments and hence non-

ambiguous, are disqualified as real idioms. Such requirements establish disinformation potential as another key criterion of idiomaticity for Makkai. Consequently, disinformation needs to be distinguished from misinformation, a feature of homonyms, Makkai's example of such a homonymous expression being *She bears children*, 'carries', 'gives birth to'. According to Makkai, the disinformation potential of idioms of decoding allows for the possibility that the hearer 'will decode the idiom in a logical yet sememically erroneous way' (ibid.: 122).

Makkai classifies idioms of decoding as *lexemic* and *sememic*, giving greater attention to the structure of the lexemic variety. Six types of lexemic idioms are identified: phrasal verbs (*bring up, get away with*, etc.); tournures (*fly off the handle, rain cats and dogs*, etc.); irreversible binomials (*salt and pepper, bag and baggage*, etc.); phrasal compounds (*blackmail, high-handed*, etc.); incorporating verbs (*eavesdrop, man handle*, etc.); and pseudo-idioms (*spick and span, kith and kin*, etc.).

Sememic idioms correlate with institutionalized culturally pragmatic meanings, institutionalization being another of Makkai's criteria for establishing idiomaticity. Some of the expressions in the sememic category are proverbs (*don't count your chickens before they are hatched*, etc.); familiar quotations (*not a mouse stirring*, etc.); idioms of institutionalized politeness (*May I ... X?* with interrogative intonation for *I want to ... X*, etc.); and idioms of institutionalized understatement and hyperbole (*I wasn't too crazy about him, he won't even lift a finger*, etc.).

The main difference between lexemic and sememic idioms, both classified as idioms of decoding, appears to be functional. Sememic idioms, in contradistinction to the lexemic type, clearly have an interpersonal role, signifying as they do warnings, requests, evaluations, and so on.

In his study of idioms, Makkai adopts mainly the concepts and classification associated with stratificational grammar. The use of a specific model makes Makkai's study an early example of a highly formal approach to idioms. Makkai offers a set of precisely formulated criteria for identifying idioms as well as useful categorizations and sub-categorizations for distinguishing between them based either on structural or functional differences. However, one of his salient criteria for identifying idioms, their disinformation potential, is questionable. Cowie *et al.* (1983) also recognize figuarative idioms

5

similar to Makkai's idioms of decoding as a distinct type citing *close ranks* (1983: xii) and *burn one's boats* (ibid.: xiii) as examples, but rightly argue that ambiguity is improbable as the literal senses of such expressions 'do not survive alongside their figurative ones in normal everyday use' (ibid.: xiii) and even if they did, they may be unrelatable for some speakers. My objection to Makkai's disinformation potential as a criterion of idiomaticity is that adequate contextualization in situational and textual terms substantially reduces, if not completely dispels, the possibility of disinformation in normal discourse, spoken and written. Situational improbability, as in *rain cats and dogs*, is yet another factor working against disinformation. Despite these reservations, Makkai's observations help explain the penchant journalists show for idioms of decoding, both lexemic and sememic: their ability to function both idiomatically and non-idiomatically make them ideal for various forms of word play, especially punning, as many of the illustrative texts in the following chapters will show.

1.2.2 U. Weinreich (1969)

Originally presented as a lecture in 1966, and subsequently published in 1969, Weinreich's article, 'Problems in the Analysis of Idioms', is really a monograph in terms of the scope and depth of its treatment of the topic. Like Makkai's, Weinreich's analysis of idioms is highly formal. While Weinreich's definition of idioms shows the influence of the Soviet phraseologists named above (section 1.2), he establishes the place of this type of expression in English vocabulary using the theory, model, and terminology of transformational–generative grammar (TG). The aims of this book make a discussion of the place of idioms in a TG grammar irrelevant, especially when that grammar happens to be a very early product of the theory. The focus of my discussion of Weinreich's work will, therefore, be on his criteria for the identification and definition of idioms as well as on his exploration of their semantics.

Only multiword expressions, Weinreich's term is 'phraseological units', are accepted as idioms but not all such items qualify as idioms. One of the features of idioms is their potential ambiguity arising from their having multiword literal counterparts in other discoursal environments. *Spick and span*, though a phraseological unit, is disqualified as an idiom for this reason, as are *blow to kingdom come* and *by and large*:

> ... they would not be idioms in our theory because they do not have any literal counterparts and cannot have them in view of their ill-formedness. (1969: 68)

In attempting to identify the essential features of idioms, Weinreich distinguishes between the 'idiomaticity of expressions' and the 'stability of collocations'. Examples of the latter are *assets and liabilities*, *Latin and Greek*, and *Two wrongs don't make a right*:

> These have nothing idiomatic or even phraseological about them. They are merely stable and familiar. (ibid.: 71)

Weinreich's argument is that collocations and idioms both reflect a co-occurrence phenomenon but that the co-occurrence of words in an idiom results in a special semantic relationship not evident in the former. The nature of this relationship is exemplified in Weinreich's analysis of four examples: *by heart*, *rain cats and dogs*, *blind date*, and *red herring*. The first of these will suffice to illustrate his claim:

1   Heart 'memory' has no shared semantic components with heart 'blood pumping organ'.

2   The subsense 'from memory' arises solely as the result of a fixed co-occurrence relation between *by* and *heart*. Only when these two words occur together do we have this idiomatic meaning. *From heart*, for instance, is not an idiom.

3   The co-occurrence of *by* and *heart* yields an accepted phraseological unit with a special meaning 'from memory'; however, there is no isomorphism between the syntactic organization of this idiom and its semantic structure in the sense that *by* signifies 'from' and *heart* 'memory'. This appears to be another way of saying that a non-literal meaning may be acquired by a habitual word combination which then functions as a semantically indivisible idiom.

Analyses of the kind *by heart* is subjected to lead Weinreich to his definition of an idiom:

A phraseological unit involving at least two polysemous constituents, and in which there is a reciprocal contextual selection of subsenses will be called an idiom. (ibid.: 42)

Makkai (1972) observes that the reciprocal selection of subsenses on which Weinreich's definition of an idiom rests is untenable as such subsenses are independently non-existent. In other words, there is no genuine polysemy in, for example, *by heart* 'from memory'. This is true but Makkai's observation does not entirely invalidate Weinreich's deep exploration into the semantic structure of selected idioms providing, as it does, more evidence for the semantic opacity characterizing many such expressions. Additionally, the notion of reciprocal subsenses has more point in those idioms which have one non-literal component and another literal one as in *white lie, drop names*, etc. In such cases, polysemy is less elusive than in the case of *by heart* and other idioms analysed by Weinreich, making the concept of reciprocal subsense selection more valid.

1.2.3 B. Fraser (1970)

In discussing Fraser's article, 'Idioms within a Transformational Grammar', I shall apply the same selectivity as I did in discussing the work of Makkai (1972) and Weinreich (1969): those aspects of Fraser's article chosen for discussion are the ones most relevant to the concerns of this book. Fraser's definition of idioms reflects an oft invoked property:

> ... I shall regard an idiom as a constituent or a series of constituents for which the semantic interpretation is not a compositional function of the formatives of which it is composed. (1970: 22)

Using this criterion, his only one, he identifies such expressions as *figure out, make love to, pass the buck, has the cat got your tongue?*, etc. as idioms.

As the title of his article indicates, Fraser's main concern is to explore the transformational potential of idioms, which he notes differs widely. In order to capture these differences, Fraser proposes a six-level hierarchy or scale:

L 6 – Unrestricted
L 5 – Reconstitution
L 4 – Extraction
L 3 – Permutation
L 2 – Insertion

L 1 – Adjunction
L 0 – Completely frozen

While idioms like *kick the bucket* take only the gerundive transformation and are, therefore, at L 1, others like *read the riot act* appear to qualify for L 6: they can undergo indirect object movement, two types of passive transformation, the gerundive and action nominalization transformations.

Fraser's work on the transformational behaviour of idioms has resulted in practical applications evident in the two volumes of the *Oxford Dictionary of Current Idiomatic English* (ODCIE) (1975, 1983) and the *Longman Dictionary of English Idioms* (LDEI) (1979), which indicate the transformational constraints on all the idioms listed. Fraser's work is useful in another way: by drawing attention to the variations an idiom may or may not undergo, he has also incidentally drawn attention to the stylistic effects that transformations of idioms, especially the less common ones, can achieve.

1.2.4 A. P. Cowie and R. Mackin (1975); A. P. Cowie, R. Mackin, and I. R. McCaig (1983)

There are several collections of idioms aimed at giving the English language-user, particularly the foreign user, guidance in this most distinctive as well as most opaque part of the vocabulary. Many of these works such as, for example, the three collections of idioms by F. T. Wood, *English Prepositional Idioms* (1969a), *English Verbal Idioms* (1966), and *English Colloquial Idioms* (1969b), or W. McMordie's *English Idioms* (1972) are organized in ways very similar to one another: an idiom, a paraphrase meaning, the source, and one or more illustrative examples. The type of expression identified as an idiom conforms to the *OED* definition. The following from McMordie is typical. Idiomaticity arises from

> peculiar uses of particular words, and also particular phrases or turns of expression which, from long usage, have become stereotyped in English. (1972: 5)

The most characteristic feature of idioms is identified as lexical integrity:

> As a general rule an idiomatic phrase cannot be altered; no other

synonymous word can be substituted for any word in the phrase, and the arrangement of the words can rarely be modified. (ibid.: 6)

The collections cited above provide the student of English with a wealth of information on the idioms listed but presented without the formal rigour of the scholars reviewed so far. This rigour, a characteristic feature of all those scholars who draw on modern linguistic theory, appears in the dictionaries of Cowie *et al.* (1975, 1983). Cowie *et al.* draw on both transformational as well as neo-Firthian theory in formulating the content of their entries in the two volumes of the *Oxford Dictionary of Current Idiomatic English* (ODCIE). Volume 1 (1975) covers phrasal verbs with prepositions (*abstain from*), with particles (*make up*), or with both (*make up to*). Volume 2 covers types that are both more varied and more complex: phrases (*red herring*), semi-clauses (*spill the beans, take a step*), and sentences (*The coast is clear*). The different types of idioms in these two volumes do not result in any corresponding differences in the selection of features which qualify as those defining this type of multiword expression. Consequently, both volumes will be discussed together.

The two features of the entries which serve to distinguish these dictionaries from the more traditional collections named above are the nature of the grammatical and lexical information they provide: the transformational potential of idioms, possible options in the form of idioms, and the grammatical pattern of the idiom, as well as its usual collocates, correct choice of which is necessary to produce idiomatic usage:

make it/this up to [B3 pass] (informal) give to sb in compensation for sth he has missed or suffered. *I am sorry you missed the outing. It will be **made up** to you at Christmas. When I get you home safely in the country I'll **make all this up to you**.* DC

take a step [V + O pass] act in a particular way **det:** a, the; this, that; another, such a□ *It was not just to confound their enemies that the company **took this step**. At the back of its mind was the very real fear that if the wine turned out not to be genuine it would face prosecution.* ST□ *'I reported it to the police, sir.' 'You had no right to **take such a step** without first consulting me.'*

(1975: 204)   (1983: 536)

There are other differences which set the work of Cowie *et al.* apart from that of their quasi-lexicographical predecessors, one of these being methodology. Wood. McMordie, and others working in the

10

tradition of quasi-lexicography present idioms as a given. Cowie *et al.* identify idioms using a set of 'tests' which serve to separate those multiword expressions that are idioms from those that are not. Such tests also establish what Cowie *et al.* consider to be the characteristic features of idioms or their sub-classes. In Volume l, for example, the particle deletion test when applied to phrasal verb idioms such as *take off* 'mimic' gives the unacceptable **Bill took Winston Churchill to perfection*. This kind of lexical integrity is noted by traditional scholars, but they do not set out to demonstrate and prove such integrity by the methodology and mode of argumentation adopted by Cowie *et al.* Nor does this traditional approach to idioms seek to accommodate their lexico-grammatical variability, which range from the virtually unchangeable to those that allow restricted variation.

The formal and semantic features Cowie *et al.* select, as characterizing idioms after scrutiny of a number of illustrative data, are compositeness and semantic unity:

> We can begin the discussion of idiomaticity with a simple and familiar assumption: an idiom is a combination of two or more words which function as a unit of meaning. (1975: viii–ix)

> The view taken here—as in Volume 1—is that idiomaticity is largely a semantic matter, and that it is manifested in much the same way in expressions of different structural types. (1983: xi)

Such semantic unity, Cowie *et al.* argue, is demonstrable by the fact that idioms, in this case phrasal verbs, can be matched with a single word synonym: *take off* 'mimic', 'imitate' (1975: ix). This test is not necessarily applicable to all idioms; it is, in fact, not used in Volume 2 of the *ODCIE*.

The most original contribution Cowie *et al.* make to the study of idioms does not lie in an exploration of their semantics alone but rather in their analysis of how grammar and meaning complement each other to create idiomaticity, on the one hand, and of how idioms vary in their lexical integrity with varying consequences for their idiomaticity on the other. Thus, Cowie *et al.* state:

> This approach has the descriptive advantage of enabling us to speak of *make up* (*one's face*) etc. as a unit of meaning while leaving us free to speak of the grammatical separability, or mobil-

ity of its parts (as in *make up one's face/make one's face up*). (1975: xii)

... the meaning of a combination may be related to those of its components in a variety of ways, and must take account also of the possibility of internal variation, or substitution of part for part. (1983: xii)

The approach adopted by Cowie *et al.* enables identification of an important class of multi-word expressions, namely semi-idioms. In Volume 1, this recognition of variations in the lexical integrity of idioms enables inclusion of items like *abstain (from) develop (from) (into)* which have optional prepositions: if removed they do not affect meaning but are included in Volume 1 because of their strong tendency to co-occur with the verb (1975: xi). In Volume 2, these semi-idioms are of two types: those that have figurative senses in the non-literal member of the combination, for example, *jog* in *jog sb's memory* and those that allow restricted lexical variations as in *cardinal error/sin/virtue* and *grace*. Semi-idioms point to the difficulty of drawing a sharp dividing line between idioms and non-idioms; as descriptively useful as their recognition of semi-idioms is the recognition by Cowie *et al.* of a number of intermediate categories between pure or *par excellence* idioms and borderline idioms suggestive of a hierarchical scale. The borderline cases are termed 'open collocations' in contradistinction to the restricted ones, which are termed 'semi-idioms'. Open collocations are expressions with freely recombinable elements: *fill/empty/drain the sink* and *fill the sink/basin/bucket* (1983: xiii).

The principal contribution of Cowie *et al.* to the study of idiomaticity lies in the attention they draw to the permissible variability of idioms and to the proper use of their collocates, or 'the company words keep' to borrow Firth's definition (1951). Their use of naturally-occurring data demonstrates authentic usage in terms of the collocates, the allowable transformations and the semantics of the idiom in question. Cowie *et al.* comment briefly on idiom functions and idioms as markers of style and register. Such information is also included in their entries. The Introductions to both dictionaries contain much useful information on idioms and idiomaticity in addition to showing how contemporary linguistic theory can be given practical applications in advanced language-learning.

1.2.5 J. Strassler (1982)

Strassler's aims in *Idioms in English: A Pragmatic Analysis*, a book deriving from a doctoral thesis, are twofold:

1 The identification of idiom functions, hence Strassler's choice of pragmatic theories in terms of which to analyse idiom use.
2 The identification of the special features of idioms which set them apart from the rest of the vocabulary, features which also constitute their raison d'être.

Strassler's thesis reflect these two aims:

> ... every idiom has a non-idiomatic synonym on the semantic level. The question now remains as to why idioms exist and why they can only be used under certain circumstances ... . I trust I shall find elements within idioms which they do not share with their literal counterparts. (Strassler 1982: 85)

The different social implications of *She died* and *She snuffed it* (ibid.: 119–120) are used by Strassler, along with other types of evidence, in support of his thesis.

What I have noted so far concerning Strassler's study of idioms should make it clear that it differs quite strikingly from the work already reviewed. Strassler explores idiom structure primarily through his review of scholarly work (the Soviet phraseologists (see section 1.2), Makkai 1972, Weinreich 1969, Fraser 1970, Healey 1968, etc.), not through any independent investigation of his own. However, his comments on this work pinpoint what are to him the significant features of idioms:

> ... the fact that the meaning of an idiom is not deducible from its constituents entails certain barriers to structural changes. (Strassler 1982: 24)

Like Makkai (1972), Strassler cites sense 3a of the *OED* definition of *idiom* (quoted in section 1.2) claiming it provides 'the best framework for categorizing the different notions of idiomaticity' (Strassler 1982: 13). He does, however, give his own working definition of an idiom:

> An *idiom* is a concatenation of more than one lexeme whose mean-

ing is not derived from the meanings of its constituents and which does not consist of a verb plus an adverbial particle or preposition. The concatenation as such then constitutes a lexeme in its own right and should be entered as such in the lexicon. (ibid.: 79)

Strassler's definition is noteworthy for its exclusion of 'a verb plus an adverbial particle or preposition' since an idiom dictionary (the *ODCIE* Vol. 1 1975) devoted primarily to such expressions exists, a fact acknowledged by him. No reasons for such an exclusion are offered other than 'practical reasons' not elaborated on.

Strassler's study is the first major work to appear on the functions of idioms. Such a task requires corpus substantiation, in this case one that takes into consideration a number of socially significant variables: 'social status, age, education and profession, and wherever possible, the gap between the partners with respect to these parameters' (ibid.: 78). Strassler's data is only of the conversational sort gathered from 'transcripts of trials, recordings of therapeutic sessions, and excerpts from the White House transcripts' (ibid.) totalling approximately 106,000 words and yielding 92 idioms.

Strassler argues that:

> ... when using an idiom the speaker conveys more information than its semantic content. He either establishes a social hierarchy or he tests the hearer's opinion in this matter. (ibid.: 116)

Demonstrating the workings of such a social hierarchy by analysing the deictic use of idioms in conversation between participants of equal or higher/lower social status in a variety of situations constitutes the most insightful part of Strassler's book.

Strassler notes that the deictic use of idioms covers personal reference (first person idioms), reference to the communicative partner (second person idioms), and to a third person or object. Examples are given of all these types of deixis (ibid.: 85–9). Strassler states that third person deixis is the commonest identifiable function of idioms in his conversational data and concludes on this evidence that such usage is unmarked and neutral (ibid.: 89). Idioms used for first and second person reference are marked. The reason for this markedness lies in the social relations between conversational partners, what Strassler calls social deixis. Examination of a variety of participant exchanges in different situations (court–accused, therapist–patient, US President–communicative partners in the White House transcripts, etc.) lead Strassler to conclude that the deictic use of idioms is determined by the social status of the users in relation to their conversational partners:

> The 2nd person idiom is restricted to the communicative partner of higher status, the 1st person idiom to the lower status partner. This pattern is so strong that there are hardly any exceptions to be found. (ibid.: 101)

Third person idioms being neutral are unrestricted and so may be used by anybody unless the status difference between participants is too great as in the case of a patient and his therapist. Similarly, the use of first person idioms is open to anybody but is avoided by dominating speakers as, according to Strassler, they have a 'self-abasement effect' (ibid.: 103). Second person idioms are the most restricted as their use is socially acceptable only among peers. Strassler, therefore, concludes that idioms function as status markers and, accordingly their use or non-use among conversational partners is a form of social membershipping. These deictic elements are not present in the literal synonyms of idioms: consequently, the additional deictic information idioms convey constitute their functional *raison d'être* while at the same time accounting for their presence or their absence in different situations.

Strassler's thesis that idioms convey information absent in their denotative semantic component, a component they share with their non-idiomatic synonyms, is probably correct: so are his observations on the distribution of deictic idioms. There is nothing to contradict Strassler's evidence in the much bigger corpora I have used for my own study. What is wanting in Strassler's study is a more precise and fuller account of the nature of the special information conveyed by idioms but not by their non-idiomatic synonyms. The use of idioms is a stylistic strategy made possible by the expressive meanings present in idioms but not in their non-idiomatic synonyms: *snuff it*, like *kick the bucket*, are marked as slang and convey an irreverent jocularity which the unmarked *die* does not (see Fernando 1981). Additionally, the kind of idioms Strassler's corpus contains are strongly evaluative: negative + *worth shit, have a chip on one's shoulder, have an axe to grind*, etc. Avoidance of evaluation, whether good or bad, could very well explain the distribution of idioms in personal and social deixis. The strength of Strassler's study lies in its focus on the deictic functions of idioms; its weakness is the absence of a fuller analysis of the special information he rightly claims idioms convey such as, for instance, why the self-referential use of idioms could have a 'self-abasement effect'.

1.2.6 Conclusions

The introduction (section 1.1) to this chapter draws attention to the variety of multiword expressions identified as idioms as well as to their centrality in English. Both these factors require the idiomatologist to define idioms in such a way that the definition captures this range and accordingly their centrality without being at the same time a catch-all for every word combination in a language. Some scholars (Makkai 1972; Weinreich 1969) use the absence of a literal counterpart to exclude certain expressions from the domain of the idiomatic. Others (Strassler 1982) arbitrarily exclude phrasal verbs. All the scholars reviewed are to a greater or lesser extent influenced by the *OED* definition of idioms, though this is much more evident in the work of some (Makkai 1972; Strassler 1982) than in that of others. It is the least evident in Cowie *et al.* (1975, 1983). The semantic peculiarities of idioms receive the most attention from Weinreich (1969), while the variability of idiom forms is most fully explored by Fraser (1970) and by Cowie *et al.* (1975, 1983). Cowie *et al.* not only note variations: they also link such variations to the practicalities of language use.

While Makkai (1972) and Cowie *et al.* (1975, 1983) comment briefly on the functions of idioms, the most detailed treatment of this topic comes from Strassler (1982), who analyses the pragmatic functions of idioms, drawing, like Cowie *et al.*, on a body of naturally-occurring data.

That idiomaticity does not appear in the same degree in all multiword expressions is recognized by a number of scholars. Multiword expressions range from those that qualify as pure or *par excellence* idioms through semi-idioms to various types of collocations with marginal idiomatic status. The best means of accommodating such a phenomenon is a scale, scales being common to several language models: transformational (Fraser 1970), functional (Halliday 1978), and structural (Bolinger 1975). A scale of idiomaticity such as that first used for idioms by Cowie *et al.* (1975, 1983), permits discussion of expressions as diverse as *make up, put up with, spill the beans, take a step, a blue film/joke*, etc., *a chequered career/history*, etc., *(just) for the record, arm in arm*, and *opt in favour of/for*, all of which appear in either Volume 1 (1975) or Volume 2 (1983) of the *ODCIE*. The inclusion of expressions like a *chequered career/history* in these dictionaries make possible discussion of a class of freer expressions idiomatic only in the sense of being predictable collocations in English as, for example, *addled eggs/brains* (see Chapter 2) or *violent campaign/backlash, peace talks*, etc. both of which are familiar combinations in media reportage (see Chapter 6). Acceptance of such predictable, often recombinable, collocations as marginally idiomatic makes identification of an interface possible between idioms and semi-idioms on the one hand and the *ad hoc* collocations of the rest of the vocabulary on the other as I have done in Chapter 6.

In the section that follows, I look at work that analyses idioms as peculiarities of encoding, that is as non-canonical, grammatical idiosyncrasies in contradistinction to the mostly regular types of word combinations discussed above, or as idiosyncrasies exemplifying the genius of a particular language.

1.3 Idiosyncratic idioms

1.3.1 M. H. Roberts (1944); L. P. Smith (1925); O. Jespersen (1924); C. Fillmore, P. Kay, and M. C. O'Connor (1988)

My discussion of work on idioms and idiomaticity so far has focused on studies which approach the topic in ways essentially consistent with sense 3a of the *OED* definition of the term *idiom*, though the orientation and interests of each scholar reviewed have been different. This section draws attention to work exemplifying another sense of idiom, also listed in the *OED*, sense 2, allied to sense 3a but foregrounding other aspects of idioms and idiomaticity:

The specific character, property or genius of any language; the manner of expression which is natural or peculiar to it.

A work giving a very clear exposition of this sense of *idiom*, though not specifically with English, is the article by Roberts (1944): 'The

Science of Idiom: A Method of Inquiry into the Cognitive Design of Language'. Idiom, Roberts observes, is the manifestation of a specific inner design or structure of thought communicated via a given language code, the most striking manifestation of which is 'the idiosyncrasy of permutation which a given language exhibits in contradistinction to all languages or a given period exhibits in contradistinction to all periods' (Roberts 1944: 300). Roberts is not concerned with establishing such idiosyncrasies or peculiarities as idioms by means of a set of tests in the manner of Makkai (1972) or Cowie *et al.* (1975): to him, they are idioms because they are peculiar to one language in contrast to another and as such serve as a mirror of its cognitive design accounting for interlingual differences in usage. Roberts supports his thesis by drawing on illustrative examples from a number of languages, including English, Russian, and Spanish, in other words, by an exercise in comparative linguistics.

Particularly interesting, because it throws light on the process of conventionalization, is Roberts' use of the Saussurean *langue/parole* dichotomy: individual creativity (*parole*) becomes in time part of the common system of elements (*langue*) that comprise a language. Every idiom is the result of a personal innovation at a particular point in time. An expression created in this way could then be adopted by the community, an institutionalization, to become part of the vocabulary of that speech community.

If Roberts' article is an exposition of what idiosyncrasies tell us about deferring usages in language in general, L.P. Smith's book, *Words and Idioms* (1925), is an exposition of what English idiosyncrasies tell us about usage in that language. Though Smith's analysis of idioms is more characteristic of the scholarly lover of English than of later theoretical model-oriented linguists with their formal methodologies, he anticipates some of their observations, as, for instance, Malkiel's (1959) on binomials and Makkai's (1972) on idioms of encoding.

Smith's definition of idiom derives from sense 3a of the *OED*:

We also use 'idiom' for ... those forms of expression, of grammatical construction, or of phrasing, which are peculiar to a language, and approved by its usage, although the meanings they convey are often different from their grammatical or logical signification. (Smith 1925: 167)

18

Such a definition enables Smith to classify many expressions, different in their degree of semantic unity and in their structure as idioms. Smith pays more attention to interlingual structural peculiarities ('idiosyncrasies') and intralingual ones ('idiomatic transgressions') than to the semantics of idioms. To him, idioms are essentially those forms peculiar to a language, whether they are literal or not. In view of this approach, it is hardly surprising that Smith selects English word combinations comprising verb + particle/preposition as well as other sorts of prepositional phrases in the language as one of its most striking peculiarities. Such word combinations range from 'terse adverbial phrases' such as *at hand, by far, of late, on hand*, etc., to those vast numbers of phrasal verbs such as *keep down, set up, put through*, that English is so rich in. The second type of idiosyncrasy Smith singles out for special mention are *habitual collocations*, a specific sub-class of which has since been termed *binomial* by Malkiel (1959). Apart from binomials such as *heart and soul, bag and baggage, milk and honey*, etc., Smith also includes familiar similes, *as plain as a pikestaff*, and proverbs, *out of sight, out of mind*, within this category of habitual collocations.

In addition to such idiosyncrasies, Smith also identifies expressions he terms *idiomatic transgressions*, breaking the rules of grammar (*it's me, who did you see?, try and go*, etc.) on the one hand, and the rules of logic on the other (*to keep one's head above water, to curry favour*, etc.). *Idiomatic transgressions* of this type are regarded much more tolerantly by today's linguistic scholars than by Smith, who was writing from an older, prescriptive viewpoint.

Smith's observations on this particular class of non-literal, 'illogical' idioms are brief. Such idioms are figurative and while some, such as *to keep one's head above water, to sail too near the wind*, etc., are, perhaps, semi-opaque, others are completely opaque because their origins are obscure except to the scholar. Among the latter are expressions such as *to curry favour, to peter out, to go the whole hog*, etc.

A good part of Smith's account of idioms is devoted to their classification on the basis of their imagery: the sea, the military, hunting, cattle, sheep, swine, birds, woods, and trees, etc. Body part idioms are singled out as being dominant in English imagistically: 'about fifty parts of the human body ... are all put to vivid expressive uses'; verb + particle combinations (*pull through, keep up*, etc.)

suggestive of kinaesthetic metaphors arousing imagined sensations of muscular effort are similarly singled out as being a noteworthy part of English. Another insightful observation from Smith is that so many English idioms are used as 'expressions of determination, of exasperation, and vituperation'. Such observations draw attention to what Roberts (1944) calls the 'cognitive design' of a language and identify one of Smith's contributions to vocabulary studies as being a description of how the peculiar genius of English shows itself in its idioms.

I shall conclude this section by presenting two other contributions to our understanding of English idiosyncrasies, some multiword, others single. One way in which idiosyncrasies arise is fossilization and the subsequent unproductivity of a pattern. Jespersen (1975: 21) contrasts the productivity of the *-ness* suffix with the unproductivity of *-lock*, the sole instance noted by Jespersen being *wedlock*; the contemporary *deadlock* is another example. A similarly unproductive suffix is *-th* as in *wealth, stealth, health, width*, and *breadth*. Despite John Ruskin's attempt to popularize his construction of *illth* on the analogy of *health*, neither *illth* nor any other similar word has been adopted into general use in English for centuries (Jespersen 1975: 21). Milton's *heighth* to parallel *depth* could also be added to the list of non-adoptions. There are probably many other inventions of this type which have not been taken up.

Some idiosyncrasies arise from unusual grammatical patternings. Social formulae of this type are often associated with institutionalized situational contexts: ceremonies (*Long live the Queen!*), official procedure (*The motion is carried*), legal documents (*This is the last will and testament of me* followed by the name of the testator), etc. (Jespersen 1975; Yorio 1980). Variables mark the non-formulaic portions of the expressions: *Long live* + restricted variable (*the King/President*, etc.). While idiosyncratic formulaic expressions are still part of the living language, the type itself is dead. Thus, *Late live the king* or *Soon come the train* are not customary (Jespersen 1975: 20). *Long live sb* is an unproductive pattern confined to this one formulaic saying.

Idiosyncrasies are not always confined to unproductive patterns as Fillmore *et al.* (1988) show. They classify idioms into those that are grammatical—characterized as being substantive or lexically filled (e.g. *kick the bucket, spill the beans*)—and those which are extra-grammatical—characterized as being formal and lexically open (e.g.

X-er the Y-er, X *neg let alone* Y). Grammatical idioms have 'words filling proper and familiar grammatical structures' (Fillmore *et al.* 1988: 505), extragrammatical ones 'anomalous structures'. The latter have empty slots available to be filled by variables, hence their characterization as being lexically open.

As examples of the *X-er* the *Y-er* construction Fillmore *et al.* cite the ad hoc: *The more carefully you do your work the easier it will get* and the set expression: *The bigger they come, the harder they fall.* Fillmore *et al.* observe:

> This use of the comparative construction is unique: the use of the definite article that we find in this construction is not, so far as we can tell, found generally elsewhere in the language: nor is the two-part structure uniting the two atypical *the*-phrases found in any of the standard syntactic forms in English. (1988: 507)

They go on to note that despite this pattern hosting a number of set expressions, it is fully productive, a claim that can be substantiated by the large number of *ad hoc* sentences such as *The more you eat, the fatter you get* that can be constructed on this pattern. Semantically, the pattern exemplifies an entailment relationship where given the truth of one proposition, the other follows.

The other pattern analysed by Fillmore *et al.* is the *let alone* construction, which though unique in its pattern belongs to a functionally similar 'family' comprising *much less, not to mention, never mind, if not*, etc. (ibid.: 533). *Let alone* functions as a type of connective and incorporates a syntactic 'fragment' into its structure: a full clause + *let alone* + phrase as in

A: Did the kids get their breakfast on time this morning?
B: I barely got up in time to eat lunch let alone cook breakfast.
(ibid.: 512)

Semantically, *let alone* is designated as 'a negative polarity item' (ibid.). Thus, *I wouldn't pay five dollars for it, let alone ten dollars* is glossed as 'You want to know whether I'd pay ten dollars for it? Well, I'll have you know that I wouldn't even pay five dollars for it.' Constructions of this sort, Fillmore *et al.* (ibid.: 533) argue, convey two propositions which 'identify distinct points on a scale' with the stronger point presented first.

1.3.2 Conclusions

The idiosyncrasies of a language constitute either its specific character or genius or its intralingual irregularities. The preponderance of verb + particle/preposition constructions and body part idioms are good examples of the special genius of English. Its intralingual irregularities comprise a variety of expressions: binomials with unique items (*kith and kin, to and fro*, etc.), unusual collocations (*hell for leather, mind your Ps and Qs*, etc.), unusual patterns of deletion (*the more the merrier, shall do*, etc.), and unusual combinations of the various parts of speech (*nothing loath, fancy free*, etc.). Such non-canonical, unproductive combinations could be very problematical for foreign learners. Native speakers' repertoires of idioms differ from one person to another and within various social groups (especially age groups), so some of the more unusual English idioms are learned as 'brute' facts even by native speakers of English, sometimes by asking, sometimes from reference works. However, as the discussion above of idiosyncratic idioms shows, not all idiosyncrasies are unproductive. Atypical but productive items (e.g. *the X-er, the Y-er*) form an interface between those idioms which conform to regular grammar such as *smell a rat, make up, The coast is clear*, etc., and those that are grammatically atypical and also unproductive (e.g. *long live sb, nothing loath*). To describe both semantically anomalous but grammatically regular idioms and semantically regular but grammatically anomalous ones is part of the task of the lexicologist. But while expressions like *long live sb, the more the merrier*, etc. constitute a kind of appendix to the lexicogrammar of English, those like *X let alone Y*, etc. lend themselves to systematic description and suggest a scale of grammaticality for multiword expressions with grammatically regular idioms showing productive patterns (*smell a rat, make up, the coast is clear*, etc.) at the top through anomalous patterns also productive (*X-er, Y-er*, etc.) to anomalous unproductive patterns (*long live* sb, etc.). Such a scale highlights the range of productive and unproductive elements in a language, in this case English, and throws light on why grammatical multiword expressions lend themselves more readily to variation than anomalous ones: not surprisingly, the more grammatically anomalous and idiosyncratic the expression, the more fixed it is. The extent of variation a given expression may be subjected to as well as the fixity of others will be evident in the following chapters.

1.4 About this book

The nature of idiomatic word combinations, both idioms and habitual collocations, is the concern of Chapters 2 and 6. These chapters support the core of this book, the first introducing, the latter reiterating its main theme: the interplay between the habitual and conventionalized on the one hand, and the novel and *ad hoc* on the other, characterizing so much language-use, noted also by other scholars (Cowie 1988, Nattinger and DeCarrico 1992, etc.).

Demonstrating how the conventional and the novel interact in discourse requires two kinds of evidence:

1 An adequate corpus of naturally-occurring data.

2 A theoretical framework which can explain the particularities of language-use in specific contexts, provided for this study by the higher level macro-functions derived from Halliday (1973, 1985), identified here as ideational, interpersonal, and relational, as well as one enabling an analysis of communicative strategies. Both explanatory and analytical adequacy is achievable using Hallidayan functional theory.

Chapters 3 to 5 show how various expressions identified as idioms in terms of the criteria presented in Chapter 2 are used ideationally, interpersonally, and relationally in a range of discourses. These analyses show up the semantic complexities of idioms and the ways in which novel variations in the habitual form of idioms are employed by language-users as a type of communicative strategy as well as the ways in which an idiom is used conventionally, equally a communicative strategy, but one drawing less attention to itself. The idiom functions I discuss in these chapters are not only more numerous than those presented by Makkai (1972), Cowie *et al.* (1975, 1983), and Strassler (1982), but they are also analysed in much more detail.

Neither a comprehensive classification of idiom functions nor an adequate analysis of how they are used is possible without suitable data. It is to these data, their sources, methods of collection, and the principles guiding their presentation that I now turn.

The data for this study comes from two sources:

1 My own corpus built up primarily during two periods (1975–81, 1989–94) of intensive collecting from newspapers, a major but not the only source, general reading, literary and academic, personal correspondence, conversation, the electronic media, and seminars. No word count is possible but the volume of language I was exposed to in these two periods probably amounted to billions of words. The number of individual idioms collected numbered approximately 1,000–1,100, and were listed on cards or stored in the form of newspaper clippings, copies of transcripts of conversations, and of talk-back radio. Unless stated, these idioms do not belong to a specific variety of English, such as British, American, or Australian English, but are part of a common heritage.

2 The Birmingham Collection of English Text (BCET) approximated 20 million words at the time of consultation (1990).

My own corpus was built up on the basis of a kind of random sampling; this was also the method used in retrieving data from the (BCET). In both cases, I took what came my way.

The data I obtained both from (BCET) and my own collection supported my initially tentative conclusions regarding the various functions of idioms or gave me new insights into their semantic complexities as well as revealed the kind of variations possible in their forms. Since the main purpose of my analyses in Chapters 3 to 5 is to extend understanding of how idioms are used in discourse, what I looked for was the apt illustrative example.

The frequency of a specific idiom is an indicator of its current status and its topicality, both useful criteria in selecting idioms for teaching, but it does not necessarily illuminate the ideational, interpersonal, or relational function of an idiom. Besides, drawing conclusions on the statistics valid for a specific corpus is not especially satisfactory as statistics for a particular item can vary between corpora. A corpus is not necessarily representative of a language as a whole: that is to say that relatively low-frequency items may not be particularly well represented. The account given by Mackin (Cowie *et al.* 1983: vi) is illuminating in this connection: a research group looking out for occurrences of *red herring* collected 50 instances 'in a period of several months. Yet in all my years of collecting from written sources I had not come across more than three or four occurrences of this expression.'

The two corpora used in my study of idioms yielded 52 occurrences of *red herring*, 13 from the (BCET) and 39 from my collection. There were occasions when I heard the idiom or came across it in my reading but did not record it; consequently 52 is only an approximate figure for this idiom.

Data sources could be a determinant of frequency. Newspapers were the commonest source not only for *red herring* but also for a large number of other ideational idioms. That the occurrence of items like *red herring* in the spoken discourses of my corpora was much lower could be purely fortuitous. Consequently, any conclusions I offer in the following chapters regarding which sections of a speech community use specific types of idioms in contradistinction to other sections are tentative. They are valid for my corpora but not necessarily outside them.

In this chapter, I have attempted to give my study of idioms and idiomaticity the perspective necessary to establish what its contribution is to the field. Some of the concerns referred to here will be taken up in subsequent chapters. Many of the issues to be discussed, however, have not been concerns of the scholars reviewed above largely due to their preoccupation with form rather than with function. When function has been a major interest, a different theoretical orientation as well as different data sources have led to a portrayal of the form and functions of idioms very different from mine. The description and analysis of idioms presented in this book aim to enhance our understanding of how language-users function in their roles of observer/reporter (the ideational function), interlocutor (the interpersonal function), and thinker (the relational function), idioms being a significant part of the lexicogrammar necessary for producing not only coherent discourse but also discourse that is socially acceptable as well as precise, lively, and interesting.

2
Conventional ways
of saying

The simplest, at least the most economical, method of conveying some sort of grammatical notion is to juxtapose two or more words in a definite sequence ...
(Edward Sapir, *Language* 1921)

This invasion of one's mind by ready-made phrases (*lay the foundations, acquire a radical transformation*) can only be prevented if one is constantly on guard against them, and every such phrase anaesthetizes a portion of one's brain.
(George Orwell, *Politics and the English Language* 1946)

2.1 The novel and the conventional in language

2.1.1 Introduction

If idioms are a relatively neglected area in lexical studies (the observation which began the previous chapter), it can also be said that the lexis itself has been relatively neglected in language studies. Such neglect could be ascribed to the vocabulary being viewed as the non-generative component, the rules of sentence construction being the generative and, consequently, the creative component (Chomsky 1965). Terms like *generative* suggest a transformational generative model of language with its stress on novelty and creativity; however, whatever the model adopted, structuralist, transformational generative, or functional, the vocabulary has tended to be a Cinderella in relation to sentence construction and the grammatical categories (mood, tense, concord, etc.) relevant to sentence-construction.

The commonest view of the vocabulary is that it is an inventory of words and it is as an inventory of words that it is displayed in that institutionalized repository of the word stock, the dictionary. Though this view of the vocabulary obscures the systematic, interdependent nature of words in use and the way language-users perceive these interdependent relationships as reflecting conceptual associative organization (e.g. pairings such as *night/day*, *king/queen*, etc., or semantically related groups such as *brainchild, -storm, -wash, -wave*, etc.), it is not entirely unjustified. Words and multi-word expressions on the one hand, and sentences on the other, are interdependent yet two different phenomena. There are differences between producing and responding to new sentences and to new words (McIntosh 1966). People continually recognize and produce novel, or at least partly novel, sentences in terms of their information content; many of these also show grammatical variations. But they do not habitually produce new words with anything like the same frequency. A *pre-existing* word stock and set of grammatical rules serve as a resource for the creation of new sentences. The examples below will clarify these observations:

(1) B: They arouse in me pleasurable feelings when I see them.
     A: It ... well it depends if your beauty's in the eye of the beholder.
     B: Well that's just what I'm saying. [BCET]

(2) A: Yes, but you've lost sight of the moral values—this is what I mean.
     B: No, this is not the fault of the religion, this is the fault of the teachers.
     A: Well, this is what I'm saying—let's get back to the morals. [BCET]

It could be said that these sentences are novel in that though some of their underlying patterns (e.g. Subject–Verb Phrase–Object/Complement) and some words and phrases are repeated (e.g. *that's just what I'm saying; this is what I mean; that is what I mean; this is not the fault of the religion, this is the fault of the teachers*), they are not information-wise the same: the *that* of (1B) *that's just what I'm saying* and the *this* of (2A) *this is what I'm saying* refer to quite different statements and consequently are completely different in meaning. Similarly in (2B), while the patterns are virtually identical in the two juxtaposed clauses, they assert different propositions, one of which reinforces the other, both together constituting a combined assertion regarding the cause of a particular social phenomenon. All the sentences, excluding lexicalized multiword sentential expressions (e.g. *beauty's in the eye of the beholder*), are one-offs (nonce forms).

Their meanings while being intelligible are not predictable, despite the repeated patterns; in other words, it is not possible to say in advance what propositions S–V (Phr)–O/C, etc. will produce. Nor are there comprehensive collections of sentences serving as a resource, the way words, single, compound, and multiword, do in a dictionary. We learn individual words and the rules for combining them into acceptable sentences but not the individual sentences themselves. The meanings of these sentences are deduced on the basis of familiar words and rules.

The emphasis throughout the 1960s and the 1970s was on creativity and novelty, and consequently syntax (sentence construction) was the major preoccupation of the analyst. Such a view tended to give the lexicon stepmotherly treatment since it consists of prefabricated and hence familiar elements. This relative neglect of the vocabulary is now being redressed with more attention being paid to the familiar elements of language, a development resulting in the vocabulary becoming an increasingly important domain of investigation in its own right, not simply an appendage to the grammar. (For an overview of the vocabulary see Carter 1987 and Carter and McCarthy 1988.)

Predictably, it is the vocabulary that is invoked when it is argued that very little that is novel is actually said (Bolinger 1976; Halliday 1978; Pawley and Syder 1983; Pawley 1986). What must be emphasized in order to maintain a proper balance is that both the novel and the familiar are present in language-use because both are indispensable to the proper functioning and purpose of communication: we speak and write most of the time in order to inform others of what they do not know: say only what is *newsworthy* is one of the Gricean Conversational Maxims (see Chapter 3); the message content or the way of communicating it or both can be new; on the other hand, familiar elements, the word-stock, enable language-users to be rapid and fluent in constructing their utterances and their addressees to process these pieces of discourse on Zipf's principle of least effort, least effort being a psychological necessity in normal communication, especially in speech, rarely the only activity going on (Gibbs and Gonzales 1985; Gibbs 1980). Generally, speech accompanies other activities such as cooking, driving, eating, etc. Though literary-minded individuals like George Orwell may deplore the dominance of the familiar in language, recourse to such a resource is inevitable

28

considering the conditions in which the addresser and addressee function. Additionally, even the familiar can be used in new contexts leading to the development of new meanings (see *sangre azur*, section 2.1.3).

Interest in the familiar aspects of language-use began in modern linguistics with J. R. Firth. The bases for extending the study of the vocabulary beyond traditional preoccupations (e.g. semi-productive processes of word-formation, sense-relations such as synonymy and antonymy, figurative language, etc.) was laid as early as the 1950s when Firth established the concept of collocation ('the company words keep') in linguistic theory. Collocation simultaneously foregrounds the significance of co-occurrence relations in establishing recurrent lexical patterns as well as the routinized nature of language. The concept of collocation and its various applications has since been more extensively explored in the work of Halliday (1966); Sinclair (1966, 1987); McIntosh (1966); Mitchell (1975); Cowie and Mackin (1975); Mackin (1978); Cowie (1981); and Cowie *et al.* (1983), among others.

Some of the first reactions against novelty as the most salient characteristics of language came from Hymes (1971); Bolinger (1976); and Halliday (1978) who all three imply that the familiar is at least as prominent as the novel in discourse:

> ... the human mind is less remarkable for its creativity than for the fact that it remembers everything.
> (Bolinger 1976: 2)

More recently, Coulmas (1979); Pawley and Syder (1983); Pawley (1986); and Tannen (1989) have also highlighted the abundance of familiar conventionalized word combinations in discourse. These familiar combinations, which include idioms and habitual collocations, can be described as realizations of what Sinclair (1987) calls the 'idiom principle', although such realizations vary from strong in the case of idioms to weak in collocations. Implicit in such a gradation is the notion of a scale of idiomaticity (see Table 2.1 below) in which items at the bottom, such as various types of collocations, are only marginally idiomatic.

2.1.2 Idioms and idiomaticity

Idioms and idiomaticity, while closely related, are not identical. The basis of both is the habitual and, therefore, predictable co-occurrence of specific words, but with *idioms* signifying a narrower range of word combinations than *idiomaticity*. Idioms are indivisible units whose components cannot be varied or varied only within definable limits. No other words can be substituted for those comprising, for example, *smell a rat* or *seize/grasp the nettle*, which take either of these two verbs but no others: thus *grab* is unacceptable. Nor are the words of an idiom usually recombinable.

All idioms, of course, show idiomaticity. However, all word combinations showing idiomaticity, for instance, *habitual collocations* such as *rosy cheeks, sallow complexion, black coffee*, or *catch a bus*, etc., are not idioms for they are relatively unrestricted in their adjectival and nominal variants: *rosy/plump cheeks, rosy dawn*, and *a sallow skin* are all possible. Similarly, we can have *strong coffee* and *catch a tram*. All these variations yield idiomatic expressions exemplifying idiomaticity, but they are not idioms. Idiomaticity is exemplified not only in idioms and conventional *ad hoc* collocations, but also in conventional lexicogrammatical sequencing most apparent in longer text fragments: *those smooth, plump, rosy cheeks will one day be shrunken, shrivelled, and withered*. This *ad hoc* sequence of adjectival modifiers preceding and following *cheeks* exemplifies idiomaticity in both selection and sequencing, but there are no combinations within the sequence qualifying as idioms. Such an *ad hoc* sequence can be compared with *tall dark and handsome*, an idiom both lexically and sequentially fixed.

That conventionalized co-occurrence is the usual basis of idiomatic expressions is evident in the unacceptable sequencing of **butter and bread issue, *rosy, plump, smooth cheeks*, or **little, three adorable girls*. More strikingly, Chomsky's famous **Colourless green ideas sleep furiously* illustrate a different kind of unacceptable co-occurrance, a semantically unconventional collocation.

All idioms are not grammatically regular, a fact already established in section 1.3. Non-canonical conventionalized word orders and semantics are possible as in *nothing loath, footloose and fancy free, beside oneself, curry favour*, etc.

In sum, while habitual co-occurrence produces idiomatic expressions, both canonical and non-canonical, only those expressions which become conventionally fixed in a specific order and lexical form, or have only a restricted set of variants, acquire the status of idioms and are recorded in idiom dictionaries as *bread and butter* and *footloose and fancy free*. Combinations, showing a relatively high degree of variability, especially in the matter of lexical replacement such as *catch a bus, catch a train*, etc., are not regarded as idioms, though they exemplify idiomaticity by virtue of habitual co-occurrence: *catch* meaning 'be in time for' co-occurs usually with a mode of transport, though *catch the post* is also possible.

The existence of conventionalized multiword expressions, or idioms, showing invariance or only restricted variation and habitual collocations, restricted or unrestricted in their variability, calls for a scale of idiomaticity. Several other scholars (Cowie and Mackin 1975; Cowie *et al.* 1983; Alexander 1984; Carter 1987; Nattinger and DeCarrico 1992; etc.) have all used scales to demonstrate the shading off of sub-classes of idioms into one another as well as the overlap between idioms and their lexical kin, collocations. The scale presented in Table 2.1 has most in common with that of Cowie *et al.* (1983) but is probably less delicate than theirs.

The rationale underlying the combination of scalar and columnar format in Table 2.1 is that it makes possible:

1   A clear presentation of idioms and habitual collocations as related, but two different lexical types.

2   A clear presentation of the basis of this difference: the degree of variability, a lexicogrammatical feature, distinguishing these two lexical types. The semantics of idioms and collocations, though important, is not crucial as the examples cited in Table 2.1 show. There are both literal and non-literal expresssions in the two columns, whereas only variable items occur in the collocations column.

The items at the top of the Idioms column (Ia), are both invariant and non-literal, while Ib shows restricted variance and non-literalness. Ia and b are classed as pure idioms. IIa and b repeat the features invariant/variant evident in Ia and b, but are semi-literal and so are classed as semi-literal idioms. This set, as the arrow shows, overlaps

31

Idioms	Habitual collocations
I Pure idioms **invariant, non-literal** a. devil-may-care, backlash, chin wag, red herring, make off with, spick and span, smell a rat, the coast is clear, etc. **Restricted variance, non-literal** b. pitter-patter/pit-a-pat, take/have forty winks, seize/grasp the nettle, get/have/cold feet, etc.	
II Semi-literal idioms **invariant** a. drop names, catch fire, kith and kin, foot the bill, fat chance you've got, etc. **Restricted variance** b. chequered career/history, blue film/story/joke/gag/comedian, good morning/day, etc.	**I Restricted variance, semi-literal** explode a myth/theory/notion/idea/belief, catch the post/mail, thin/flimsy excuse, etc.
III Literal idioms **invariant** a. on foot, one day; in sum; in the meantime; on the contrary; arm in arm; very important person (VIP); potato crisps; tall, dark and handsome; waste not, want not; happy New Year, etc. **Restricted variance** b. opt in favour of/for, for example/instance, in order that/to, happy/merry Christmas, etc.	**II Restricted variance, literal** addled brains/eggs, in-the-not-too distant past/future, for certain/sure, potato/corn/wood, etc. chips, etc. **III Unrestricted variance, semi-literal** catch a bus/plane/ferry, etc. train, run a business/company, etc. theatre, by dint of hard work/patience/repetition, etc. **IV Unrestricted variance, literal** beautiful/lovely, etc. sweet woman, smooth/plump, etc. glowing/rosy cheeks, etc.
Literal idioms **IV Restricted variance, optional elements** abstain (from), (even) worse, worse (still), develop (from) (into), etc.	**V Restricted variance, literal, optional elements** shrug (one's shoulders), nod (one's head), clap (one's hands), etc.

Table 2.1: Multiword expressions

with a sub-class of collocations (I). IIIa and b (the Idioms column), both variant and invariant, are literal idioms of which IIIb overlaps with the literal collocations marked II. The idioms in IV are also literal with prepositions, which though optional, usually co-occur with their verbs (see section 1.2.4).

The various classes of idioms listed above are not as neatly differentiated as they appear to be in Table 2.1. The fuzziness characterizing their interfaces are looked at in section 2.1.3.

The salient characteristic of habitual collocations is that all the items there show variance, restricted as in I: *explode a myth*, etc., or relatively unrestricted as in IV: *beautiful/lovely*, etc. *woman*. Some of these collocations have one item with a non-literal subsense as *explode* 'debunk' *a myth* or *catch* 'be in time for' *a train/plane*, etc. do. Others are literal, for example, *addled eggs/brains*. The bracketed items in V tend to be omitted and in this respect are more strongly optional than those optional items in the Idioms column IV.

A word regarding terminology: *idioms* is used as a cover term for the various sub-classes of idioms looked at in greater detail in section 2.1.3. *Idioms* is also used in a similarly general way when contrasted with non-idioms. Specific classificatory terms, for example, *pure idioms*, are used where necessary. The same practice is followed for *collocations*: the term is used generally, with the type of collocation specified where necessary.

2.1.3 Idioms, semi-idioms, literal idioms, and habitual collocations

The vocabulary consists of single words and multiword expressions. Though multiword expressions differ formally and semantically in many ways, they can be categorized into two major lexical types: idioms and habitual collocations (see Table 2.1 above). It is the nature of the first of these two lexical types, idioms, that make up the subject matter of this chapter.

Idioms (*While the cat is away, the mice will play; the coast is clear; that's a good question; guess what?; smell a rat; red herring; bread and butter; at the same time; as good as gold; the simple life; a war of attrition;* etc.) would not exist were it not for the tendency of words to co-occur, yet any juxtaposition does not result in locutions having the status of conventionalized multiword expressions in a language. Four factors appear to favour the acquisition of such a status. They are discussed below.

Multiword expressions need to conform to the grammatical rules of the language. *The purplish to eating* (Determiner (Det) + Adjective (Adj) + Verb (V) or *lock the luckily* (V + Det + Adverb (Adv)) are not likely candidates for multiword expressions, though grammatical idiosyncrasies do appear in some well-known ones: *waste not want not, long time no see, guess what?, be that as it may, beside oneself, white lie, foot the bill, fancy free*, etc. However, these are not as flagrant in their non-canonical grammar as the invented ones cited above; their unusualness arises from deletion (*waste not want not, guess what?*, etc.), illogicality (*beside onself*), figurative use (*white lie*), or the presence of a specialized subsense (*foot* the bill) 'pay' in a restricted context. *Nothing loath, happy-go-lucky*, etc. are examples of more extreme departures which, like the others, are conventionalized by usage.

The majority of multiword expressions in English conform to the grammatical rules of the language as even a cursory scan of collections of idioms and dictionaries will show. Adj + Noun (N) (*sacred cow, white elephant, red herring*, etc.) is a common pattern of many phrasal multiword expressions conventionalized by usage. Commonest, perhaps, is the semi-clausal pattern V + Det + N (*pass the buck, smell a rat, spill the beans, catch one's breath, do one's bit, tighten one's belt*, etc.). Less frequent is Preposition (Prep) + N + Prep (*on behalf of, by way of, by dint of sth., in case of sth., in the name of sb/sth.*, etc.). Prep + Adj ... Prep + Adj (*at best ... at worst*) is an infrequent pattern in the formation of conventionalized multiword expressions.

Invariance or the fixity of the words making up the expression, combined with non-literalness in many cases, are two other factors favouring conventionalized multiword status. Such fixity and non-literalness are a matter of degree. Consequently, multiword expressions can range from the completely fixed, semantically non-literal, e.g. *pins and needles* 'the tingling sensation following numbness', through the possibility of some grammatical changes like those for tense, e.g. *spill/spilled the beans* 'commit an indiscretion', to lexical variation from the restricted and semi-literal, e.g. *blue film/joke*, etc. 'obscene', *explode a myth/belief/theory/notion/idea* 'debunk', to the unrestricted semi-literal, e.g. *catch a bus/train*, etc. 'be in time for'.

34

The fourth factor favouring the emergence of multiword expressions is culturally salient encodings (Pawley 1986), that is, the expression captures some phenomenon prominent in the collective consciousness. *Blue blood* (*le sangre azur*) was originally used to signify the blue veins of the Spanish showing through their white skins in contrast to the invisibility of those of the swarthy Moors. Later on, it came to signify 'aristocratic birth' regardless of colour. Current locutions on the way to gaining status as conventionalized multiword expressions are *fat cat* 'person in a sinecure position', *compassion fatigue* 'reluctance to continue charity', *a war of attrition* 'a war which will continue indefinitely as neither side is strong enough for victory'. These expressions could qualify as conventionalized multiword expressions for they are likely to be recognized 'by members of the language community as a standard way of referring to a familiar concept or situation' (Pawley 1986: 101).

The multiword expressions cited above show a variety of structural types: compounds (*happy-go-lucky*), phrases of various types (*red herring, bread and butter, on behalf of, at best ... at worst*), semi-clauses of various types (*guess what?; waste not, want not; do one's bit, spill the beans*), and full clauses of various types (*the coast is clear; while the cat is away, the mice will play*). These structural types may also be categorized as lexical types, a categorization which, from the point of view of how people use words, is much more illuminating: idioms and their sub-classes as well as collocations and their sub-classes (Cowie 1981; Cowie *et al.* 1983). What these lexical types all have in common is that they show the regular co-occurrence of words in a specific form and order, habitual word combinations, so much so that the presence of one sets up an expectancy of the other (Firth 1957; Halliday 1966; Mitchell 1975; Mackin 1978; Cowie 1981). Thus, *waste not* will very likely elicit *want not* from anyone familiar with English; *fat chance* will elicit only *you've got*; *at best* will be followed by *at worst*, etc. If variable, such variations occur only within definable constraints. For example, *catch a* ... will elicit either a word signifying some form of public transport *bus/train*, etc. or an ailment, such as *cold*.

Idioms yield three sub-classes: pure idioms, semi-idioms, and literal idioms. A working definition of a pure idiom which is adequate for the present is 'a type of conventionalized, non-literal

35

multiword expression'. *Spill the beans*, for example, has nothing to do with *beans*. In contrast to its literal counterpart meaning 'letting fall leguminous seeds', a non-literal meaning is imposed on the idiom as a whole: 'commit an indiscretion'.

A semi-idiom (Weinreich 1969; Cowie 1981) has one or more literal constituents and at least one with a non-literal subsense, usually special to that co-occurrence relation and no other: *drop* has the meaning 'overuse' only when it co-occurs with *names*. Other examples are *catch one's breath* 'check', *foot the bill* 'pay', etc. Some of these semi-idioms, like their kin, restricted collocations with specialized subsenses, permit lexical variation, for example, *blue* 'obscene' *film/joke/gag/story/comedian*.

Literal idioms (*on foot; tall, dark and handsome; waste not, want not; on the contrary; a (very) happy birthday; a merry Christmas and a happy New Year*, etc.) meet the salient criterion for idioms: invariance or restricted variation. They are, however, less semantically complex then pure and semi-idioms.

Some collocations, like idioms, show a habitual co-occurrence of words but these are multiword expressions which permit lexical alternatives as a matter of course, either restricted or unrestricted: *addled eggs/brains, in the-not-too-distant past/future (restricted)*; *by dint of hard work/perseverance/repetition/application/patience/ persistence*, etc. *catch a bus/train/tram*, etc. (unrestricted). The last example is the most unrestricted collocation of the cited examples, but this is only in relation to the others. *Catch* in the context of items signifying public transport has the specialized subsense 'be in time for', as it does with the *post* (*catch the post*). New forms of public transport can be added to the set of possible alternatives (e.g. *hydrofoil/hovercraft*), but some restrictions exist as with *ship*, though not with *boat*. *Catch* does not generally co-occur with forms of private transport (*bicycle/car/yacht/dinghy/helicopter*, etc.) though *taxi* (*catch a taxi*) is an exception. Although *catch* is unrestricted in relation to restricted collocations such as those cited above, it is relatively restricted itself when compared with some other habitual co-occurrences such as Adj + *coffee*: *strong/weak/black/white/Irish/ Turkish/Brazilian/hot/iced/sweet/bitter*, etc. *coffee*. However, numerous as are the adjectives that can co-occur with *coffee*, there are limits: *coffee* can be *strong* but not *powerful* or *vital*, *weak* but not *limp*, *Irish* 'coffee laced with whisky', but not *British*, and so on.

36

Despite such limits, the generous openness of this collocation apparent in the wide range of possible adjective options it has, places it at the lower end of a scale of idiomaticity (habitual collocations, IV, Table 2.1) in contrast to *smell a rat, white lie, catch fire*, etc., which are lexically invariant and non-literal, completely or partially.

It is difficult to maintain a strict division between pure idioms, semi-idioms, literal idioms, restricted and unrestricted collocations (as Table 2.1 shows). The range of alternatives that can co-occur with *blue* 'obscene' (*film/joke*, etc.) may lead to this expression being seen as both a semi-idiom like *white lie* and a restricted collocation like *explode* 'debunk' *a myth/theory/notion/idea/belief*, especially as both have specialized subsenses; 'obscene' and 'debunk', which are non-literal. Consequently, semi-idioms and restricted collocations can be regarded as overlapping as in Cowie (1981). However, *explode a myth* because of its several options has less unity as a multiword expression than the invariant *catch one's breath* 'check' or *catch fire* 'ignite', 'be enthused'. Looked at in this way, *explode a myth*, etc. belongs more with *catch a bus*, etc., the chief difference being that the first is relatively restricted, the second relatively unrestricted. A pure idiom such as *get cold feet* can take two other options (*have/give*), a flexibility which establishes links between it and restricted collocations. This kind of fuzziness afflicts taxonomies in every area of language. The elements of a language cannot all be lumped together—differences do exist—nor can they be inflexibly categorized, as shared features are also present. What we have in the linguistic universe, as in the material one, is a mix of pure breds and hybrids. Following other scholars, I have already suggested a graduated scale (see Table 2.1) as the best means of accommodating such diversity. A scale enables us to discuss lexical types such as collocations, which show some of the features of idioms, without being idioms themselves. *Idiomatic expressions and conventionalized multiword expressions* are the terms of widest general reference in this book, being cover terms for idioms and habitual collocations of all types.

2.1.4 Conclusions

The *raison d'être* of multiword expressions rests on the tendency of words to co-occur initially in *ad hoc*, novel ways. Some of these *ad hoc* word combinations turn into lexicalized multiword expressions showing differing possibilities of variation. In other words, habitual co-occurence, the basis of idiomaticity, leads to:

1   the formation of pure idioms, semi-idioms, or literal idioms showing resistance in varying degrees to internal lexical substitutions and functioning, therefore, as single lexical units even though such units are multiword expressions: compounds, phrases, semi-clauses, and clauses;

2   non-literalness as a result of pure idioms losing the meaning of their constituent words over time and so having an external meaning imposed on the unit as a whole, or in the case of semi-idioms certain of their words developing specialized subsenses in restricted contexts.

Some of these expressions could very well be filtered out of a more rigorously defined class of idioms on the grounds of their simply being a type of unrestricted or open collocation (e.g. *catch a bus*, etc.) or variable locutions (*Sorry to have kept you waiting/My apologies for keeping you waiting*, etc.) and therefore neither invariant nor restricted in their variations in the way idioms are. The abundance of such expressions in English makes the recognition of an 'idiom principle', strongly realized in idioms, weakly in collocations, very useful as an explanation of the way an important part of the vocabulary works: the language-user is sensitive to word combinations, not merely words as self-contained isolates and employs such combinations, some of which are idioms, for various purposes.

2.2 The lexicogrammar of idioms

2.2.1 Introduction

A working definition of an idiom has already been given (see section 1.1) and is repeated here for convenience: 'conventionalized multiword expressions often, but not always, non-literal'.

The following text gives some idea of the variety of items employed by the language-user that are candidates for classification as common multiword expressions, but does this mean they are also idioms?

(3)   [a personal letter]
      Now comes the hoot. At the beginning of July, quite *out of the blue*, came an important-looking letter *one morning* marked *OHMS*. *Guess what*: an invitation to a *Buffet Supper* with the members of the *Royal Commission … Talk about feeling a VIP*—it was marvellous after the first shock *died off* though being me it was a bit difficult to *keep up* the VIP image. [A]

To this set of italicized expressions in example (3) many of those already cited in the foregoing sections as well as new ones can be added, so that a set of criteria for separating idioms from those expressions that are only marginally idiomatic, or not at all, may be established.

Multiword expressions vary in size from compounds (e.g. *foxglove, happy-go-lucky*), and phrases (e.g. *die off, red herring, run away with, out of the blue, first and foremost, OHMS, VIP*), through to semi- and full clauses (e.g. *guess what; spill the beans; talk of __ing sth; the coast is clear; while the cat is away, the mice will play*); they vary in degrees of non-literalness (e.g. *smell a rat, drop names, look out, say no more, a dog's life, the facts of life, arm in arm, first and foremost, what I'm saying is*), and in the possibility of lexical substitution, or in other words, degrees of lexical invariance (e.g. *pins and needles, catch fire, spill the beans, burn one's bridges/boats, head/leave/set out for, potato crisps, potato/corn/wood, etc. chips, addled eggs/brains, catch a bus/train, etc.*). Despite the differences in size, and differences in degrees of non-literalness and invariance, all the cited items show features of idiomaticity. The question, already raised, is what gives some of these expressions the lexical status of idioms, but not others? What separates *one morning, buffet supper, Royal Commission*, etc., together with other habitual expressions such as *rosy cheeks, shrug one's shoulders, wag its/their tail(s), strong coffee, addled brains/eggs, a week elapsed*, etc. and common locutions like *Can I take a message?* or *Take one tablet three times a day* from idioms, for example, *smell a rat* or *drop names* or *arm in arm*? Explication of the nature of the difference amounts to an explication of the nature of idioms. It can be argued that an idiom and idiom categories, like many other 'entities' and categories in linguistic theory, are theoretical constructs (Weinreich 1969; Pawley 1986). Language-users produce many sorts of expressions. Identifying idioms is simply an attempt to differentiate and label one class of common expressions with specific functions from others on the basis of criteria which strike the analyst as being the most illuminating. Consequently, it is inevitable that different analysts will come up with somewhat different criteria and different identifications. The criteria and identifications favoured in this study are presented below and draw on a number of insights common to general linguistic theory.

2.2.2 Compounds, phrases, semi-clauses, and clauses

Lexicogrammatical features characteristic of idioms are primarily those of *form* (Healey 1968; Weinreich 1969; Fraser 1970; Makkai 1972; etc.). These formal features constitute, along with others of a semantic nature, a basis for separating idioms from non-idioms.

While some scholars (Katz and Postal 1963; Fraser 1970) following Hockett (1958) accept even single words as idioms this is a minority view. Others (Wood 1966, 1969a, 1969b; Cowie *et al.* 1975, 1983; Long *et al.* 1979) and (Smith 1925; Malkiel 1959; Weinreich 1969; Makkai 1972; Fernando and Flavell 1981; Strassler 1982; Pawley and Syder 1983; Pawley 1986) favour only multiword expressions as candidates for recognition as idioms. Conventionalized multiword expressions have lexicogrammatical and semantic features that single words and *ad hoc* expressions do not, and consequently a distinction on this basis is fundamental for idiomatology.

Idioms are multiword expressions but there are limits on their size. Ad hoc constructions, on the other hand, do not have such limits on size apart from those imposed by contextual appropriateness and memory limitations. Non-idioms can range from short phrases like *very true, rosy cheeks, one morning*, etc. to multiple modifying recursive structures, for example, *In heman America*, or *In heman, twofisted, broncobusting, poker-playing, stockjuggling America* (John Dos Passos, USA), or recursive multiple-clause structures such as *well this is what I'm saying let's get back to the morals* (BCET), both of which are potentially extendable. The same is true of common locutions like *Come here* or *Please/do come right here or come right up and straight in here*, etc. Idioms do not permit such extensions; they are conventionalized expressions and, if variable, are variable only within definite constraints.

The lower limit for idioms is established by the compound. Though not generally included in dictionaries of idioms, compounds show many of the characterizing features of idioms. They are multiword expressions and represent habitual co-occurrences between two or more words (e.g. *foxglove, overtake, pitter-patter/pit-a-pat, happy-go-lucky, devil-may-care*).

Compounds are classifiable into the parts of speech which categorize the content words of the vocabulary: nouns (*baby-sitter*), adjectives (*devil-may-care*), verbs (*overtake*), and adverbs (*pitter-patter/pit-a-pat*). Relational forms like *however, moreover, therefore, none the less, nevertheless*, etc. though consisting of two or more independent forms are, like complex prepositions (e.g. *inside, outside*), accepted as single words and listed as such in dictionaries.

In speech, compounds are identified by distinctive stress patterns which differentiate them from homonymous free constructions, if these exist. Primary stress in compounds always falls on the first part of the compound: *si'lver screen* 'film industry' vs. *silver scre'en* 'a silver-coloured screen'. By this criterion, not only *si'lver screen* but other expressions like it that are orthographically spaced (*bi'rth control, inco'me tax*, etc.) are also compounds despite the difference in writing conventions (Huddleston 1984: 45). The presence of the space as opposed to hyphenation or closed juxtaposition reflects different degrees of institutionalization in the recognition of the expression as a compound as opposed to a phrasal sequence (ibid.). Like larger idioms, compounds can be both literal (e.g. *mother-in-law*), semi-literal (e.g. *baby-sitter, sickroom*), or non-literal (e.g. *foxglove, eavesdrop, pick-me-up*).

Some semi-clausal idioms can be transformed into compounds, e.g. *lick sb's boots* → *boot-licker*; *break the ice* → *ice-breaker*, etc.

These features have led many scholars working in the field of idiomatology to accept compounds, such as those cited above, as idioms (Hockett 1958; Healey 1968; Katz and Postal 1963; Fraser 1970; Makkai 1972; Fernando and Flavell 1981).

If the compound is the recognized lower limit for idioms as far as size goes, the complex clause is the recognized upper one in dictionaries of idioms, and citations by scholars: *when the cat is away, the mice will play* 'uninhibited behaviour'; *don't count your chickens before they are hatched* 'ill-advised optimism'; etc. There are no idioms, whatever their sub-classes, that consist of more than two subordinating clauses. In fact, longer expressions such as those quoted are often shortened: *don't count your chickens*, *red herring* (originally *trail a red herring across the path*), etc. Short expressions that are easily remembered are the commonest; what matters is not the number of clauses but the length as is evident in *I came, I saw, I conquered*, a saying that has acquired the status of an idiom.

The most favoured type of construction evident in English idioms, in terms of both size and form, going on collections in dictionaries and other works, appear to be the verb + particle(s) constructions (e.g. *put up, put up with*) and the semi-clause (e.g. *spill the beans, smell a rat*, etc.).

2.3 Idioms and transformations

2.3.1 Introduction

Though grammatical patterns *per se* are not crucial in distinguishing between idioms and non-idioms, form needs to be considered in examining idioms. There are many idioms whose lexicogrammar is the same as that of *ad hoc* constructions: *spill the beans* 'commit an indiscretion', 'let fall the leguminous seeds'; *do a U-turn* 'reversal of policy or opinion', 'turn a vehicle around'. Such expressions display constructional homonymity with their parallel literal counterparts. These are idioms of decoding (Makkai 1972) and may in certain contexts result in ambiguity and misinterpretation. Idioms that do not show constructional homonymity are idioms of encoding (Makkai 1972). They represent the idiosyncrasies or irregularities of a language, e.g. *nothing loath; easy does it; waste not, want not*; etc.

One of the purposes of examining the lexicogrammar of idioms is to identify those elements which make up the essential parts of an idiom as opposed to those that are optional. Thus, in

(4) a. [a seminar participant]
Can I throw in *a red herring*? [A]

the determiner slot can be realized variously without affecting the status of the expression, as in (4b.) below, where the indefinite article is replaced with 'zero article', *red herring* becoming plural:

b. *Red herrings and the Iraki breakfast*
(*The Australian*, 4 March 1976: 6)

Similarly, *somebody* in *give somebody the cold shoulder* represents a variable indirect object slot (*Tom/Jill/my boss/this woman/that bastard*, etc.) and not a lexically fixed part of the idiom.

However, replacement of characteristic lexis within an idiom is either not possible (e.g. *tighten one's belt *girdle, kick the bucket *pail*), or, if possible, the range of options is restricted (e.g. *a lot of water flows/passes/goes under the bridge*). Such constraints on replacing the words of an idiom with others, even ones that are synonymous, is an important feature separating idioms from non-idioms normally open to a wide range of word replacements: *a second/minute/month/year*, etc. *elapsed/passed/went by*, etc.; *a buffet supper/dinner/lunch*, etc.; *Royal/Senate/University/Grants*, etc. *Commission*, and so on. These expressions are unrestricted collocations like *catch a bus/train*, etc. or *potato/corn/wood*, etc. *chips* and other similar expressions. Being unrestricted, they exemplify English idiomaticity but are not idioms for a number of reasons (see section 2.3.6 for a more detailed discussion of such expressions).

OHMS and *VIP*, like *RSVP* and *ASAP*, are acronyms for *On Her/His Majesty's Service* and *Very Important Person* respectively. Though literal, they are fixed expressions and so have claim to be regarded as idioms, especially since they encode culturally salient phenomena. This raises the question of other acronyms which are titles of organizations like UNESCO and the UN. Since these are very similar to proper names, they could be excluded.

Apart from constraints on word replacement, there are other types of constraints on idioms which make them fixed or invariant, for example, in respect of their word order: *pins and needles, spick and span, fancy free, fat chance you've got*, etc. However, most idioms can be manipulated or transformed in various ways according to the communicative needs of the language-user. What these ways are will be looked at in the sections that follow.

2.3.2 Replacements or substitutions

Variation of the parts of an idiom could be in terms of number and tense (inflectional changes) or the replacement of one structure word like an article by another or by zero, or it could be lexical, one content word being replaced by another. Additionally, there are built-in variables such as *one's* or *somebody's (sb's)* e.g. *tighten one's belt or twist sb's arm* which allow replacement by any appropriate noun.

Variations in tense are permitted in many verb idioms and are therefore common. Tense in verb idioms usually mirrors the time-frame of the discourse:

(5) a. He *smelt a rat* and he *kept* mum.
         (past tense, past time)
         (*The Oxford Dictionary of Current Idiomatic English* 1983)
         Everybody *smells a rat* in a doctored obituary, even the widow.
         (present tense indicating a timeless truth)
         (*The Oxford Dictionary of Current Idiomatic English* 1983)

     b. Yet some of his excuses for his absence lately *had been* pretty thin. Some women *would have begun to smell a rat.*
         (past time with the infinitive *to smell a rat* governed by the past form *would*, a modal expressing certainty)
         (*Sparkling Cyanide*, Agatha Christie 1957: 50, Pan)

There are idioms with verbs which resist even such minimal variations. Proverbs, expressing as they do general truths, normally retain their original form: *a watched pot never boils*; *a stitch in time saves nine*; *if wishes were horses, beggars would ride*; etc. *A stitch in time saved nine*, for example, would not be acceptable as an idiom. However, the same is not true for proverbs subjected to word play. These can undergo many changes (see example 25). Most discourse formulae: *You were telling me* or *You could say that again* mean something different from the original *You're telling me* and *You can say that again*.

Number functions in many idioms with the same freedom as tense does:

(6) a. Student: Can I throw in *a red herring*?
         Tutor: Several.

     b. *Red herrings* and the Iraki breakfast
         But Mr Whitlam has to talk about these things—*any red herring* will do ...
         (*The Australian* 4 March 1976: 6)

(7) a. We went there one evening. I *twisted Richie's arm* I said he's
         your brother-in-law too but they weren't in. [A]

     b. If you can't turn up let us know—if necessary I *can twist the
         arms* of a few friends and get them to come. [A]

By contrast, pluralization is not possible in *kick the bucket* (*It was
quite sudden—poor old Bill's *kicked the buckets*) or in *smell a rat*
(*Bill's a shrewd bloke—he'd *smell the rats* at once), though both
permit tense variation. If plurals are not possible in some idioms,
neither are singulars in others: **twiddle one's thumb* (*twiddle one's
thumbs*), **raining a cat and a dog* (*raining cats and dogs*), cf. *a cat
and dog life* (**cats and dogs lives*).

   Inflections apart, what of the individual words in an idiom? Can
these be varied? As already noted, some idioms admit no lexical
substitutions: *tighten one's belt/*girdle, smell a rat/*mouse, say no
more/*nothing, see red/*scarlet*, etc. Such lexical co-occurrence
constraints would also be true of a number of habitual collocations
which are idiomatic English but do not have the status of idioms: *she
shrugged (her shoulders), he nodded (his head), the dog wagged its
tail*, etc. While some expressions, idiomatic and idioms proper, do
not permit substitutions, others do in varying degrees. *Burn one's
boats/bridges* and *get/give/have cold feet* are examples of idioms that
permit a choice of restricted variants. Unrestricted choice reduces the
fixity of an expression and so brings it closer to an *ad hoc* construction. Open expressions of this sort are *catch a train/tram/bus/
ferry/plane/hydrofoil*, etc. 'be in time for', *catch cold/mumps/
measles/bronchitis*, etc. 'be infected with', *take a trip/a holiday/a
vacation/leave/a week-end off*, etc. Though, as noted earlier, the
collocates of *catch* 'be in time for' do not extend to private transport
(**catch a motor cycle/bicycle/car/scooter*, etc.) *catch* in this combination has a predictable meaning which ensures that any new form
of public transport could be added to the list, for example, *hover-
craft*. Similarly, any new disease could be added to the cluster of
existing collocates for *catch* 'be infected with'. This feature of unrestrictedness is one that *catch*, in the two senses given above, shares
with verbs like *eat/drink/gobble/fill/chew*, etc. + *up*. In these examples, *up* has the meaning of 'completely'. Such unrestrictedness
contrasts with the single collocate of *catch* in *catch fire* 'ignite', or
parts of an idiom such as *by* in *by heart* 'memorize', or *by* in *by the*

way 'incidentally', or *by* in *by-law* 'law operative only in a specific area', 'subsidiary law'. In each of these instances, *by*, together with the other parts of the idioms, convey their given meanings only in this combination. The overall meaning of the combination overrides that of the individual parts. Similarly, *the cat* of *set the cat among the pigeons* 'cause an outcry in conventional circles' has no more connection with *let the cat out of the bag* 'disclose a secret especially at the wrong time' than either has with a real cat. While idiomatic expressions like *catch measles*, etc. or *eat/drink up*, etc. are instances of analogical productivity, *par excellence* idioms (*by heart, let the cat out of the bag, drop names, arm in arm*, etc.) have no such generative potential, that is, they cannot be produced according to predictable rules.

Expressions using polysemous words like *thin* 'of small breadth', 'lean', 'meagre', 'transparent' or *slender* 'of small breadth', 'slight', 'scanty': *thin arm/wrist/slice of bread/excuse/alibi*, etc. or *slender arm/wrist/means/resources/chance*, etc., are best classed as restricted collocations (see Table 2.1). The abstract collocates (*excuse*, etc. or *chance*, etc.) that both *thin* and *slender* go with result in a transfer of one of the attributes of *thin* and *slender* to the accompanying word, for example, a *thin excuse* or *alibi* means a flimsy or transparent one; *slender resources* means scanty resources. In other words, the literal meanings of these words help the language-user to decode them in their non-literal uses. It is interesting to compare an idiomatic expression such as *slender chance* or *your chances are slender* for the insights it gives into the differences between idiomatic expressions such as these and semi-literal idioms like *fat chance you've got* which means the same thing but behaves differently. *Fat chance* is not part of a cluster as the parallel polysemous word *fat* appearing in *fat arm/cheeks/bank balance*, etc. is. Additionally, it is part of a fixed expression and consequently cannot be transformed in any way: **You've got a fat chance* or **Your chances are fat* are unacceptable (cf. *your chances are slender*, above). The idioms in the naturally-occurring examples that have so far been looked at contain only permissible inflectional or lexical substitutions.

As already indicated above, there are many idioms which permit only minimal variation (*kick the bucket* for tense) or are totally invariant (*fat chance you've got*). But language-users are innovative.

They make their own idiosyncratic substitutions in an idiom while contriving to retain its idiomaticity.

(8)   ... we should not entirely rely on *the Japanese even when they are not bearing gifts.*
      (trust not the Greeks when they come bearing gifts)
      (*The Australian* 28 November 1975)

(9) a. *Is Arafat his* brother's keeper?
         (*The Jerusalem Post*, syndicated article in *The Australian* 4 March 1989: 16)

     b. ... In Denmark *no one is his sister's* keeper.
         (I am not my brother's keeper.)
         (*The Australian* 28 November 1975)

(10)   ... critics have had 150 years to do what they wanted with *Sandition* and they did nothing. So *Marie stepped in where Janeites fear to tread.*
       (fools rush in where angels fear to tread)
       (*The Australian* 2 August 1975: 20)

In all these instances, language-users assume they are addressing a readership familiar with the original allusions or sayings which now have idiom status. No change is intended in the meaning of the idiom; there is only an attempt to make it more precisely applicable to a particular situation by using appropriate substitutions.

A telling instance of the resistance of an idiom's conventional meaning to an inappropriate substitution in the original construction is cited by Tannen (1989). *Every* was substituted for *no* in *leave no stone unturned* by a spokesman for an investigation team at a press conference, an obvious slip of performance under pressure, as the substitution signified the exact reverse of the idiom's meaning: he would not stop the investigation until *every stone was unturned.* What is interesting is that this speaker was understood as intending the conventional meaning of *leave no stone unturned*: 'explore every avenue'; do everything possible to achieve a goal.

2.3.3 Additions

Except for those needed to give idioms correct form (e.g. *twist sb's arm → sb's arm was twisted*) additions are not normally permitted within an idiom. But as with novel substitutions, language-users may introduce extraneous elements into idioms to make their messages more precise:

(11)   Rudyard Kipling took the *art world bull by the horns* when he wrote , "It's clever, but is it art?"
       (*The Sydney Morning Herald* 4 December 1978: 1)

(12)   Professor McDonald also suggested (*with his tongue only partly in his cheek*) that the current state of Australia's economy could be attributed to analysts not being able to interpret data ... .
       (*Macquarie University News* Nov/Dec 1987: 16)

Much more interesting as examples of innovation are those instances where an added adjective is treated as if it were literal, whereas what is really intended is the idiomatic meaning.

(13)   It is very easy for those academics to look out of their *carpeted ivory towers* across the quagmire of business stagnation.
       (*The Australian* 8 December 1975)

(14)   One of his examiners said that this was *a feather in his cap* but he said it was a small *feather*. [A]

This emphasis on the literal 'face' of an idiom by means of an extraneous adjective is a variety of word play.

Whatever the nature of the innovative addition, it requires a certain intuitive feel for the limits beyond which the idiomatic cannot be pushed.

(15)   I am certain the majority of parents are completely *in the dark* about what is happening.
       (*The Australian* 20 December 1975)

In this example, the addition of *pitch* (*in the pitch dark*) would not make the idiom unacceptable, whereas *when the lights are out* would. In other words, any addition to an idiom must be designed to reinforce its meaning and not simply elaborate on the expression *per se*. Some idioms (e.g. *kick the bucket, smell a rat*, etc.) are unlikely to tolerate any additions, even innovative ones.

2.3.4 Permutations

The possibility of rearranging the words of an idiom as we do those in non-idiomatic constructions (Jack killed the giant → the giant was killed by Jack) varies from idiom to idiom just as substitution and addition do.

Some idioms have no permutational possibilities in terms of their internal grammar. If transformed, such idioms lose their idiomaticity: *say no more* → **no more was said, John smelt a rat* → **John is a rat-smeller*, etc. Some common types of permutation that transformable idioms are capable of undergoing are discussed below.

Particle shift is a permutation that can be optional as in *they beat up people* or *they beat people up*. It becomes obligatory when the intervening object is a pronoun:

(16) Airliner *blown up*

  Seven masked separatists ... forced an Air France airliner to an isolated area ... and *blew it up*.
  (*The Sydney Morning Herald* 9 September 1976: 5)

While the optional permutation is a matter of free variation, the obligatory permutation realizes an invariant rule of the language.

(17) a. *To split* hairs over these cases being civil or criminal offences is unworthy of us all.
    (*The Oxford Dictionary of Current Idiomatic English* 1983)

  b. .... the jury lost itself in the minutiae of legal argument and *hair-splitting* rather than using common sense.
    (*The Australian* 15 April 1989: 6)

This kind of transformation is quite common with both idioms and non-idioms:

(18) [radio news report]
  Baby-kissing, handshaking, backslapping and signing autographs were the order of the day when the Prime Minister visited Brisbane yesterday. [A]

A similar permutation of elements can also convert a verb + object predicate into a nominal in both idioms and non-idioms: *sb writes a letter* → *a letter writer, sb drops a brick* (idiom) → *a brick dropper*. This kind of structure is very like, but not the same as, the gerundive compounds of (17) and (18), being as it is a pure nominal in form:

(19) a. [an advertiser's caption]
           Opening this will *open your eyes*. [A]

      b. This '*eye-opener*', according to Tass, showed that the
          President was not for office.
          (An article in *The Guardian* printed in *The Sydney
          Morning Herald* 28 May 1988: 17)

(20) a. **D.B.** Those people are hoping they don't have Arthur as
           chairman.
           Y.M. Oh I don't know it served to *break the ice*. [A]
           (it refers to 'Arthur's opening speech')

      b. He thinks a party would be a good *ice-breaker*.
          (*The Raj Quartet* by Paul Scott, Vol. 3, 1971: 350)

These 'compressions' are generally used unconsciously by the
speaker/writer and do not strike the hearer as being unusual. They
indicate the ease and fluency which mark the native speaker or the
competent foreigner in handling the language.

   Another very common form of permutation is passivization:

(21) a. On the one hand he's got *crocodile's tears* about interest
           rates ... .
      (*The Sydney Morning Herald* 1 April 1989: 1)

      b. Buckets of *crocodile tears have been shed* at dozens of
          public rallies ... .
          (*The Sydney Morning Herald* 14 May 1988)

The usual form is either *weep* or *shed crocodile tears* but the speaker
has made an idiosyncractic substitution (*got*) here, which could very
well be a slip of performance of the sort that so often characterizes
speech.

(22) a. Gorbachev *leaves no stone unturned* at the PR summit.
           (*The Sydney Morning Herald* 28 May 1988: 1)

      b. [radio news report]
          He released a statement saying that *no stone would be left
          unturned* to find the culprits. [A]

Passivization is a permissible transformation which can be carried
out on some idioms such as those above.

Language-users may also sometimes reverse subject and object in order to create a foregrounded one-off variation of an idiom:

(23) For a while in Hobart this week it looked faintly as if *the canary had swallowed the cat.*
(*The Australian* 16 August 1975)

This kind of reversal seems to be on the analogy of *the tail wagging the dog* where the reversal is the normal form of the idiom and constitutes its meaning and its point.

2.3.5 Deletions

While some idioms are well established in their truncated forms so much so that these forms are now the norm (e.g. *red herring* from *draw/trail a red herring across the track/path, a rolling stone* from *a rolling stone gathers no moss*), others rely on the hearer's knowledge of the original for comprehension.

Deletion is a process common at all levels of language though different sorts of levels require that other terms (e.g. elision, contraction) be used to describe its effects: the absence of an element normally present. Idioms that are current in the language in their full form but which appear with parts deleted, as with permuted 'compressions' (e.g. *hair-splitting*), indicate the confidence and fluency of the language-user. Non-native speakers whose knowledge of idioms has been derived from dictionaries may find such deletions impeding identification and interpretation of particular idioms. *The idol has feet of clay* becomes *X has clay feet*; *dangle a carrot before the donkey* is reduced to *dangle a carrot* or simply to *carrot* with an appropriate modifier:

(24) a. Sunshine dangles *an issue carrot* (headline)
          (*The Australian* 15 November 1975: 12)

      b. Thatcher waves *trade carrot* (headline)
          (*The Australian* 6 August 1988: 3)

      c. The Prime Minister has offered some very appealing *political carrots* in his economic program.
          (*The Australian* 28 November 1975: 10)

In (24b and c) deletion is accompanied by the substitution of *wave* and *offer* for *dangle*.

(25)   Hold up guns all *bark*, no *bite* (headline)
       (*The Australian* 10 September 1975)

This example, like (24) functions as an allusion to an idiom, *barking dogs seldom bite*, rather than as the idiom itself so great is the degree of deletion. Other examples, less radical, are:

(26)   [a conversation]
       This fellow thought the Professor would drop him like a hot potato so he preferred *a bird in the hand*.
       (a bird in the hand is worth two in the bush)

(27)   Alba (1981) in his study of American Catholics, notes that the ethnic revival was largely '*an-eye-of-the-beholder effect*' ...
       (*beauty lies in the eye of the beholder*)
       (*Language, Society and Identity*, by John Edwards 1985: 107)

(28)   While this *home fire burns* Bob Hawke can relax, feel safe ...
       [A]
       (*keep the home fires burning*)

(29)   Norman Sherry is the epitome of the *no-stone-unturned* school of biographers ...
       (*leave no stone unturned*)
       (*The Sydney Morning Herald* 10 June 1989: 85)

Though deletion is possible in idioms, such as those cited above, there are large numbers of idioms, especially those made up of verb + preposition/particle, where deletion is unlikely, even impossible: *see through sb, bring the house down, get in touch with sb, so much so, you're telling me*, etc. One of the reasons for deletion in the newspaper examples given above is that space-saving can be conveniently combined with wit and humour by this means. In other instances what is evident is the principle of least effort common in most language use in one form or another. It is, however, impossible to predict those features likely to lead to deletion as usage, rather than form.

2.3.6 Summary and conclusions on the transformations in idioms

The two most important features of the lexicogrammatical composition of idioms are (1) compositeness and (2) the fixity or the relative fixity of the words making up the idiom. In other words, the less the possibility of replacing the words of an idiom, the stronger its status as a word-like unit. *Smell a rat, make off with*, *pins and needles*, etc., being invariant, will be at the top of any idiom scale exemplifying lexical substitutability. While pure idioms at the top of the scale (see Ia, Table 2.1) are invariant expressions, others allow minimal variations (e.g. *burn one's boats/bridges*) as do restricted collocations (e.g. *grip/seize/catch/capture one's imagination*). Such restricted collocations overlap with semi-idioms. But as the options for replacement increase, we move towards unrestricted collocations (e.g. *catch flu/pneumonia/bronchitis/measles*, etc.). An expression such as this is not unlike *Jill was asked to roll up her stockings/socks/hose/the bottoms of her trousers/the carpet/the sheets of paper lying on the floor*, etc. However, the difference between *catch flu*, etc. and the example just given, is that the possible replacements for *catch flu*, etc. function as members of a very common cluster of habitual collocates and are therefore predictable. *Catch* functions either with words denoting *public transport* (*bus*, etc.), *diseases* (*catch flu*, etc.) or is restricted to *fire* (*catch fire*), and *breath* (*catch one's breath*), whereas the collocates of *roll up* are *ad hoc* one-offs and not part of an established habitual collocational cluster.

The possibility of replacing the words of an idiom by others is the transformation most likely to reduce its status as a composite unit. Looked at from the perspective of fixity alone, *fat chance you've got, all gone, arm in arm*, or *on foot* are higher on the scale of idioms than idioms like *give/have/get cold feet* or *burn one's boats/bridges* despite their being near literal or completely literal.

There are, of course, other kinds of transformations idioms can undergo. While some idioms (e.g. *say no more*; *fat chance you've got*; *waste not, want not*; *pins and needles*) allow no additions or deletions even in the form of inflectional variations for tense or number as the case may be, others inflect readily in order that the idiom appears in its correct form in terms of number concord (*I twisted Richie's arm/I can twist the arms of a few friends* (7a. and b.)) or in terms of the correspondence between time and tense (*This bloke got such a fright he kicked the bucket!*). Such alterations of tense and number can be regarded as a form of replacement of the original grammatical category by another, if looked at from a different perspective, that of change, which is general enough to subsume the processes of addition, deletion, and permutation.

In terms of lexical status, deletion of parts of an idiom has the least effect compared with other transformational processes. This is why some idioms rarely appear in their full forms (e.g. *draw/trail a red herring across the path/track* → *red herring*). Reduction of proverbs, if they are used, is not uncommon (see section 2.3.5). Permutation is like substitution and addition with regard to decreasing an idiom's retention of its status. Like addition, permutation too may be regarded as the replacement of the original form of the idiom with another.

The transformational variations (substitution, addition, permutation, and deletion) discussed above are of two sorts: normal variations which are part of the language system, and variations which show innovative, rule-breaking novelty. Both types of variations suit the communicative purposes of language-users. Conventional grammatical transformations enable them to produce the correct form of the idiom demanded by the linguistic context; innovation enables them to display their wit and skill in handling the vocabulary.

While the range of grammatical structures spanning idioms and the dynamics of their transformational behaviour need to be described in order that the learner may become aware of constraints on the use of idioms, grammatical patterns *per se*, whatever the idiom sub-class, are not what makes an idiom an idiom. What is crucial in the syntactic domain is the fact that certain sequences of words (co-occurrences) over time become composite units (idioms), which then function as if they were single words. The degree of compositeness differs: some idioms are more unified than others. Despite such differences, it is this compositeness brought about by lexicalization that unites idioms as structurally different as *foxglove, arm in arm,* and *never put off till tomorrow what you can do today*) and as functionally different in a discourse as *blah blah blah, how are you?, not bad,* or *in fact.* Such examples show that idioms exemplify a heterogeneous phenomenon and that the various expressions identified as idioms need to be seen as shading off into one another rather like a graduated scale (see Table 2.1). Looking at specific language phenomena in terms of a scale or gradient is not a novel idea in language studies. Bolinger's view (1976) is that gradience is an in-built feature of language and appears at all levels. Halliday's model of language (1961) uses the notion of cline similar to that of scale. The concept of scale has also been adopted by other scholars (see section 2.2) in describing the pervasiveness of idiomaticity in English.

It has been indicated above that substitution of various kinds, whether of one grammatical category for another, one word order for another, or one word for another affects the status of some idioms as lexicalized multiword expressions. The substitution of one word for another is, however, different from the two other substitutions referred to. The replacement of one type of grammatical category with another, for example, present into past tense or singular into plural in an idiom, is an indicator of the sensitivity of the language-user to co-text: an idiom needs to be given its correct form to fit into its linguistic environment. Similarly, considerations of style may lead the language-user to replace one word order with another, for example, active into passive, resulting in the fronting of a different element from that in the original. The substitution of one word for another in some idioms is, however, an indication of the possibility of restricted free variation of the sort that exists at other levels of language.

In the introduction to this discussion of idioms and idiomaticity (see section 2.2.1), the problem of habitual co-occurrences such as *shrug one's shoulders, wag its/their tail(s), addled eggs/brains*, etc. was raised. Why should not such expressions be classed as idioms? Though these have the semblance of idioms, by virtue of the criteria adopted in the foregoing discussion and in the following one (see section 2.2.2), they are not really idioms. Such expressions are the products of the narrow co-occurrence range of one of their constituent words: *shrug* which co-occurs only with *shoulders* or *addled* which co-occurs only with *brains* and *eggs* (see also section 2.3.1). Consequently, they only exemplify idiomaticity as a type of restricted collocation (see II, V Table 2.1).

Such collocations, being habitual, share the feature of predictable co-occurrence with idioms in respect of their components, especially in this case with variant literal idioms, being literal themselves. However, they differ in their lexicogrammatical behaviour from the literal idioms of IIIb and IV (see Table 2.1). *Shrug one's shoulders* or *nod one's head*, like most other verbs taking body part objects, can occur without these objects and so appear as single items (*He/She shrugged/nodded*), as the relevant objects are easily inferrable.

The collocates of an item like *wag* are more complex. *Chin wag* 'intimate conversation' and *set tongues wagging* 'cause gossip' are invariant, non-literal pure idioms; the combination of *wag* with *head, finger,* and *tail* gives a set of restricted literal collocations: *Heads wagging in denial, the Bloggs protested their innocence, Joe Bloggs wagged his finger admonishingly, Tail wagging joyfully the pup ran out, The pup wagged its tail,* etc.

Also complex is the use of an expression like *potato crisps/chips* which is culturally determined: *chips,* in British idiom is reserved for expressions such as *fish and/'n chips* (a meal), while *crisps* are packaged and eaten as a snack and hence the term is not a variant for *chips.* Consequently, I have classed *potato crisps* as an invariant literal idiom (see IIIa Table 2.1).

Addled eggs/brains are collocationally very restricted but their claim as idioms is weakened by the possibility of permutation as in *Bacon that's rancid and eggs that are addled, I won't eat* or *What Bloggs has done means only one thing—his bloody brains are well and truly addled.* An idiom in the correspond-class (IIIb, Table 2.1) with a parallel Adj + Noun structure such as *a happy/merry Christmas* cannot be transformed into *a Christmas that's merry/happy* and function as a greeting.

For all these reasons expressions such as *addled eggs/brains, shrug one's shoulders,* etc. do not have a place on a scale of idioms; however, since they exemplify idiomaticity, they appear in a class of restricted collocations (II, V Table 2.1) related to literal idioms (IIIb, IV Table 2.1).

2.4 The collocability of idioms

The compositeness and lexical fixity of an idiom has been referred to throughout this chapter so far as being its salient features; however, they are not the only features which need to be taken into account in considering the nature of idioms. As already stated, though they are composite units, idioms function as single words do. In normal language use all words conform to the linear principle of language structure and so co-occur or collocate with other words.

Collocation has already been defined as the company words keep. If one is sufficiently familiar with a language, the co-text of many words can be accurately predicted or at least what kind of co-text they are unlikely to occur in. While a large number of collocations are casual, for example, *the green and purple dress* or *the tall, angular, black man*, others are predictable and stable as *nod (one's head)* or *weak/strong, etc. tea* are. These expressions show idiomaticity in terms of the English language without being idioms as they are not lexicalized units (see section 2.3.6 above). While all words need to be semantically compatible with one another, in the case of idioms, an awareness of such compatibility depends on the language user's responding to the semantic unity of the idiom, hence its idiomatic meaning (see section 2.1.3). This will be virtually automatic if he/she already knows the idiom. Such a response is supported by the co-text of an idiom usually containing many words which harmonize semantically with it, in other words, predictable collocates. A more detailed examination of the relations idioms contract with other words throws light simultaneously on both idioms and collocational relations generally.

A number of text fragments in which the idiom *turn/put back the clock* appears are cited below in an attempt to identify the typical collocates of this idiom. Halliday (1966: 159) points out that any investigation of collocation requires the study of very large samples of text in order to detect collocates that are sufficiently regular to constitute a pattern. This would depend, arguably, on the word being considered. Common words *like man, woman, cat, tree*, etc. would indeed require very large samples of text for their typical collocates to be identified. Such a requirement would not hold to the same degree for relatively less common words such as *turn/put back the clock*. In the analysis below, only content words (i.e. nouns, verbs, adjectives, and adverbs) are counted in establishing the collocates of *turn/put back the clock*. Structure words (articles, pronouns, prepositions, conjunctions, etc.) are not since their use with all kinds of content words is unavoidable and therefore their appearance as collocates tells us little that is semantically significant about the item under consideration.

A series of text fragments appear below, followed by an examination of the typical collocates of *turn/put back the clock* in the set:

(30) a. But the *communists have managed* to <u>*turn the clock back*</u>
           at *least* to the *latter years* of the *Malayan Emergency*.
           (*The Australian* 9 October 1975: 9)

b. It is not a *licence to put the clock back*: no one *wants* to go *back* to the *boredom* of the *23 years* before we thought it was time for a change.
(*The Australian* 15 December 1975: 8)

c. Labor turns back the clock (headline)
The *Labor Party has returned* to the *negativism* of the *sixties* after its leadership ballot in Canberra yesterday.
(*The Australian* 28 January 76: 1)

d. The Whitlam years simply cannot be erased. *The clock cannot be put back* to *Menzies-time*.
(*The Australian* 21 February 1976: 5)

e. Patricia Kennedy and *Frederick Parslow* lead the *small cast*, and *Ray Lawler turning the clock back* to *20 years* directs.
(*The Sydney Morning Herald* 8 September 1976: 7)

f. *The clock turned back a few years* in *King's Cross yesterday* when the *American Navy* came to town.
(*The Sydney Morning Herald* 2 November 1976: 3)

g. The Council's main worry is that the *proposed changes* to the *Marriage Act will be used* to *put the clock back* and *remove* some of the *more enlightened parts* of the *Family Law Act*.
(*The Australian* 4 May 1976: 9)

h. *Mrs Whitehouse* was in *favour of repressive censorship* and *wanted* to *turn the clock back* to the *19th century*.
(*The Sydney Morning Herald* 4 September 1978: 1)

i. He [i.e. Fraser] is *trying* to *turn the clock back* to the *pre-Whitlam era*. [A]

j. Both the *United States* and *Britain put their clocks back one hour today* in the *face* of *approaching* winter as Australians put theirs forward an hour to enjoy more spring sunshine.
(*The Sydney Morning Herald* 30 October 1978: 5)

Sinclair (1966) notes the extent to which casual collocation dominates discourse. Despite this limitation, even a small sample for certain types of expressions, for example, idioms, can yield one or two recurrent, and, therefore, significant collocations, as this one does. In general terms, *turn/put back the clock* collocates with time adverbials. More specifically, if literal, it collocates with time adverbials such as minutes or hours (30j.) or, if idiomatic, with much larger periods of time such years or centuries (30a., b., d., e., and f.). This sample of ten text fragments yields five occurrences of *years* and one occurrence of *century* (30h.). There are also four instances of quantifying numerals both cardinal and ordinal: *23*, *sixties*, *twenty*, and *19th*. Less predictably, we have the unusual *Whitlam years*, *pre-Whitlam era*, and *Menzies time*. Practically all the collocates of *turn/put back the* clock strongly indicate that the clock in question does not refer to a real one but is rather a figurative way of indicating various kinds of temporal regression—social, political, economic, etc. The agents instrumental in turning back the clock in these texts, together with the time adverbials quoted above, leads the addressee to the signification 'return to the past, restore the institutions and values of the past'. *The communists, the boredom of the 23 years before, negativism of the sixties, remove more enlightened parts, repressive censorship of the 19th century* carry a negative evaluation.

This examination of some of the typical collocates of *turn/put back the clock* shows that idioms in the matter of their external collocational behaviour are no different from non-idioms. The salient difference between idioms and other words is that an idiom is a multiword expression which then enters into further linear relationships not only strengthening the interconnections between the parts of a text but also creating various modifications of meaning both at the local and global levels. Because of establishing such predictable cohesive links, collocates establish regular co-occurrence patterns, at least the typical ones identified here do. Such patterns help language-users to create new sentences using familiar elements; they also help comprehension by contextualizing the idiom and so narrowing down the range of its possible meanings.

2.5 The semantics of pure and semi-idioms

2.5.1 Semantic unity

Pure and semi-idioms are non-literal and, consequently, could be opaque to language-users in respect of all or some of the words that make them up. Mitchell (1975) sees an idiom as 'a cumulate association' and as an 'assemblage of roots', roots being his term for the base word forms (morphs) constituting the idiom. In other words, an idiom is formally a multiword expression (an 'assemblage of roots') functioning as a single semantic unit ('a cumulate association'). (See also Weinreich 1969; Makkai 1972; Cowie *et al.* 1975, 1983; Strassler 1982; Pawley 1986, etc.) *Smell a rat* being a pure idiom and not an *ad hoc* construction, like *the cat sat on the mat*, means 'become suspicious', not 'sense rodent with olefactory organs'. Other examples of such opaque non-literal pure idioms are: *twist sb's arm* 'coerce', 'cajole'; *break the ice* 'deformalize'; *pins and needles* 'the tingling sensation following numbness'; *by heart* 'memorize'; *pick up* 'collect', 'improve in health', etc., *you can say that again* 'one agrees', etc. What is evident in all these idioms is that a single meaning different from the separate meanings of each word is imposed on the whole unit. Though this sort of semantic unity is most clearly seen in pure idioms, it is also evident in semi-idioms. Thus, the semi-idiom *blue film* has the specialized sense 'obscene film' only when these two words occur together. This kind of unity brought on by habitual co-occurrence is also seen in the pure idioms *by heart* 'memorize'; *red herring* 'decoy'; or the semi-idiom *rain cats and dogs* 'rain heavily'. The typical result of such semantic unity in all these idioms is non-literalness complete in pure idioms, partial in semi-idioms. Yet even a completely literal idiom such as *try, try and try again* because of its currency in this fixed form has become a synonym of 'persevere' in the same way that the non-literal *you can say that again* signifies 'one agrees'. There is, of course, a difference between literal and non-literal idioms. Literal idioms (e.g. *on foot*; *try, try and try again*, etc.) can be interpreted on the basis of their parts: they are transparent; non-literal pure or semi-idioms (e.g. *smell a rat, blue film, foot the bill*, etc.) are opaque, completely or partially.

Non-literalness, and its result, semantic opacity, has already been identified as a salient, though not invariant feature of idioms. There are many literal expressions which are regarded as idioms only on the criteria of compositeness and fixity (e.g. *try, try and try again*; *zoom along*; *arm in arm*); on the other hand, there are also large numbers of common idioms which have the additional property of partial or complete non-literalness (e.g. *rain cats and dogs, red herring, at the same time, blue film, drop names*, etc.). It is these wholly non-literal pure idioms that will be looked at below.

2.5.2 Non-literalness

There are many pure idioms which do not easily show connections between the literal meanings of the *individual words* which make them up and the idiomatic one applicable to the *whole expression*:

(31) Yet some of his excuses for his absence lately had been pretty thin. Some women would have begun to *smell a rat*. Thank goodness Sandra wasn't a suspicious woman. (become suspicious)
(*Sparkling Cyanide* by Agatha Christie)

(32) ... the Australian public, until Mr Menadue *let the cat out of the bag*, did not realise just what "the department" was up to. (disclose a secret, esp. at the wrong time)
(*The Sydney Morning Herald* 30 March 1981: 6)

(33) [TV presenter introducing a film]
a. I won't mention the character in case *I spill the beans*. (commit an indiscretion) [A]

b. Now the Tax Office *spills the beans*.
(*The Sydney Morning Herald* 8 February 1991: 1)

(34) a. Something very strange about the statement somebody can be tired of life and not tired of poetry because the connections between poetry and life are surely pretty warm and important. *At the same time* I think there may be something in the way Strachey wrote that ... [BCET]

b. ... Anyway the unsuspecting bit of me realized it was a trap when I saw the wolf and the bear fighting. They turned round and saw me *at the same time* and sort of ran up or loped up and started to attack me (literal). [BCET]

The words making up each of these pure idioms are semantically void ((34b.) is the exception, being literal), in that they do not carry any independent meaning of their own. If the words in idioms of this type were given their independent meanings, the result in relation to the rest of the text would be semantic oddness, cohesive irregularity, or situational irrelevancy:

(35) "Children dying of AIDS are *brushed under the carpet*," she said.
(*The Sydney Morning Herald* 13 January 1990: 1)

Brush under the carpet used as a pure idiom in this text means 'evade difficult or embarrassing issues', semantically compatible and situationally appropriate; literally it is absurd. Similarly, *at the same time* in (34a.) is used as a concessive conjunction qualifying the idea expressed in the preceding clause; the same expression in (34b.) means 'simultaneously', a meaning logically inappropriate in (34a.). Only the idiomatic meaning, which the unit as a whole carries, makes sense in examples (31 to 34), the exception being the non-idiom (34b.).

Though the original literal meanings of *smell a rat, spill the beans, kick the bucket*, etc. are now only known to the etymologist, there are other pure idioms in which the literal meanings of the words making up the idiom are still partly operative, though, of course, the idiomatic meaning is the dominant one. *Red carpet*, with its variants, *roll out the red carpet* and *red carpet welcome/treatment*, is one such example. An idiom like *red carpet* is different from one like *smell a rat* in that *red carpet* is likelier to be used literally to refer to a real red carpet than *smell a rat* would be to refer to the presence of a real rat:

(36) a. They smiled and made a well synchronized procession along the *red carpet* that tumbled down the stairs and across the lawn in front of the birch, cedar and chestnut trees.
(*The Sydney Morning Herald* 9 July 1978: 5)

      b. *Red carpet* out as Sydney crowds greet Li Xiannian (headline)
The *red carpet* was rolled out, ... The Vice-Premier of China, Mr Li Xiannian, noted the sumptuous proceedings and thanked everyone.
(*The Sydney Morning Herald* 12 May 1980: 3)

c. ... the pub did not have a suitable *red carpet* to roll out for the distinguished visitor. Happily ... the Sheraton Wentworth ... loaned its stretch of *claret broadloom*.
    (*The Australian* 6 August 1988: 20)

The pure idiom, *red carpet*, even when used to refer to a real carpet as at public functions, is a symbol of respect and deference; though literal, it differs from the reference to a red carpet in somebody's house. In other words, when the idiom refers to a real carpet, the carpet is confined to public functions. However, *red carpet* can be used in a purely figurative sense in a variety of situations. Like the literal *hand in hand* or *arm in arm*, both of which symbolize 'mutual closeness' or the similar *bread and butter* meaning 'basic part of English breakfast or tea', 'ordinary means of livelihood', or 'plain and wholesome', the common meanings of *red carpet* have strong symbolic overtones:

a symbol of respectful or deferential reception and attention
(*The Oxford Dictionary of Current Idiomatic* English 1983)

especially good treatment
(*The Longman Dictionary of English Idioms* 1979)

In (36a. and b.) the *red carpet* refers to the floor-covering put down for royalty or VIPs to walk on during an official visit. The meaning the idiom conveys additionally is 'a symbol of respect and deference'. That a real carpet is present is evident in the reference to *the red carpet that tumbled along the stairs* in (36a.) and the synonymous nonce variant *claret broadloom* in (36c.) The two uses of *red carpet* in (36d. and e.) make it a less straightforward idiom. The headline in (36b.) conveys the meaning 'especially good treatment'. The following text describes this lavish treatment, part of the lavishness being the presence of a carpet, additionally a symbol of respect. However, if the idiom is used in the sense of 'especially good treatment' a red carpet need not actually be there, particularly if the idiom is used to refer to ordinary persons as in (36e.):

(36) d. Boris Yeltsin has been given the *red carpet* treatment reserved only for heads of state.
      (*BBC World News* 20 December 1991) [A]

e. When I married the second time, it was to a man actually younger than me and suddenly the red carpet was whipped from under my feet. Now I was just a youngish wife married to a youngish husband.
(*Nova*, November 1974, quoted in *The Longman Dictionary of English Idioms* 1979)

These texts, (36 a.–e.) exemplify constructional homonymity, i.e. the presence of two expressions using the same sequence of words but to convey different meanings. There are many pure idioms which show such constructional homonymity with non-idiomatic *ad hoc* constructions: *pull up one's socks* 'lift up foot-covering' (non-idiom) or 'make a greater effort' (idiom); *kick the bucket* 'strike pail with foot' (non-idiom) or 'die' (idiom). These are all examples of idioms of decoding conforming to the lexicogrammatical regularities of the language. They contrast with the conventionalized irregularities (e.g. *guess what*; *nothing loath*; *waste not, want not*), the idioms of encoding.

2.5.3 Summary and conclusions on the semantics of idioms

Several features relating to the semantics of idioms, with the focus being on pure idioms, have been discussed in the foregoing sections. The most salient semantic feature of a pure or semi-idiom is its semantic unity: the *par excellence* or pure idiom is a composite unit consisting of semantically 'empty' words; consequently, a new meaning—different from what the same unit would have had if each word were not void—is now associated with the idiom, e.g. *spill the beans*, 'commit an indiscretion' (the non-literal idiomatic meaning) as opposed to the literal non-idiomatic meaning, 'let fall leguminous seeds'. While the non-idiomatic *He spilled the beans on the floor* means just that and has a specific sort of syntactic behaviour (*The beans were spilled on the floor*, passive) the idiom as in

Mystery man spills the beans on Fiji arms cache
(*The Australian* 20 May 1989)

means something different and is not passivized when used in this sense.

Since large numbers of idioms are non-literal these may offer difficulties of interpretation to language learners, native and non-native; if unfamiliar, they would be semantically opaque and, if so, incongruous in terms of the co-text even to competent language-users as no one knows all the words of a language. The property of non-literalness has been frequently invoked in this discussion. While non-literalness and opacity are closely linked they are not identical, nor is there a necessary cause-and-effect relationship between them. People can encounter a new wholly or partly non-literal idiom for the first time and understand it in much the same way as they would any new word or longer, composite expressions such as *sleep that knits up the ravell'd sleeve of care* (Shakespeare, *Macbeth* II.i).

I have referred to opacity in connection with decoding idioms. It can be argued that opacity is only an incidental feature of pure or semi-idioms and as such may or may not be present for the language-user. It is a variable relating to the perceptions of the language-user and does not reside in the idiom *per se*. Non-literalness, on the other hand, when it appears in an idiom is intrinsic to the idiom regardless of the language-user. However, not all idioms are non-literal. This means that idioms can be ranked in terms of degrees of non-literalness just as they can be ranked in terms of degrees of lexical fixity (see Table 2.1). This second scale of non-literalness, while corresponding to the first in respect of some idioms, does not in the case of others. The fixity of an idiom in terms of its component words (lexical fixity) and its non-literalness have no inherent connection; however, it must be noted that over time fixity bestows semantic unity on an expression and such unity could lead to this expression becoming less and less connected to its original reference, e.g. the idiom *blue blood* (*sangre azur* in section 2.1.3). *Red carpet* now refers not only to a carpet that is red but much more saliently to 'especially good treatment', 'respectful or deferential reception and attention'. These latter meanings hold whether a red carpet is present or not. In many idioms the literal meaning dominates: *by hand, arm in arm, on foot, fancy free, a good question, OHMS, VIP*, etc. Such expressions are regarded as idioms by virtue of being fixed multi-word expressions. But as a result of such conventionalized co-occurrence many of these 'literal' idioms have developed strong connotational meanings: *by hand* 'urgency', 'confidentiality'; *arm in arm* 'intimacy'; *on foot* 'effort', 'exertion'; *fancy free* 'unconstrained', 'insouciance'; *a good question* 'approval'; *OHMS* 'official'; *VIP* 'power and status'.

The *composite* nature of idioms, together with their total or partial *fixity*, affects their semantics, whether this is a matter of signification or connotation, in that the semantic unity of idioms is strongly linked to these two lexicogrammatical features.

2.6 Idioms: indicators of conventionality

2.6.1 Introduction

The lexicalization of multiword expressions is an indication that these items have entered the vocabulary and as such function as words despite their compositeness. As such, they are different from novel *ad hoc* constructions ranging from the idiosyncratic *a grief ago* to more ordinary phrases (*a pearly-grey sky, a mild day, is there such a thing as a clean nuclear bomb?*) and familiar collocations, sometimes termed clichés (*the wonders of nature, the marvels of science, the clink of glasses, a just war*, etc.). The key differences between *ad hoc* constructions and idioms are, on the one hand, the various syntactic constraints on idioms, especially that of lexical replacement (cf. *the marvels of nature/the wonders of science* as against **sniff a rat*) and on the other, the special semantic features of many idioms, especially that of idiosyncratic form/meaning pairings, that is, the meaning imposed on an idiom is different from what its constituent words have in other contexts. Additionally, conventionality is also an important feature of idioms: idioms are *conventionalized* multiword expressions as opposed to *ad hoc*, flexible multiword ones such as those cited above. This raises the question of what conventionality means in relation to idioms.

2.6.2 Conventionality and currency

The conventionality of an idiom is related to its currency in the speech community and conventionality is, therefore, not a linguistic property in the way an idiom's lexicogrammatical and semantic features are; currency is a sociolinguistic feature aiding conventionality (Fernando and Flavell 1981). The currency of idioms varies. Two examples will make this clear. At one extreme is the 'private idiom' current maybe between just two people or within a family. Hockett (1958) cites the hypothetical example of a husband with a limited colour vocabulary who incorrectly identifies the colour of his wife's blouse of an indeterminate blue-green shade as blue. 'That's a nice shade of blue' is thereafter used as an 'idiom' by the wife to signify her husband's ignorance of colour terminology. At the other extreme is the 'public idiom' which appears even in general dictionaries and so could be regarded as belonging to the core vocabulary of the language: *crack down, put in for, play it by ear, fall short, smell a rat,* etc. (*The Penguin English Dictionary* 1979). The core vocabulary is relatively free of contextual restrictions and so has great freedom of occurrence in discourse, both spoken and written. It is neutral (Carter 1987) in its privilege of occurrence in terms of register.

In between these two extremes of 'private' and 'public' idioms, we have idioms of varying degrees of currency depending on who uses them and where. These restricted idioms are usually associated with specialist areas of discourse and constitute part of the jargon of various activities (registers): *black box, soft/hardware, hard copy,* and *data base* will immediately be recognized by those who are computer literate as belonging to that technology; *pseudo-cleft sentence, transformational generative, affix-hopping,* etc. by the initiated as belonging to linguistics. Restricted idioms are just like other marked forms in the vocabulary, for example, nautical terminology: *port, starboard, fore and aft, knots,* etc. (Carter 1987).

Apart from the 'jargon' of different activities ranging from computer technology to navigation and the specialist terminologies of everyday activities such as cooking and gardening, there is also the vocabulary of 'anti-languages', the 'dialects' created by anti-social and non-conformist groups like drop-outs, criminals, political terrorists, etc. The following terms, though marked as belonging to an 'anti-language' and so opaque to the outsider, are commonplace to the Australian street-kids who use them: *roll a joint* 'steal sth from a shop'; *right off* 'muck around'; *B's and E's* 'break and enter'; *rack it* 'steal'; *throw ups* 'a quick graffiti drawing'; *a job* 'doing a break-and-enter'; *snowdrop* 'steal clothes off the line'; etc. (from a feature article on street-kids, Simpson and Lumby (1989: 81)).

All these words are non-core in relation to the total vocabulary of English. But to be non-core is precisely their function. Their opacity hives off the group that uses them by excluding the non-initiates, the outsiders. Such sub-vocabularies within a language exemplify idiom in the broader sense of the term: 'the variety of a language peculiar to a ... class of people' (*OED*, sense 1b), 'the language proper or peculiar to a people, or to a district, community or class' (Webster's *Third New International Dictionary* 1965). This sense of idiom is related to the sense in which it was presented earlier, 'the genius of any language; the manner or expression which is natural or peculiar to it' (*OED*, sense 2), in other words, its usage—the sense that will be illustrated in the discussion of verb formations, bracketing and deletion in English and German and English and Sinhala respectively (see sections 2.9 to 2.9.3). The idioms cited above are peculiar to a specific group and its culture, that of drop-outs, and therefore limited in their currency, though not 'private' in the way of 'family idioms' (see the reference to Hockett 1958, above). Though limited in their currency they are in use among a group or class of people and so have sociolinguistic viability.

2.6.3 Conventionality and frequency

The frequency of a word is an indicator of the extent of its currency. A multiword expression is conventional by virtue of not being a one-off form; it is used by the speech community in a specific form or within prescribed variations. The extent of its currency in these prescribed forms marks its vitality in the speech community, the fact that it is not obsolete. Frequency checks on idioms are now made relatively easy by the existence of computer corpora. Thus, the sequence *what I am, etc. saying* has a total of 708 occurrences in The Birmingham Collection of English Text of 20 million words at the time of consultation (1990), which as far as multiword expressions go is a relatively substantial figure. *Not to worry* has 5 occurrences in the same corpus. However, frequency is not a necessary criterion for inclusion in idiom dictionaries: *not to worry* is listed in the *Oxford Dictionary of Current Idiomatic English* (1983) but not *what I am, etc. saying*, though it appears to be more frequent. The variability of the pronoun in this expression is not an issue as the *Oxford Dictionary of Current Idiomatic English* (1983) lists many expressions which contain variable elements, for example, *what could be more natural/reasonable, etc. (than sth)*. Both expressions contain variables, both are literal and both have anaphoric reference to a preceding statement. As already observed, the recognition of multiword sequences as being idioms or not is, especially in borderline cases, a matter of theoretical orientation. No problems arise with pure idioms like *smell a rat, spill the beans, kick the bucket, red herring, make off with*, etc. No idiomatologist would exclude such expressions from an idiom dictionary, even though relatively infrequent: *smell a rat* has one occurrence in the BCET, yet it is listed both in the *Oxford Dictionary of Current Idiomatic English* and in *The Penguin English Dictionary*. *What I am, etc. saying* is listed in neither. What such an omission indicates is that selection is an arbitrary matter when it comes to certain classes of expression like connectives and discourse formulae, admitted to the domain of idioms only relatively recently, largely as a result of collocation-oriented dictionaries (Cowie *et al.* 1983, etc.), collections for second language learners (Peaty 1983; McLay 1987, etc.), studies in English language teaching (Alexander 1984), and advances in idiomatology (Makkai 1972; Pawley 1986, etc.). Such works provide a rationale for going beyond traditional idioms (e.g. *smell a rat, curry favour, red herring*, etc.) and accepting a wide range of multiword expressions (e.g. *not to worry, first and foremost*) as also being idioms as they show some or all of the characteristics of the 'traditional' ones.

2.7 Categorizing idioms

2.7.1 Lexicogrammatical categorizations

Scalar categorizations, other than the one given in Table 2.1, are possible and many such exist, each reflecting the theoretical bias of their creators. Fraser's scalar categorization (1970) reflects a transformational orientation and Makkai's (1972) which is non-scalar, a stratificational one. Cowie *et al.* (1983) offer a scalar categorization showing the influence of general linguistics, but one which has no specific theoretical bias. These have already been looked at in Chapter 1.

The lexicogrammatical categorizations presented in this section show no specific model-orientation using as they do the kinds of descriptive categories found in general linguistic theory as exemplified in the work of Cowie *et al.* (1983) and those concepts in Makkai's work (1972) that are not special to the stratificational model. Alexander (1984) offers a categorization overlapping with

Makkai's in some respects but taking in an even greater range of multiword or 'fixed expressions' as he terms them. Being orientated towards English language teaching, his categories range from idioms (binomials, compounds, full and semi-idioms) through proverbs, stock phrases, allusions, quotations, and idiomatic similes to various types of discoursal expressions (social formulae, connectives, conversational gambits, stylistic formulae, and stereotypes).

The summary of fixed expressions presented by Carter (1987: 63–4), given below in a modified form, covers a multitude of multiword expressions, some of which have been cited in the preceding discussion. His three scales exemplify the three features most frequently invoked in identifying multiword expressions as idioms in this chapter:

1 Collocational restriction:
   a. unrestricted, e.g. *run a business*;
   b. semi-restricted, e.g. *harbour doubt/grudges/uncertainty/ suspicion*;
   c. familiar, e.g. *lukewarm reception*;
   d. restricted, e.g. *pitch black*.

2 Lexicogrammatical structure:
   a. flexible, e.g. *break sb's heart*;
   b. regular with certain constraints, e.g. *smell a rat*;
   c. irregular, e.g. *the more the merrier*.

3 Semantic opacity:
   a. transparent, e.g. *long time no see*;
   b. semi-idioms, e.g. *a fat salary*;
   c. semi-transparent , e.g. *a watched pot never boils*;
   d. opaque   (i) overt, e.g. *OK*;
           (ii) covert, e.g. *kick the bucket*.

The categorization I give below focuses on a feature that has received special attention in earlier discussion (see sections 2.3 to 2.3.2): the impossibility or possibility of lexical replacement in multiword expressions. Lexical invariance or variance more than any other lexicogrammatical feature strengthens or weakens the status of multiword expressions as idioms, yet has never been fully exemplified in a scale before:

Degrees of lexical variance in pure idioms, semi-idioms, literal idioms and collocations (restricted and unrestricted)

1   Invariant and non-literal:
spill the beans, smell a rat, say no more, you're telling me, on the one hand ... on the other, etc.

2   Invariant and literal:
nothing loath, fancy free, be that as it may, upside down, inside out, etc.

3   Invariant and both literal and non-literal:
roll out the red carpet, do a U-turn, a fat cat, kick off, the tip of the iceberg, at the same time, etc.

4   Variant and non-literal:
rain/pour cats and dogs, a lot of water has flowed/passed/gone under/run under the bridge, pitch black/dark, etc.

5   Variant and both literal and non-literal:
a dog's breakfast/dinner, a lone wolf/bird, the loose ends/threads, I'll/you'll/she'll, etc. live/survive, etc.

6   Invariant with a specialized subsense in one item:
catch one's breath, *drop* names, *foot* the bill, *move* house, *short* list, a *white* lie, *fat* chance you've got, etc.

7   Variant (restricted) with a specialized subsense in one item:
keep one's cool/temper, a *thumbnail* portrait/sketch, *explode* a myth/belief/theory/notion/idea, a *blue* film/gag/joke/story/comedian, *thin/flimsy* excuse, etc.

8   Invariant and literal with specialized connotations:
hammer and sickle; the simple life; poor little rich girl; an only child; try, try and try again; first and foremost; last but not least; a good question; arm in arm; on foot; by hand; OHMS; VIP; etc.

9   Variant (restricted) and literal:
a crash course/programme, dodge/duck the issue, one's pet hate/aversion, prove one's case/point, for certain/sure, do the necessary/needful, to be exact/precise, etc.

10 Collocations: restricted and literal:
addled eggs/brains, a gust of wind/emotion, shrug one's shoulders, stark naked, etc.

11 Unrestricted with a specialized subsense:
catch a bus/tram/train/ferry/plane/boat, etc., *run* a business/
company/firm/shop/theatre, etc.

12 Unrestricted and literal:
weak/strong/black/white/sweet/bitter/Turkish, etc. coffee, etc.

2.7.2 Functional categorizations

Though the categorizations above are termed lexicogrammatical, they
contain functional categories as well. The inclusion of sememic idioms
(Makkai 1972) and discoursal expressions (Alexander 1984; Carter
1987) in idiom categorizations extends the scope of idiomatology
beyond a relatively narrow focus on lexicogrammatical classes (e.g.
compounds, phrasal verbs, binomials, 'tournures', and collocations) to
functional types (e.g. proverbs, allusions, quotations, greetings, farewells, and other sorts of discoursal expressions). Such an extension
paves the way for a comprehensive study of what speakers do with
idioms in discourse. Identifying the specific uses of idioms also reveals
their more general role as conventional, familiar ways of saying: idioms
are not one-offs as their recurrence in the same type of context shows.

The functional categorization based on Halliday (1985) given
below is intended only as a pointer to the chapters on the uses of
idioms that follow, and, consequently, is concerned only with
common domains and features of usage. It is not intended to be
exhaustive in its sub-categorizations. (See Chapters 3 to 5 for many
of these idioms in their source texts.)

Ideational or 'the state and way of the world' idioms

Ideational idioms either signify *message content*, experiential
phenomena including the sensory, the affective, and the evaluative,
or they characterize the *nature of the message*, for example, as being
specific or non-specific.

Message content

1 **Actions:** tear down, mess about with, do a U-turn, twist sb's arm,
   spill the beans, wear different hats, give sb an inch (and he'll take
   a mile, etc.), wave/offer/hold out the olive branch, etc.

2 **Events:** turning point, the straw that breaks the camel's back, out
   of the mouth of babes, have blood on one's hands, etc.

3 **Situations:** be in Queer Street, be in a pickle, be up a gum tree, etc.

4 **People and things:** a back-seat driver, a man about town, a scarlet woman, a fat cat, a red herring, a lounge lizard, etc.

5 **Attributes:** cut-and-dried, matter-of-fact, lily-white, as green as grass, from A to Z, etc.

6 **Evaluations:** turn back the clock; it is a pity; matter-of-fact; cut-and-dried; lily-livered; beauty is/lies in the eye of the beholder; waste not, want not; a watched pot never boils; if you can't stand the heat get out of the kitchen; a Trojan horse; I am not my brother's keeper; etc.

7 **Emotions:** green with envy, have one's heart in one's mouth, a lump in one's throat, lose one's heart, for one's blood to boil, walk on air, down in the dumps, tear one's hair, etc.

Characterizing the message

1 **Specific information:** to be exact/precise, for example, that is, the question is, what I am saying is, my guess is, I felt like saying, etc.

2 **Non-specific information:** kind of/sort of, or something, such and such, and so on, etcetera, etcetera, blah blah blah, etc.

Interpersonal idioms

Interpersonal idioms fulfil either an interactional function or they characterize the nature of the message. In their interpersonal function they initiate, maintain, and close an exchange and are closely associated with politeness routines. In such roles these idioms exemplify the mores of social interactions. They can also exemplify the operation of some of the maxims of Grice's Co-operative Principle: sincerity, newsworthiness, and brevity, which characterize the nature of the message.

Interactional strategies

1 **Greetings and farewells:** good morning, how are you?, see you later, bye for now, etc.

2 **Directives:** let's face it, tell you what, say no more, believe you me, not to worry/don't worry, never mind, do you mind, etc.

3 **Agreement:** that's true, you're telling me, say no more, (that's) a good question, etc.

4 **'Feelers', eliciting opinions:** what do you think?, how do you feel?, etc.

5 **Rejections:** you're kidding/joking, come off it, tell it to the Marines, I wasn't born yesterday, etc.

Characterizing the message

1 **Newsworthiness:** guess what; what do you know; what, you ask?; etc.

2 **Sincerity:** quite seriously, believe you me, as a matter of fact, etc.

3 **Calls for brevity:** cut the cackle, get to the point, etc.

4 **Uncertainty:** I daresay, mind you, etc.

Relational idioms
Relational or textual idioms ensure the cohesion, and can therefore aid the coherence of discourse. They can accordingly be grouped along with conjunctions, for example, *and, but, or, and so, because, if ... then*, etc., as having a textual function. They may be categorized into those which integrate information and those which sequence information (Pawley and Syder 1983):

Integrative

1 **Adversative:** on the contrary, far from, etc.

2 **Comparison:** on the one hand ... on the other, etc.

3 **Causal:** so that when, the more X ... the more Y, no wonder, etc.

4 **Concessive:** at the same time, etc.

5 **Addition:** in addition to, what is more, etc. (the last item also clinches an argument)

Sequencing or chaining information
Sequencing meta-discoursal information, e.g. in the first place, last but not least, etc.
Sequencing temporal information, e.g. one day, a long time ago, up to now, etc.

2.8 Conclusions on idioms

The distinctive feature of idioms is that though they are multiword expressions, they are also lexicalized: they have the semantic unity of single words but the grammatical flexibility, though in varying degrees, of phrases, semi-clauses, and clauses, which indeed the majority are. Hence, they need to be described by means of the descriptive procedures common to both the grammar and the vocabulary. The transformational changes that can be rung on idioms reveal their lexicogrammatical nature, and additionally, their amenability to the communicative needs of the language-user (see sections 2.2 to 2.3.6). Their semantic unity and the corollary of such unity, non-literalness, and opacity (see sections 2.5 to 2.5.3) also serve the communicative needs of the language-user by adding to the synonymic resources of the language forms which are connotatively different and whose composite nature makes them specially suited to different forms of word play. They serve, accordingly, both the conventional and the novel purposes of the language-user. Their conventional uses, however, dominate over their novel ones. Conventional forms are easier to use for communicating concisely, intelligibly, and fluently with the minimum effort.

Sections 2.3 to 2.7.2 deal with those features that characterize idioms or lexicalized multiword expressions and the categorizations of such expressions. The sections that follow deal with English idioms from another perspective, related to but not identical with what has preceded.

2.9 Idiomatic usage: an exercise in comparative usage

2.9.1 Introduction

Does a language favour specific types of multiword expressions (verb + particle(s), reduplications, etc.) and specific types of syntactic processes (degrees of bracketing, deletion, etc.)? Most languages do, and it is these preferred combinations and processes which bestow on it its 'specific character, property or genius' (*OED* 1989, sense 2 of *idiom*, see section 1.3). What is prominent in one or more languages may be absent in others: verb + particle(s) combinations, though not identical in their constituents, are prominent in German and English, two close kin, but not in Sinhala, a language of Sri Lanka, also a member of the Indo-European family. Consideration of idioms as exemplifying the specific character or usage of the language they occur in allows us to go beyond multiword expressions to consider various syntactic processes relevant to idiomaticity but different from the transformations discussed above in connection with the variability of idioms. In other words, the sections that follow deal with aspects of acceptable usage in terms of the norms of a language or of a language variety.

2.9.2 English verb formations and bracketing in relation to German

To see the vocabulary as being composed of two types of items, content and structural, is a traditional distinction and still a useful one. These two types combine in various ways. The focus in the following sections is on verb (content) + adverb/prepositional particle (structural) combinations where such particles occur singly in combination with verbs (run + away), in doubles make + off + with) or as heads of prepositional phrases (*turn on one's heel/on one's opponents*) (Witton 1979).

The following text fragments give some idea of the range of uses the ubiquitous particle is put to in English and German:

(37) So if you are *interested in leaving* your worldly troubles aside for a couple of hours a week, if you like to enjoy yourself whilst *mixing with* a great group of people, and if you can (or would like to) sing soprano, alto, tenor or bass, then why not *come along to* a rehearsal and *join in*!
      (Sirius, Summer, 1990: 5)

(38) a. *ablehnen* [refuse]
          Nujoma *lehnte* das *ab*.
          [Nujoma refused that.]

      b. *einstellen* [stop]
          Gorbatschow: Sowjetunion *stellt* Uran-Produktion *für* militärische Zweke *ein*.
          [Gorbachev: The Soviet Union suspends uranium production for military purposes.]

      c. *zunehmen* [increase, grow]
          Unterdessen *nimmt in* Windhoek der Besucherreigen *von* Politikern *aus* der Bundesrepublik Deutschland *zu*.
          [Meanwhile the flood in Windhoek of politicians from the German Federal Republic is increasing.]
          (Frankfurter Allgemeine 4 August 1989: 1–2)

In view of the emphasis placed on the regular co-occurrences of words and the resulting multiword units in English in the earlier

discussion of idiomaticity, the emphasis in these sections will like-
wise be on similar patternings but an emphasis intended to highlight
the different usage of English and German in a specific area.

The strongest co-occurrence patterns between verb and particle
emerge in those cases where a particle or a phrase headed by a particle is structurally obligatory to complete the verb when it is used to
specify particular meanings:

(39) Jack *stepped aside/back*, etc. to let Jill pass. [I]
      (moved out of the way)

is the acceptable form, whereas **Jack stepped to let Jill pass* is
ungrammatical. Other English verb + particle combinations of this
sort are *stride over/across/along*, etc., *sally forth/out, believe in sth,
think of sth, plod along, plod away at sth*, etc. More complex examples of such obligatory complements are provided by verbs such as
keep 'store' and *put/place* 'set down', which require adverbial locative phrases as complements:

(40) a. Jill *keeps* her jewellery *in the drawer*. [I]
      b. **Jill keeps her jewellery. [I]
      c. Jack put/placed the books *on the table*. [I]
      d. **Jack put/placed the books. [I]

German also requires that similar verbs need to be complemented by
an appropriate particle or noun phrase:

(41) a. Lwow *liegt am Ende der Welt.*
          [Lwow is situated at the end of the world.]
          (*Frankfurter Allgemeine* 4 August 1989)
      b. Er *schritt durch* die Halle. [I]
          [He strode through the hall.]
      c. George Bush *glaubt an* Gott. [I]
          [George Bush believes in God.]
      d. Gretel *bewahrt* die Dokumente *an der Schublade auf*. [I]
          [Gretel put the documents in the drawer.]
      e. *Treten* Sie *beiseite*! [I]
          [(You) Step aside!]

While *treten beiseite* and *auf bewahren* structurally parallel *step
aside* (verb + adverb particle) as conventionalized units, *liegen, schre-*

iten, and *glauben* parallel the English *keep*, *place*, and *put* in requiring an adverbial complement of an acceptable sort, but are not in themselves conventionalized units. For example, in English, as with the German equivalent, *believe* can take a range of noun phrases apart from *in God: in peace/war/in religion/in preserving the environment*, etc. These are *ad hoc* constructions. Other parallel German verbs of this sort are *nachdenken über* 'think/ponder about sth', *vorbereiten auf* 'prepare for sth', 'get ready for', or 'train for sth', etc.

Co-occurrence patterns are potentially weaker where there is a possibility of structurally optional elements as in cases where the use of particles with verbs is optional. In these cases, the language-user can choose whether or not to use an adverbial adjunct to elaborate on the circumstances (direction, place, manner, etc.) in which an event takes place:

(42) a. Why not come (along) (to a rehearsal).
          (*Sirius*, Summer 1990: 5)

      b. Jill went (away/off). [I]

      c. We joined the two ends (together). [I]

      d. They had to queue (up). [I]

Parallel constructions in German are:

(43) a. George ging (weg/fort). [I]
          [George went (away/forth).]

      b. Hans saß (auf der Mauer). [I]
          [Hans sat (on the wall).]

In each of these sentences the particle or particle-headed phrase adds either emphasis (go *away/off*) or precision to the event (*join together, on the wall*) by defining or delimiting, but its presence or absence does not affect the grammaticality of the sentence.

In the following texts, the presence or absence of a particle or particle-headed phrase creates a difference in meaning and therefore different contextual conditions of use. When present, such elements are a means of vocabulary building:

(44) a. Georgy Porgy *ran*. 'move swiftly over the ground using one's feet alternately.

78

    b.   When the boys came out to play
         Georgy Porgy *ran away*. 'flee'
         (An English nursery rhyme)

    c.   The little dog laughed to see such sport
         And the dish *ran away with* the spoon. 'elope'
         (An English nursery rhyme)

(45) a.   Why not come along to the rehearsal and *join us*? 'meet up with' [I]

     b.   Why not come along to a rehearsal and *join in*? 'participate'
         (Sirius, Summer 1990: 5)

(46) a.   Oil and water don't *mix*. 'combine' [I]

     b   .... if you like to enjoy yourself whilst *mixing with* a great group of people ... 'interact socially'
         (Sirius, Summer 1990: 5)

(47) a.   Leave your bags here. 'put' [I]

     b.   If you are interested in leaving your worldly troubles aside ... 'stop thinking about' (Sirius, Summer 1990: 5)

The change of meaning occasioned by the presence or absence of a particle in these examples is also one of literal vs. non-literal meaning but a non-literal meaning does not necessarily follow from the addition of a particle: *queue/queue up, seek/seek for,* etc. remain literal regardless of the presence or absence of the particle.

    The examples from (42) to (47) show verb + particle constructions that use particles in both their adverb and preposition functions, e.g. *aside* (39) and *away* (42b.) are adverbs, while *with* in *with a great group of people* (37) and *ran away with* (44b.) is a preposition. In English, whether a particle functions as an adverb or a preposition is not a decisive factor in determining the semantics of verb + particle constructions. Thus, *they went into the tunnel, they went into the problem,* and *they went into politics* have identical constructions (verb + prepositional particle + noun phrase), but the relationship of the verb to the following preposition-headed phrase is nevertheless quite different and results in different meanings in each case: *go into the tunnel* 'enter'; *go into the problem* 'investigate'; *go into politics* 'adopt as a career'. In these three instances, the differences in meaning result from the noun phrases that habitually co-occur with *go* + *into* + (Noun Phrase): a locative (*the tunnel*) gives the meaning 'enter', nouns which imply reasoning (*problem/issue/evidence/pros and cons*, etc.) give the meaning 'investigate', and institutionalized activities (*the Civil Service/Army/Navy/politics*, etc.) give the meaning 'adopt as a career'. Such co-occurrences are predictable and are a manifestation of idiomaticity.

German too shows a similar constructional design in the matter of vocabulary building by means of particles, but the semantic subtleties of German co-occurrence relationships will not be taken up here:

(48) a. *blasen* [blow]
Jurgen *blies* die Trompete. [I]
[Jurgen blew the trumpet.]

   b. *abblasen* [off-blow, call off]
Jurgen *blies* das Projekt *ab*. [I]
[Jurgen called the project off.]

(49) a. *bringen* [bring]
Hans *brachte* die Zeitung. [I]
[Hans brought the newspaper.]

   b. *umbringen* [kill, bump off]
Al Capone *brachte* viele Menschen um. [I]
[Al Capone bumped off many people.]

(50) a. *kommen* [come]
Hans *kam* gestern nach Hause. [I]
[Hans came home yesterday.]

   b. *ankommen* [come to, arrive]
Gretel *kommt* morgen *an*. [I]
[Gretel is arriving tomorrow.]

   c. *auf* etwas *ankommen* [depend on sth]
Es *kommt auf* das Wetter *an*. [I]
[It depends on the weather.]

All German particles are formally categorized in virtually every grammar as separable (see (38a.–c.) or as both separable and inseparable (Law 1964; van der Helder and McGlashan 1970). In relation to English this distinction may be more usefully restated as a similarity, on the one hand, between German adverb particles which can be prefixed to verbs (*um*gehen, *wieder*holen, *über*setzen, etc.) and English prefixed ones (*over*take, *under*go, *out*do, etc.); and on the other, between those formations in which English and German adverb particles follow the verb, when this is possible, generally with a change of meaning:

(51) a. *overtake* 'to pass another (vehicle, etc.)'
          The car *overtook* the bus on the highway. [I]

      b. *take over* (from) 'assume direction or control'
          John Smith & Company *took over* the business. [I]

(52) a. *umgehen* [go around]
          Er *umging* die Vorschriften. [I]
          [He circumvented (went around) the regulations.]

      b. Das Gerucht *ging um*. [I]
          [The rumour was going around.]

Comparison between verbs such as *overtake* and *take over* draws attention to the different degrees of productivity of these two verb types in English. The verb + particle construction type (*take over*, etc.) is much more productive than the particle + verb construction one (*overtake*, etc.). In other words, the adverb particles (*up*, *over*, *down*, etc.) producing phrasal verbs in English (*take up*, *take over*, *take down*, etc.) give a far higher yield than those producing prefixed verbs as a scan of any dictionary will show. Moderately productive prefixed particles are *fore-*, contracted from *before*: *fore-cast*, *-see*, *-stall*, *-tell*, etc. *For* is even less productive: *forbear*, *-bid*, *-give*, *-judge*, etc. More prolific are *over* as in *overawe*, *-come*, *-draw*, *-dress*, *-flow*, *-hang*, *-pay*, *-populate*, *-react*, *-sleep*, *-trade*, etc.; *under* as in *underachieve*, *-buy*, *-cut*, *-develop*, *-pay*, *-rate*, etc; *out* as in *outclass*, *-do*, *-date*, *-law*, *-run*, *-sell*, etc. The dominant type of formation in English is verb + particle(s) (see example (37). Further evidence for this dominance is provided by the presence of dictionaries devoted entirely to verb + particle(s) constructions, as for example, the *Oxford Dictionary of Current Idiomatic English* (1975) is. No equivalent work exists for the particle + verb type of formation.

So far, the emphasis has been on the similarities between complex verb formations in English and German. Predictably, various differences exist in this aspect of the two languages. The German examples (49 and 50) exemplify how the addition of a particle (adverb) or particles (adverb + preposition) result in the creation of different words as in the case of English, e.g. *run/run away/run away with*. But it cannot be assumed that the correspondence carries over to the particularities of word formation, that is, the elements that compose these verb + particle constructions are often different in the two languages. While *hinausgehen* in *Er ging hinaus* 'He went outside' and *ausgehen* in *Er ging aus* 'He went out', with the implication of going out socially, are lexicogrammatically parallel to the corresponding English utterances (*go outside* and *go out*); *durchfallen* 'fail'; *abblasen* 'call off'; *umbringen* 'kill', 'bump off'; and *auf etwas enkommen* 'to depend on sth' are not. Even when the elements in the verb + particle are similar in form, their meanings are not. Thus, the English verb + particle construction *fall through* is paralleled by the German *durchfallen* 'throughfall', but their different meanings appear in their different collocates: *durchfallen* 'fail' (*an exam*) and *fall through* 'fail', 'come to nothing' (*plans, negotiations,* etc.). The German equivalent of the English *fall through* in its figurative sense is *fehlschlagen* 'come to nothing', not *durchfallen*. Other differences exist in the complex verb constructions of the two languages. Thus, though both English and German verb constructions are complex, one element (e.g. *call off, abblasen* 'offblow') or both (e.g. *bump off, umbringen* 'roundbring') can be different.

The feature that provides the most interesting basis for comparison in the syntax associated with complex formations made up of verbs and particles in English and German is bracketing. In English, bracketing is achieved in verb + particle constructions by optional particle movement round a nominal direct object and its appendages, e.g. *So if you are interested in leaving (your worldly troubles) aside*, (*Sirius* 1990) vs. *leaving aside your worldly troubles*. Where the particle is obligatorily separated from the verb (*pull sb up* 'reprimand'; *pull sth apart* 'dismember'; *show sb in* 'usher'; etc.) bracketing is usual (cf. the unidiomatic **She pulled up Jack*). However, these divorced particles are united with their verb partners in passive constructions: *Jack was pulled up* 'reprimanded' *by Jill*. The majority of verb + particle constructions in English permit particle movement. In German, particle movement is permitted with 'separable' verbs with the particle, the non-finite element, moving to the end of a clause. The result in both languages is a bracket comprising a finite verb and a non-finite particle: *leaving* (...) *aside* (47b.), *lehnte* (...) *ab, stellt* (...) *ein* (38a. and b.).

While both English and German have bracketing, what the bracket can encompass differs quite strikingly in the two languages. In English, the verb (...) particle bracket favours one-unit interpolations, typically a short noun phrase or a pronoun (in which latter case, bracketing is obligatory):

(53) a. The girl *knocked* twenty-five pence *off* because it was shop-soiled.
      (*The Oxford Dictionary of Current Idiomatic English*, Vol. 1 1975)

     b. They kept saying over and over again, "We're going to *blow* you up."
      (*The Sydney Morning Herald* 14 September 1976: 4)

Longer stretches of material result in the particle remaining with its verb partner as the preferred option even though bracketing effected by moving the particle round the direct object and its 'appendages' is usually not ungrammatical. Such potential bracketings may, however, strike the language-user as unwieldy:

(53) c. Milorad Brabic in a statement from the dock, said he had only tried to break up the fight between his father and Mr Christian.
      (*break* the fight up; ? *break* the fight between his father and Mr Christian *up*)
      (*The Sydney Morning Herald* 20 August 1976: 1)

     d. The Marine Operations Centre in Canberra *called off* a sea and air search last night for a Sydney fisherman missing at sea since last Thursday.
      (*called* a sea and air search *off*)
      (*The Sydney Morning Herald* 9 August 1976: 12)

     e. ... tonight he will *kick off* the toughest game of his life.
      (*kick the toughest game of his life *off*)
      (*The Sydney Morning Herald* 9 August 1976: 51)

The following example, however, demonstrates a pattern in which the object, even when consisting of a single noun, is obligatorily placed after the particle. If a pronoun can be substituted (and in this case it cannot), the pronoun precedes the particle (see Cowie *et al.* 1975: 1i).

> f. In November he will take up residence in one of London's most delightful inner suburbs ...
> (**take* residence *up*)
> (*The Sydney Morning Herald* 9 September 1976: 7)

The structural design of German does not inhibit large bracketings as a result of verb and particle separation. On the contrary, such bracketings are common and constitute a sufficiently distinctive feature of German idiom to be the butt of the humorist:

> The German has another kind of parenthesis, which they make up by splitting the verb in two and putting half of it at the beginning of an exciting chapter and the other half at the end of it.
> (Mark Twain, *The Awful German Language*, p.356)

The bracketings in German range from a single element such as in the already quoted (38a.) *Nujoma lehnte (das) ab* to the longer (38c.), repeated as (54a.), and others that are even more complex:

(54) a. *zunehmen* [increase]
      Unterdessen *nimmt* (in Windhuk der Besucherreigen von Politikern aus der Bundesrepublik Deutschland) *zu*.
      [Meanwhile the flood in Windhoek of politicians from the German Federal Republic is increasing.]

   b. *herstellen* [reinstate]
      Mit ihrer Anordnung *stellten* (die Alliierten für ihre früheren Kriegsalliierten dann das Prinzip der Freizügigkeit in Groß-Berlin wieder) *her*.
      [With their regulation the allies reinstated the principle of freedom for their former war allies in Greater Berlin.]
      (Both texts come from *Frankfurter Allgemeine* 4 August 1989: 2)

The comparison of English and German presented above, even though confined to selected features, serves to highlight the common design features of the two languages, but at the same time shows the differences that have resulted over time despite their common origin.

Complex verb constructions with particles exist in both languages but differ not only in their individual composition but also in the way the information in the clause is distributed within the bracket formed by the separation of verb and particle.

2.9.3 Sinhala: verb formations and deletion in relation to English

Sinhala, the major language of Sri Lanka, is a descendant of Sanskrit and so by virtue of belonging to the Indo-European language family becomes a distant cousin of both English and German. There are no phrasal verbs in Sinhala and in this respect it is closer to French and Spanish where verb + adverbial particle combinations are rare (Spanish) or virtually non-existent (French). However, Sinhala has productive complex verb formations made up of noun + verb or verb stem + verb combinations.

English has a number of high frequency verbs (*make, go, catch*, etc.) which pattern with nouns. The resulting combinations yield semi-literal phrases: *make war/peace/love/a fuss*, etc.; *go mad/nuts/ bonkers/crackers/berserk*, etc.; *catch fever/measles*, etc., which have the status of conventional collocations. This lexicogrammatical pattern is a very productive one in English. Sinhala, too, has broadly similar constructions containing high frequency verbs, but the Sinhala sets are different in morphological composition: noun/nominal stem or verb stem + verb. As in English, these constructions group themselves into sets containing a common verb. One such set (noun + verb) is shown below, some of the items being literal and the others figurative:

[hulɑːŋ]	(wind)		'blow'
[ɑːdə]	(sound)	[gɑːhɑːnəvɑː]	'call'
[kelə]	(spit))	(strike)	'spit'
[poðə]	(drops)		'drizzle'
[pɑːssə]	(back)		'retreat', 'reverse' (of car)
[muːnə]	(face), etc.		'encounter'

A similar pattern but consisting of a verb stem + a full verb gives two sets of contrasting verb contructions. The contrast hinges on two different full verbs: verb stem + /gɑːnnəvɑː/ meaning 'do sth for oneself' and verb stem + /denəvɑː/ meaning 'do sth for another' (MacDougal and de Abrew 1979):

[hɑːfɑː]	(make)	
[kɑːpɑː]	(cut)	
[hojɑː]	(search)	[gɑːnnəvɑː] → 'do sth for oneself'
[ujɑː]	(cook)	or
[liɑː]	(write)	[ðenəvɑː] → 'do sth for another'
[hoːðɑː]	(wash)	

A distinction between 'self-service' and service to others, culturally more salient than in English, is given lexicogrammatical encoding in these contrasting full verb forms.

Deletion (ellipsis) is a widespread transformational practice across languages and within them. However, languages differ in the elements that can be acceptably deleted and in the conditions which make such a process acceptable. English, for example, permits deletion of all but the item(s) giving the desired information in linked adjacency pairs (e.g. question and answer or request and response):

(55) a. What's Mum doing?
       (She's) Cooking. [I]
      b. Don't forget to post my letter.
       (You're) Not to worry. (I) Shall do (it). [I]

Not to worry and *Shall do* are customary forms and have the status of conventionalized multiword expressions in English. However, such deletions of the subject and the auxiliary verb as are evident in (56a. and b.) would not normally be acceptable in a 'free' declarative clause (e.g. *Don't assume I won't write, I will*) or in a negative question form (e.g. *Don't you want a drink?*), where deletion would obscure or change the meaning, though it is possible in a non-negative question (e.g. *(Would you) Like a drink?*).

A parallel usage exists in Sinhala: in fact, the deleted form is the more idiomatic one and consequently is the commoner, especially in a question sequence such as the equivalent of the English:

(56) A: amma: koheðdə? [I]
         Mum   where Q marker
      B: kussije
         (She's) in (the) kitchen.

      A: ujənəva: ðə   huŋga:k vela: ðə
          cooking   Q   long   time   Q
                     marker   marker

In English, stating the subject of the clause is not unidiomatic in the answers to a series of questions, though the option of deletion is there, whereas in Sinhala the repeated statement of the subject in such a question series would be grammatical but unidiomatic. The effect in Sinhala would be similar to repeating an identical subject in a series of co-ordinated declaratives in English:

(57)   I went to the bank and then *I went* to the shops and then *I went* to the Homer's for coffee and cake. [I]

Unlike in English, deletion would also be possible in negative Sinhala questions:

(58)   a.   (Do)n't (you have) the book? [I]
                      poθə   næððə
                      not Q.   marker
         b.   Give (me) the book. [I]
                      poθə   ðennə (give)

where in English the ellipsis of the object pronoun is both ungrammatical and unidiomatic.

The usage in the three languages looked at here with regard to complex verb constructions and selected syntactic processes, shows that while similarities exist at a certain level of generality, they diminish when it comes to particularities. The similarities are predictably much stronger between German and English than between English and Sinhala, especially in complex verb constructions. In the areas of bracketing and deletion English is moderate, whereas these processes assume a more extreme form in German (bracketing) and Sinhala (deletion).

The sections that follow continue the theme of idioms as exemplifying the character or usage of a given language. What is different is that the discussion focuses on English and two of its many regional varieties.

2.9.4 Lankan English

English was the official language of Sri Lanka from 1802 to 1956 and is still one of the languages of the Westernized upper and middle classes, apart from being a compulsory second language from Grade 3 upwards in secondary school. Consequently, though not a native language of Sri Lanka, it cannot be regarded as a foreign one either, the way French, Hindi, or Russian are. Hence the term *Lankan English* suggesting as it does a distinctive local variety.

The character of Lankan English is partly the result of the influence of the vernaculars, Sinhala and Tamil, on the English of these two ethnic groups, partly that of innovation consistent with the English language system to meet the cultural needs of a non-British community in a non-British environment. The focus in the following discussion is on the English of the Sinhala majority, more specifically in sociolinguistic terms, the English-speaking mesolectal group of this community. Apart from pronunciation and a few minor lexicogrammatical 'deviations', the acrolectal group speaks Standard British English.

Deletion is common both in English and Sinhala but each has a different usage in this respect as already demonstrated (see section 2.9.3). Sinhala patterns of deletion are often carried over to the mesolectal group being discussed here and constitute one of the distinctive features of this middle variety of Lankan English as the following texts show:

(59)   **A:** Didn't you get yesterday's *Daily News*?
       B: *Got, got, got.* [A]

(60)   **A:** They distributed land among themselves.
       B: I deny that also.
       A: *You deny.* I will reveal how you distributed land among yourselves.
       B: I am awaiting your revelations.
       (The Sri Lankan *Hansard*, 19 May 1978: 466. Part of a Parliamentary debate.)

(61)   [a personal letter]
       One day he carried the armchair alone! Again did marketing and got hernia badly. So went to the surgeon. He luckily put it right and asked not to carry weights etc. If he is careful he can carry on. [A]

A holophrastic use of *got*, a single verb instead of *I've got it* appears in (59). Evident here is the influence of Sinhala, which allows a single verb to function as an independent declarative clause. Noteworthy too is the reduplication of a form, in this case *got*, a tendency

88

common in South Asian English (Kachru 1986). Deletion of the mandatory object in (60) *You deny ( )* is a very common type of deletion in Lankan English. Several subject deletions are shown in (61). In Standard English, subject deletions are permissible in co-ordinated clauses but not in independent ones constituting separate sentences. The latter type of deletion is possible in Sinhala.

Apart from differences in common syntactic processes putting their stamp on a language variety and so constituting part of its usage, there are also locutions peculiar to it. Preference is given in this discussion to conventionalized multiword expressions rather than single words. Such expressions may be grouped into those that enable the progression of a discourse (discourse formulae) and those that enable speakers to express their cultural semiotic. Some of these are new inventions (e.g. *rice-puller* meaning 'sth leading to several helpings of rice'); others are existing English expressions used in new senses (e.g. *it seems* meaning 'so they say' as in *Mohan got a very big dowry, it seems* (Kandiah 1985)).

Discourse formulae:
So how (how)? (greeting); *I'll go and come* (farewell); *I say* 'You there!' (i.e. a form of address); *What do you think?* (a signal that something surprising is to follow, cf. the British *What do you know*); *(You) just wait and see* (a prognosis); *Who and who* as in *Who and who were at the meeting?* (a request for more detail, Kandiah 1985); *Whose who* (is she?) (a request for details of family background), etc.

Descriptive terms:
Food: stringhoppers, egg hoppers, oil cakes, cadjunuts (cashews), ladies fingers (okra), drumsticks (an appropriately shaped vegetable), country rice, del chips, jak fruit, bread fruit, etc.

Customs and beliefs:
sb's good/bad time (astrologically auspicious or inauspicious); devil-dancer (local exorcist); devil-dancing ceremony (exorcism ceremony); light-reader (one who locates missing objects, or objects intended to cast spells by looking into an oil lamp); cousin-brother/sister, etc. The last item reflects the close kinship ties between an individual and the children of his/her parents' siblings: cousins, too, are regarded as virtual siblings.

What gives Lankan English its distinctive character is not so much a special vocabulary, but rather the way in which speakers choose to use the English language: words are selected and then combined often, though not always, in ways which while consistent with English grammar are not entirely consistent with the usage of its native forms, whether these forms are British or other varieties of Anglo-Celtic English. Thus, *You deny* (60), with its deleted direct object is paralleled by an explicitly stated object where an implicit one is more idiomatic in Standard English:

The driver drove the bus fast.
(Sri Lankan *Hansard*, 22 August 1977: 469)

Examples (59) and (61), discussed above, show other common features of Lankan usage: reduplication as in *got, got, got* and subject deletion as in so *( ) went to the surgeon*.

2.9.5 Australian English

While there is a range of opinions on the Australianness of Australian English, it is now generally accepted that an Australian variety does exist, especially since this variety has been codified in two dictionaries: *The Macquarie Dictionary* (1981) and the *Australian National Dictionary* (1988). Such works show the functional elaboration Australian English has undergone in the last two hundred years as a result of moving 'from an European-centred to an Australian-centred way of looking at the world' (Clark 1981: 11). The uniqueness of this shift in perspective is of course relative only to the European ethos, the dominant influence throughout the nineteenth century in political, social, and cultural life; the difference between the Aboriginal and the white Australian world-view is still considerable. As far as language goes, now at the end of the twentieth century with more than 200 years of 'transplantation' behind it, Australian English is sufficiently different from other Anglo-Celtic varieties to justify separate study. But different in what way? As Australian English is a native variety of English, unlike the non-native Lankan English, it does not reflect the influence of an indigenous language in its syntax. The 'Australianness' of Australian English comes from a distinctive pronunciation and a vocabulary which in certain domains (e.g. flora and fauna) has terms non-existent in other Englishes. Some of these words are adaptations of

Aboriginal ones: *kangaroo*, *koala*, *mulga* (wattle), *coolabah* (a species of native tree), etc. As far as the processes of word composition go, there are no differences of a significant sort between Australian and other Anglo-Celtic forms of English. Both single and multiword expressions are coined in ways which are consistent with the structural design or idiom of English. But though there are no qualitative differences in word-formation, the high productivity of one type of word-forming process over others could lead to quantitative differences in the output of specific types of word coinage in this variety of English in relation to others.

The most striking example of such a process in Australian English is the predominance of diminutive forms ending in *-ie*, *-o*, or *-y*, e.g. *girl/girlie*, *boy/boyo*, *duck/ducky*, etc. Since forming diminutive words from original root forms is so common in Australian English, many polysyllabic words are subject to this process. What happens in such cases is the truncation of such a word, typically down to the first syllable, followed by the addition of a diminutive suffix, the most popular being either *-ie* or *-o*, e.g. *mosquito* → *mozzie*, *afternoon* → *arvo*, etc. Some text examples follow:

(62) [noticeboard]
      There will be a lunch-hour meeting for the *lingoes* [linguists].
      Bring your *sannies* [sandwiches] and come along. [A]

(63) ... keep away from the mad opening parade of the 1988
      Spoleto Fringe Festival on *Saturday arvo* August 27.
      (*The Australian* 13 August 1988: 13)

(64) Music for an *aggro* [aggressive] culture
      (*The Sydney Morning Herald* 16 July 1988: 75)

Other common examples of this type of lexical derivation are: *wino* 'alcoholic'; *metho* 'methylated spirits'; *journo* 'journalist'; *commo* 'communist'; *smoko* 'a break from work for smoking and refreshment'; *coldie* 'cold beer'; *sickie* 'sick leave'; *postie* 'postman'; *blowie* 'a blowfly'; *drummetie* 'chicken drumstick'; etc.

From a stylistic point of view these diminutives signify informality and intimacy. They appear most frequently in casual conversation, in the personal columns and feature articles of newspapers, and in the dialogue of fiction and drama.

The vocabulary has already been identified as being the source of

Australian English idiom in the lexicogrammatical domain. In a short study such as this, the flavour of those parts of the vocabulary special to Australian English can best be captured by looking at multiword expressions using words such as *bush*, *kangaroo*, or *gum* (eucalypt) specially important in signifying the Australian ambience. Australian idiom in this sense is not 'peculiar' by virtue of its structural composition but by virtue of conveying a different cultural semiotic.

Bush is a common word in general English denoting a leafy shrub. While retaining this meaning, Australian English invests *bush* with additional meanings giving it a different connotational and collocational range. The senses of *bush* most relevant to the Australian context, both taken from *The Macquarie Dictionary* (1981), are:

5. Geo. a stretch of land covered with bushy vegetation and trees.
6. the countryside in general, as opposed to the towns.

As far as colloquial usage goes, it is 6 that is most relevant to the life and thought of the Australian for most of Australia is bush (Fernando 1985), though it is also one of the most urbanized countries in the world with the cities containing much of its population. One reason why the bush occupies the place it does in the Australian vocabulary, and by implication in the Australian consciousness, is that it is different from anything in the homeland (Britain) of the colonizers. Life in the bush today is not what it was in the nineteenth century, but the bush still imposes a life of considerable isolation devoid of the commercial and recreational amenities of urban life and a sense of vast empty spaces, the ambience of which has been captured by many Australian writers from Henry Lawson and Joseph Furphy in the nineteenth century to Patrick White in the twentieth. Most importantly, perhaps, the bush for white Australians is associated with the Aboriginal tribes and their hunter-gatherer lifestyle.

The following multiword expressions give some idea of the white Australian lifestyle associated with the *outback*, a synonym for *bush* in sense 6:

bushman 'a pioneer; a dweller in the bush'; *bush breakfast* 'a rough improvized breakfast partaken of while camping in the bush; *bush shower* 'a canvas bag to hold water, fitted with a shower nozzle, and rope for attaching it to a tree'; *bush brother* 'a person belonging to one of the Church of England brotherhoods which minister to people in the outback'; *bush band* 'a band which performs Australian folk music, usually with such instruments as the accordion, tea-chest bass, guitar, etc.; *bushmanship* 'the ability to fend for oneself in rough country'; *go bush* 'to turn one's back on civilization'.

The kangaroo is the marsupial with the strongest eco-cultural significance for Australians and also the most prolific of bush marsupials. Predictably, there are a number of multiword expressions with *kangaroo* as the headword:

kangaroo bar 'metal bar in front of vehicle as a protection against kangaroos' (cf. *cowcatcher*); *kangaroo drive* 'a kangaroo shoot, usu. at night by spotlight'; *kangaroo fence* 'a high fence to keep kangaroos out'; *kangaroo paw* 'a flower shaped like a kangaroo's paw'; *kangaroo route* 'Qantas air-route between Sydney and London, a long hop'. Other expressions with *kangaroo* are *kangaroo apple*, *-dog*, *-grass*, *-rat*, *-thorn*, etc.

If the kangaroo is the most ubiquitous member of the native fauna, the gum tree is the most ubiquitous in the domain of the flora. Consequently, the vocabulary has a number of terms for the various varieties of eucalypt that cover the countryside as well as grow in urbanized areas: *bloodwood, white-, paperbark-, blue-, ghost-, river red gum*, etc.

In addition to coinages such as those cited above, there are hundreds of others. Some of these are associated with place-names or famous people: *MacDonnell Ranges cycad, Moreton Bay fig, Port Lincoln ringneck* (a species of parrot), *Sturt's desert pea* (a flower), etc. Other expressions can be grouped into occupational registers such as sheep shearing to which *shed boss, bossaroo, drafting yards, sweatwet*, etc. belong (Gunn 1989), as well as recreational registers such as Australian Rules, surfing, Citizen's Band Radio, and so on.

The text which concludes this brief discussion of Australian English usage illustrates, as in the case of the Lankan English ones, the special flavour of Australian English. However, unlike the Lankan English texts, example (65) relies for its effect on descriptive vocabulary items seeking to evoke by this means the Australian ambience with its own special ethos and spirit of place:

(65)   There were three phases in my life you see—that of being the *wild colonial lair* up to the age of 31 ... I knew all through Western Australia *Black Velvet* was the thing ... *Stockmen* used to get out for a *"gin spree"* ... said I'm the biggest *gin-rooter* around the country myself.
('The Last Words of Xavier Herbert', *National Times* January 1985)

2.9.6 Conclusions

The foregoing discussion has been concerned with *idiom* in the sense of locutions that reflect the special cut, the different structural design of various languages (English, German, and Sinhala) and varieties of the same language (English in this case) which have developed differently either due to the influence of an indigenous language as in the case of Lankan English, or isolation from the parent language as in the case of Australian English, and which therefore show various peculiarities of usage. Usage in different languages also exemplifies how various communities of speakers have drawn in different ways on lexicogrammar, a universal property of language, so that their use of language shows, despite universally-shared features, a distinctive, though conventionalized, structural organization of elements: different kinds of complex verb formations and differences in the utilization of syntactic processes such as bracketing, deletion, and reduplication.

2.10 General conclusions: conventionalized ways of saying

Sinclair (1987) identifies two principles at work in the language: the first is the open-choice principle, which works on the assumption that language-users have a relatively free choice in composing phrases and sentences where words are concerned, constrained only by grammaticality. In other words, they are relatively individualistic in how they choose to say something.

The second priniciple, the idiom principle, works on the assumption that language-users have available to them, 'a large number of semi-preconstructed phrases that constitute single choices, even though they might appear to be analysable into segments' (ibid.).

The idiom principle referred to above is realized not only in wholly or partly 'pre-constructed phrases' of various types (*idiom*, sense 3a *OED* 1989), but also in various types of permutations peculiar to a language (*idiom*, sense 2, *OED* 1989). Conventionalized ways of saying cover multiword expressions, both idioms and habitual collocations, as well as types of idiomatic usage, those discussed in this chapter being the conventions governing bracketing and deletion phenomena arising from the structural design of English. Such idiomatic usage is simultaneously expressive of novelty in that the text fragments subjected to the processes of bracketing and deletion discussed above (sections 2.9.2 to 2.9.3) are usually *ad hoc* constructions; and of conventionality in that the constraints on bracketing and deletion show the limits of what language-users can do.

These claims can be verified by looking at stretches of discourse. While the working of the open-choice or *ad hoc* principle is borne out by the fact that few sentences are identical in such discoursal stretches (see the large number of texts cited in this chapter), the working of the idiom principle is seen in the frequency with which conventionalized multiword expressions (idioms) and various habitual collocations recur in these discourses. Normal, unmarked discourse is a mixture of the novel and the conventional, the *ad hoc* and the prefabricated produced in conformity with idiomatic usage.

Most scholars (Smith 1925; Partridge 1935; Katz and Postal 1963; Healey 1968; Fraser 1970; Makkai 1972; Strassler 1982; etc.) accept the *Oxford English Dictionary* definition of an idiom (sense 3a) in one form or another. This definition will be offered here as the classic one, not only because it is the most popular, but also because it is the one which captures the greatest variety of expressions, pure, semi-idioms, and literal idioms, habitual restricted and unrestricted collocations, all having more or less claim to exemplify idiomaticity:

A form of expression, grammatical construction, phrase, etc., peculiar to a language; a peculiarity of phraseology approved by the usage of the language, and often having a significance other than its grammatical or logical one.

What is the *raison d'être* of these peculiarities of phraseology or idioms? What can they do to serve the communicative purposes of language-users more effectively than other language elements? What idioms and their close kin, habitual collocations, do and how they do it will be the subject of the next four chapters.

3
Ideational idiomatic expressions: images of the world

The Mind, that Ocean where each kind
Does straight its own resemblance find;
Yet it creates, transcending these,
Far other Worlds, and other Seas;
(Andrew Marvell 'The Garden')

The great cliché of classicism is that imitation is the surest way to
fruitful achievement. It needs to be distinguished from straight
copying (plagiarism), in that it stresses selection and rearrange-
ment: inventive imitation.
(Walter Redfern, *Clichés and Coinages* 1989)

3.1 Vocabulary as an analogue of the world and its ways

3.1.1 Introduction

In the last chapter, two fundamental principles were seen to govern
the choice of vocabulary:

1   The open-choice principle governing the *ad hoc* lexical composi-
    tion of phrases and sentences.
2   The idiom principle governing the use of ready-made multiword
    expressions, that is, conventionalized ways of saying.

The aim of this chapter is to look at the function of what I am calling ideational idioms (see section 2.7.2). *Ideational* is the term used
by Halliday (1973, 1985) to designate the macro-function of
language realized through the clause and concerned with articulating
the speaker's or writer's experience of the world: participants,
actions, and processes, the attributes of the participants and the

circumstances associated with actions and processes, that is, transitivity. Typically, ideational idioms are realized by units smaller than the clause, units that are nominals (e.g. *backseat driver*, a semi-idiom), verbals (e.g. *make off with, smell a rat*, pure idioms), adjectivals (e.g. *tall, dark and handsome*, a literal idiom), and adverbials (e.g. *in hot water*, a pure idiom). These units function as parts of clauses. Ideational idioms can also be clauses themselves: *barking dogs seldom bite, her head rules her heart* (pure idioms), etc. The functional range of ideational idioms ensures their ubiquity in a text; they have the potential of appearing anywhere and everywhere. For example:

(1) For Gorbachev, Yeltsin was a convenient *red rag* (nominal, subject complement) to wave at the *hardliners* (nominal, in an adverbial phrase). Gorbachev would *give an inch*, Yeltsin would *take a mile* (verbal) and Gorbachev would claw back, secretly glad of the excuse to yield 100 yards.
     But it was Yeltsin, with his bluff, charismatic demagoguery, who *stole the people's hearts* (verbal). Gorbachev had become *the darling* (nominal, subject complement) of the liberals from East Berlin to West Side Manhattan but at home he was the man who had *failed to deliver* (the goods) (verbal).
     (Reprinted from *The Times* in *The Australian* 21 December 1991: 23)

Whether idioms or not, all content words (nouns, verbs, adjectives, and adverbs) have a referential function with regard to the world out there, a feature allowing speakers to produce one-word utterances or minimal phrases strung together and still achieve some intelligibility as in the early stages of first or second language acquisition:

(2) [speaker A is the course convenor; speaker B is an English language learner]
     A: What about your family?
     B: My daughter ... er in Australia ... wedding reception ... wedding ... understand wedding ... [A]

Even when listed in a dictionary or presented as citation items, words can still function as packages of information. Presented with a list such as *unicorn, eat, woman, shoe*, and *apple*, it is possible for speakers to bypass grammar and in a cognitive flash construct a meaning such as '*woman eat apple*' without actually verbalizing it in that way, excluding *unicorn* and *shoe* as edible objects because of their knowledge of the world.

If the vocabulary is a resource for talking about the world and life, real, possible, and hypothetical, what sorts of information do words convey? What does the vocabulary enable the language-user to do in contradistinction to the grammar? As Jespersen (1975) argues, grammar is allied to logic in its emphasis on structural relationships between words, relationships set up by linear groupings such as, for example, the subject–object one in *Jack killed the giant* or by the active into the passive transformation: *Jack killed the giant → The giant was killed by Jack*. Such relationships are a fact of grammar, and, consequently, exist independently of the real world out there. By contrast, the vocabulary denotes segments of experience relating to the world mediated, of course, by both collective and individual perceptions. The way in which the world is perceived and organized in the mind is very complex and seldom, if at all, precise or accurate (ibid.: 54). One of the reasons for such imprecision is that while the world offers us only 'concretissma', the specific with all the uniqueness of the fingerprint, language presents us with averages (ibid.: 63). Averages are convenient. Distinguishing between fingerprints is a necessity in criminology, but having a separate name for every fingerprint in existence is not a necessity in language. This is another way of saying that words are coined only to meet our needs.

I have already noted that one way of looking at words is to see them as packages of information. However, this information is not always packaged in the same way. In terms of form, a major difference, the one which is the focus of this study, is that between single and lexicalized multiword expressions (idioms). There are also differences in the kind of information that comprises the package. While the functions of single words and idioms are broadly the same, there are points of difference which may partly account for why idioms of the ideational sort exist. Such differences appear in the characterization of words as information packages below:

1 The general and the specific: whereas single words are either general (*creatures*), or specific (*hero*, *heroine*), ideational idioms, like *backseat driver*, etc., are typically specific, though some exceptions, *blah blah blah*, for example, exist.

2   Non-concrete phenomena are not accessible to the senses, the concrete are. Single words, whether referentially concrete or not, may or may not be imagist (*quibble*, non-concrete, non-imagist; *cat*, concrete, imagist). Ideational idioms are typically imagist whatever their referential denotation in the world out there may be: *split hairs* (non-concrete, imagist); *fat cat* (concrete, imagist); *show a clean pair of heels* (concrete, imagist).

3   The literal and the non-literal: whereas single words can be literal (*cat* 'feline') or non-literal (*cat* 'malicious woman'), though literal ideational idioms exist, those looked at here are mainly non-literal, e.g. *split hairs* 'quibble', *show a clean pair of heels* 'run away', *for sth to make one's blood boil* 'make angry' or semi-literal, e.g. *fail to deliver the goods* 'fail to fulfil expectations'.

Points 2 and 3 above overlap since the concrete imagery of ideational idioms contributes strongly to their being fully or partly non-literal.

4   The neutral and the attitudinal: single words as citation items can be neutral (*phenomenon, organism*) or they can be attitudinal (*evil, angelic*). Ideational idioms are typically attitudinal and evaluative. A proverb like *waste not, want not* even as a citation item conveys an evaluation. Evaluations can change, of course, depending on the context they are used in.

The characterization offered in points 1 to 4 profiles ideational idioms as being typically specific and impressionistic in their delineation of the world, typically non-literal, and typically evaluative.

The conventionalized nature of idioms was emphasized in the last chapter. But it must be equally emphasized that conventionality does not mean that idioms are necessarily used in a formulaic or clichéd way. Formulaic idioms like *Good morning, merry Christmas and a happy New Year* are automatized and low in information value; the majority of ideational idioms, though not *ad hoc* themselves, are high in information value and, additionally, are incorporated into novel *ad hoc* constructions so countering the principle of least effort invoked as a corollary of conventionality in the last chapter. Least effort is present, but it arises only from the fact of idioms being prefabricated and, therefore, retrievable as wholes saving the speaker or writer the trouble of the necessary *ad hoc* composition above single-word level. Least effort does not apply to the use of idioms in *ad hoc* discourse. Such use requires as much skill as single words selected on the open-choice principle do. Skill here means the ability to use words in a context-sensitive way, a requirement calling for awareness of the informational complexities of idioms and of knowing their usual collocates in addition to having a 'feel' for the less usual ones which, despite being novel, reinforce the meaning of these idioms. Context-sensitivity also means knowing in which types of discourse it is most appropriate to use ideational idioms.

The kinds of discourse in which ideational idioms are likeliest to occur are informal speech, journalism, TV and radio broadcasts, the last three powerful vehicles of the newsworthy. They are used more sparingly in academic discourse, spoken and written. To find them, for example, in legal documents or administrative regulations would be decidedly unusual.

The discussion that follows aims to show the informational complexities of idioms, their relation to the culture of the speech community, and the rhetorical skill with which they are used in discourse.

3.1.2 Images of the world: generalities

In the real world there is only the concrete, the particular, and the idiosyncratic; vocabulary categorizes and in doing so picks on the shared, unifying features in its real-life referents in order to establish superordinate classes such as *phenomena, entities, creatures,* etc. and also their sub-classes of increasing particularity, for example, *animal, human, men, women, children,* etc. Words of this sort signifying as they do a certain level of generality, underspecify to borrow a term and concept from Cruse (1977). Showing an even greater degree of underspecification and so a higher level of generality are the already cited superordinates like *phenomena, entities,* and *creatures.* I have already claimed that ideational idioms are usually specific in their referential function. Even idioms which seem general, like *every man and his dog* 'everybody' and *every Tom, Dick, and Harry* 'average people', have bits of information in their semantic make-up which constrain that generality so that these idioms do not share the same referential scope that words like *humans* and *mankind* do. Terms that underspecify and those that overspecify are marked for contextual distribution. They are not terms of usual utility (Brown 1968: 88).

101

Every man and his dog is typically used to refer to a lot of people as in *I expect every man and his dog will be at Saturday's football match*. The key semantic component is numbers, not people meaning 'humans'. The antonymous idiom *two men and a dog* 'a few people' reinforces this observation. Also present in *every man and his dog* is the contextual meaning 'ordinary' or 'common people'. The semantic component signifying ordinary becomes explicit in examples like (3) where *every man* is turned into a compound:

(3)   EVERYMAN AND HIS DOG (headline)
They are the unsung, salt-of-the earth heroes of the outback ...
(*Good Weekend* 2 November 1991: 11)

Everyman, an idiom again, refers to the attribute of humanness, especially in its moral aspects. The merging of the two idioms into one in (3) foregrounds the natural, therefore, shared attributes of people as *homo sapiens*.

In fact, idioms signifying generalities refer not to humankind, but to persons who are ordinary or average by virtue of common, and hence, commonplace qualities, the opposite of the outstanding type denoted by *tall poppy* or *high flyer*.

(4)   [seminar discussion]
a.   The knee jerk reaction of people *the man in the street* is that migrants should learn English. [A]
b.   ... and this was not only the *man in the street* but also intellectuals. [A]
(*The Fatal Attraction*, BBC TV programme on Hitler)

Every Tom, Dick, and Harry also signifies 'average', but with the additional meaning of 'no special importance', whereas *the man in the street* signifies 'average with no special knowledge or skills relevant to the matter in hand'. *Every man Jack and every mother's son (of them) (of you)* are even more bounded, used as they are of a specific male group, *Jack* and *mother's son* being used for emphasis.

Contrasting with the idioms signifying the ordinary and the average populace is *(All) the world and his wife*. Though also seeming to signify 'everybody', it is the least general in this cline of relative generality: this idiom tends to refer to the social élite.

3.1.3 Images of the world: the vague

Different from the general, but allied to it by virtue of underspecification, is the vague, the imprecise (Channell 1994). Vague idioms permit the elimination of superfluous repetition as one of their functions:

(5) Yes a large number of antibiotics are known many of them from fungal sources like penicillin tetrocyclines *et cetera et cetera*. [BCET]

(6) There'd be shadows, the underside would be darker, the upper side lighter *and so on*. [BCET]

Vague idioms also allow for the imprecision that arises from lack of specific knowledge, or that which comes from memory lapses:

(7) I think she had a nervous breakdown or *something like that*. [BCET]

(8) ... But this is something I've always just said remember we did this and remember we did that and mummy and daddy so *such and such* and does daddy do that ... as if you were my cousin *or something*. [BCET]

(9) ... for instance I was at a reading of poems I forget who it was *the other day* and it went on ... I had to walk out. [BCET]

Where the information is non-significant in itself, the vague idiom is designed to be a filler, as in (10), or it is used to refer to the approximate time where this is permissible, as it is in (11):

(10) ... and er they couldn't have been more helpful *blah blah blah* you know and I really thought after reading that ... a free lunch. [BCET]

(11) ... anyway never mind. If we can have another ten minutes *or so* that would be very helpful. [BCET]

What examples (5) to (11) show is that specific information is sometimes not available and not even always essential. The language caters for this by providing the speakers and writers with conventionalized expressions for being imprecise and vague when these speech attributes are permissible and even unavoidable, as in a casual conversation. Yet in most of the texts cited above, the general reference is clear. In (5), we know that *et cetera et cetera* refers to other types of 'fungal sources', in (7) that *something like that* restricts reference to only disorders of the nervous system. The tolerance for vagueness and imprecision has its limits: the collocates associated with idioms expressive of these qualities set the bounds.

3.1.4 Images of the world: specificities

The discussion and examples in section 3.1.2 show that even idioms with seeming general reference have restrictive components of meaning which reduce that generality in comparison with the all-encompassing reference of *phenomena, entities,* and *creatures* or the somewhat less encompassing *humans* and *people.* Thus, *man in the street,* though like *mankind* also includes women, refers only to men and women of average ability, while *every man Jack* is restricted only to men. Cruse (1977) has shown that generalizing words, for example, *animal,* underspecify in order to have as wide an application as possible in terms of animates that are non-human. *Dog* is the commonest name for canines and so categorizes on the level of usual utility being unmarked and neutral. Overspecification individualizes as *spaniel* and *terrier* do, restricting contextual distribution as a result. The generic *dogs* in *I dislike dogs* means 'all dogs'. This is different from *I dislike terriers* where the reference is only to a specific breed. Idiomatically, unless there is a special reason for doing so, it is better to choose *dog* in a statement like *Jack ran over a dog* than the more specific *spaniel.* The individualizing, overspecifying class of expressions is the focus of the discussion below.

Just as there are varying degrees of generality, there are also varying degrees of specificity: *man* and *woman* are more specific than *human,* and *man* or *woman of the world* more specific than *man* or *woman. John Kennedy was a charismatic man of the world* is even more specific by virtue of its unique referent, *John Kennedy,* and the information-adding *charismatic.* The commonest way of increasing the specificity of a word is to modify it either adjectivally or adverbially. *House,* which like *dog,* is a word of usual utility can be individualized by adding an adjective, each adding a new bit of information as in a *red-brick, four bedroomed house.* This is an *ad hoc* way of specifying. A *man of the world* 'sb with a wide experience and tolerance of life, especially that of high society' on the other hand, is inherently specific in the way single words like *spaniel*, a sub-class of *dog*, and *cottage*, a sub-class of *building*, are only more strongly so. In other words, this idiom, like all non-vague ideational idioms, overspecifies as the gloss shows. What such ideational idioms generally do is to sub-categorize a more general category: *human* can be categorized as *men* and *women*, but then there are many kinds of men and women. Whether such types are lexicalized depends on how culturally salient they are.

In most societies, men play a more active role in public and social affairs than women do. In English, this fact of life is reflected in the number of idioms sub-categorizing men into various types identifiable in the culture: *man of his word, man of letters, man of straw, man of the world, man about town, ladies' man, lounge lizard*, etc. Even idioms referring to the same domain, fashionable life, for instance, yield increasingly specific references:

man of the world	see gloss above
man about town	'a man associated with city life, esp. that of fashionable society'
lounge lizard	'a man who partners women, esp. older women for payment at fashionable social occasions'

A *man of the world* includes *a man about town*, but the latter does not include all the qualities of the former. Something of the flavour of 'the experiential gestalt', a term borrowed from Lakoff and Johnson (1980: 117), associated with these terms and the types of men they denote appears in (12), though this example refers specifically to *man about town*:

(12)   Peter Jenson, Melbourne *man about town*: "Smoking cigars is like making love to a woman. If you feel like making love, you'll make love whenever you feel like it. You don't wait till it's dark."
(*Good Weekend* 1991)

The meaning component signifying 'gigolo' in *lounge lizard* separates it from the two other idioms relating to fashionable social life listed above.

While there are many idioms identifying male types in English, those for different types of women are relatively few as any idiom dictionary shows. Standard English *offers scarlet woman, sex kitten, blue stocking, poor little rich girl,* and others, on the whole, attitudinally unfavourable. One example of this bias is found in the significations and contrasting connotations of *blue stocking* 'a scholarly unwomanly female' and *man of letters* 'a literary man whose work is likely to be of lasting worth'. If the woman scholar connotes plod and propriety, her scarlet opposite suggests boudoir and bed:

(13)   The pictures *ELLE* took of me were pretty sexy ... You want me to be the *scarlet lady*? Here look at this ... I don't feel any different whether they say I'm a *scarlet woman* or if they say I'm nice and have good apple pie recipes.
(*ELLE* December 1991)

Better half 'one's husband or wife', also Standard English, is attitudinally favourable to both sexes as *a perfect angel* is. Terms that are or once were slang (*bit o' skirt/fluff, my old woman,* etc.) are, by and large, not flattering to women. Among the reasons given by Partridge (1935) for the use of slang are the desire to be witty, picturesque, earthy, stinging, euphemistic, or arcane. While terms of praise for women are not absent in Standard English or in slang, my overall impression is that the unfavourable predominates. A possible reason could be that witty, picturesque, or stinging terms are elicited more readily by the desire to satirize, debunk, or ridicule rather than to praise.

Sometimes a particular type of person may elicit frequent discoursal references for a variety of reasons, in which case we find the idiom repeatedly used and elaborated into a profile of the type in question. An example of an idiom treated in this way is *fat cat*:

(14)   a.   Greiner's Fat Cat Tax Lurk
Who are the *fat cats*? (headline)
The *fat cats* are senior public servants, members of the Senior Executive Service. They are now the highest paid public servants ... Massive fringe benefits tax lurks are also available for *fat cats*.
(*Wastewatch* 1991)

b.   ALP plans to tighten government *fat cats*' belts.
(*The Sydney Morning Herald* 13 May 1991: 5)

c. ACT's *fat cats* set to come a cropper
(*The Sydney Morning Herald* 4 March 1989: 35)

I have argued (section 3.1) that, though conventionalized, ideational idioms are complex packages of information, often used, particularly in journalism, in ways that foreground their meaning in elaborate and stylistically lively ways. In (14), *fat cat*, 'sb who enjoys a sinecure' is presented as (1) a public servant, (2) who enjoys undeserved financial benefits and seeks to increase them further (fat), (3) is a social parasite, and (4) therefore, is not likely to be tolerated. A real-life analogy underlies this idiom in all three texts: domestic cats are fed and so spared the labour of catching mice.

Idioms such as the ones looked at so far, do not have single-word equivalents. Their *ad hoc* paraphrasal equivalents are often long-winded. However, as idioms, their lexical format (multiword) and their semantic make-up, especially that of non-literal, pure idioms, enable a great deal of information to be nutshelled into small units like phrases and semi-clauses.

One such cluster of semi-clausal pure idioms falls within the semantic scope of the general terms *behave* and *behaviour*: *skate on thin ice, spill the beans, wear different hats*, etc. *Wear different hats* 'be able to function in many different roles' is particularly complex.

(15) a. Mr P. Johnson ... said Mr Hawke was having problems *wearing three different hats* ... Mr Hawke was *wearing* the *hats* of President of ACTU, President of the ALP and yet another *hat*, that of "getting off the hook," Mr Johnson told the 450 delegates.
(*The Australian* 14 June 1976: 2)

b. I've never known anyone to *wear quite as many hats* as Anna Rutherford, except perhaps Donald Horne. Some of them are quite large, all are rather stylish ... So much for the *Danish hat*.
(*The Australian* 29 April 1989: 8)

c. [lecturer talking to author]
I'll go now and liase with EAP *a change of hat*. [A]

Wear different hats takes many variations, always a sign that the user is confident the addressee(s) will know the original form from previous encounters. This idiom is always accompanied by collocates denoting the wearer of the hats, being a semi-clause, and so needing a subject. Additionally, the kind of hat is also specified though such elaboration is optional. In this respect, *wear different hats* resembles *turn back the clock*, which typically elicits a range of time adverbials (see examples 30a. to j. in Chapter 2).

Another source of the complexity of *wear different hats* is that it can be used to signify both favourable and unfavourable attitudes to the wearer. In terms of lexical networks, this idiom can be diagrammed as shown below.

wear different hats

Good	Bad
versatile	inexpert
skilful	bungling
adroit	have too many irons in the fire
resourceful	have one's fingers in too many pies
a man of many parts	etc.
etc.	

The examples cited above illustrate both these sorts of attitudes: (15a.) is unfavourable, (15b.) favourable; how (15c.) is interpreted depends on situational context (see section 3.4 for a more detailed discussion of attitudes).

Language-users are able to remember and connect repeated vocabulary items, single or multiword, in different discourses even though these may be separate in time and place (Hoey 1991: 153–4). *Wear different hats* tends to be associated with holders of public office and *fat cats* with public servants. Apart from helping the language-user to build up elaborate meaning profiles, repeated contextualization also leads to predictable collocates allied to such items.

3.1.5 Conclusions

All the examples discussed above make it clear that ideational idioms, barring the vague class, offer only overspecific ways of talking about the world. As such, they are not vocabulary items of maximal utility in the way *people, house, dog, move, say*, etc. are. While words of intermediate generality, such as those just cited are extremely useful because unmarked, relying only on such expressions yields basic English enabling language-users to get by but not much more. So why be parsimonious when the word-forming potential of a language offers such abundant mint? Obviously, the man in the street, every Tom, Dick, and Harry, Jane and Joe Bloggs know that word mintage is everybody's privilege carrying no penalty. And since the world in all its diversity demands impressionistic representation, they have availed themselves of that privilege.

3.2 Images of the world: the politics of Jane and Joe Bloggs

3.2.1 Introduction

In the foregoing discussion I focused on ideational idioms as carriers of the kind of information needed for an impressionistic delineation of the world. The discussion that follows aims to show how experiential gestalts, such as those presented above, are made more accessible in the concrete imagist format of these idioms.

I have argued that all ideational idioms refer to specificities, even those which appear to signify generalities. The idioms examined in the following sections are in the matter of specificity similar to those discussed in section 3.1.5, but they will be looked at from a different perspective: the concrete (e.g. *offer/wave/hold out the olive branch*, *red herring*) as against the non-concrete (*make peace, conciliatory overture, decoy, misleading diversions*, etc.). While the non-idioms are literal and abstract, the corresponding ideational idioms are non-literal and imagist.

The world is not apprehended as a jumble of sense impressions, but in terms of culture-specific meaning systems made explicit particularly in the content vocabulary of a language, each word signifying an experiential gestalt. The preferred format for such gestalts, if realized as ideational idioms, is an imagist one: life experiences conceptualized as the ordinary (*fat cat, pull up one's socks, tighten one's belt*), the unusual (*swan song, hen's teeth, eat crow, tear one's hair out*), and the fantastic (*blue moon, walk on air, eat one's heart out, fly off the handle, brainwash*).

In language, an image of the real world is only a representation, it is iconic. In other words, images in language are non-physical word-pictures, only denoting concrete entities. These entities are invoked not for themselves *per se*, but because they are appropriate vehicles for other messages. There are many ways in which an image x can be used for saying something else y, but the ones I am primarily concerned with in this chapter are the figurative images which both cue addressees to the non-literalness of ideational idioms and enable knowledgeable users, if they want to, to elaborate on the figurative features of the idiom in order to foreground the message in its propositional and evaluative aspects.

I am mainly concerned with the imagery of non-literal ideational idioms because imagery concretizes the abstract more graphically than that of semi-literal and literal idioms; however, the etymology of most abstract words shows that even such words originally had concrete referents as, for example, *spirit* 'breathing', 'breath' and the allied *inspire* 'breathe in/into', a meaning still retained by this word in its sense of 'inhale' 'breathe in'. To think, at least partly, in images appears to be natural. It is certainly widespread as a consideration of the idioms of other languages as far apart as English, Chinese, and Selepet, a Papua-New Guinean language, shows (see Fernando and Flavell 1981). A possible reason for the near-universal use of imagery is that it provides a way into an abstract, conceptual universe through images of the real physical one, associated as these are with real-life experienced through the senses.

Of course, as far as non-literal or semi-literal ideational idioms go, unlike in the case of live metaphors such as Marvell's *vegetable love* or Eliot's *Christ, the tiger*, the language-user can bypass the metaphor coffined in the idiom, going directly to the living signification. But the dead metaphors implicit in idioms can be and are revived. In such cases, if the addressees are unable to recognize these revitalizations, they could miss out on the elaboration of the idiom's meaning, despite such elaborations being part of the message being communicated. Generally, grasping only the stable basic meaning of words, whether idioms or non-idioms, is not enough. If language-users want advanced compositional and comprehension skills, they must acquire the ability to create and respond to variable context-specific meanings deriving from a number of factors, including the etymological origins of words.

The thesaurus-like grouping in Table 3.1 illustrates the way in which a concept like 'strategy' is represented in the imagist format of partly synonymous idioms. 'Strategy', usually glossed as ' a method of gaining advantage in or winning a game, contest, a battle of wits, etc.' is a very complex experiential gestalt comprising persons, places, actions, and things making it, relatively speaking, much more a culture-specific concept than 'sun' or 'moon'. 'Strategy', as a concept, originates in experience, but the various components of this experience are organized in the intellect. Consequently, a strategy in its entirety cannot be seen or touched though some of its components may be visible and tangible. It is this mixture which calls forth the imagist format not only of 'strategy' but of so many other concepts as well.

Some of the idioms in Table 3.1, *do a U-turn, play cat and mouse with, a wolf in sheep's clothing*, etc., could suggest the connection their literal counterparts have to their non-literal significations because they are more transparent than *red herring* and *the emperor's new clothes* in terms of the words making up each idiom. This makes it easier to work out their meaning on an analogical basis the way we do metaphors like *vegetable love*. However, whether the dead metaphors in ideational idioms are perceived or not is variable as I have argued in sections 2.5.2 and 2.5.3, when discussing the semantics of idioms. That such variability, at least in an explicit, overt form, is indeed the case will be clear from the examples featuring *red herring* and *the emperor's new clothes* that follow. Knowledge of the origin of these idioms informs their use by the writers of several of these examples: the dead metaphor is revived and the signification of the idiom elaborated upon, especially in the case of *red herring*. Those writers who have not done so may have not known the etymology of the idiom or they may have simply opted for the basic signification.

the emperor's new clothes

Strategy

a stick with which to beat sb	throw dust into sb's eyes
do a U-turn	pull the wool over sb's eyes
endgame	under false colours
give an inch, take a mile	play cat and mouse with
dangle a carrot before a donkey	a wolf in sheep's clothing
	trail a red herring

Table 3.1

All these terms signify different strategies and are, therefore, not synonymous, a feature which emerges in their contextual distribution and the different collocates accompanying them. For example, *seeing things that aren't there* (16a.) and *exposure of fraud* (16d.) are

111

predictable collocates of *the emperor's new clothes*, while *false trails* (18b.), *divert our attention* (19), and *plots, twists and anticlimaxes* (21a.) are similarly predictable for *red herring*. Apart from perhaps *exposure of fraud* (16d.) and *false trails* (18b.), which can be interchanged as collocates of *red herring*, no other collocate was found to be interchangeable for these two idioms in the corpus used for this study.

I have selected two idioms from Table 3.1 for detailed analysis (*the emperor's new clothes* and *red herring*) focusing on the following themes:

1   Idioms are conventionalized expressions, but their use is by no means clichéd. Their collocates foreground the meaning potential of idioms in slightly different ways, sometimes in ways that are obviously novel. Such idiosyncratic uses presume a knowledge of the idiom on the part of the addressee(s).

2   The more instances of an idiom's use the analyst looks at, the clearer are its informational components, its meaning and function, the greater its capacity for helping the language-user make sense of the world he/she inhabits.

3.2.2 The politics of the Bloggs: the emperor's new clothes

The emperor's new clothes means 'deluded by others', 'acceptance of what is false as true because of the opinion of influential others'. The source of this idiom is Hans Andersen's story of that name. There is also another related idiom with a complementary meaning 'undeceived' 'fraud exposed', originating in the remark of the undeluded child in the same story: *'But the emperor has nothing on at all!'* What the child's remark shows is that the emperor is really naked, not clothed in fine garments visible only to the wise as the two swindlers who dupe him have claimed. In form, *the emperor's new clothes* and its partner are two of the most variable idioms in English as examples (16 and (17) show.

The two idioms, though related, are not synonymous as each signifies a different perspective on the situation the idiom covers:

1   *The emperor's new clothes* and its variants denote the deluded emperor and his equally deluded followers and so signifies being duped: the emperor role.

112

2 *But the emperor has nothing on at all* and its variants denote the undeluded child and so signifies being unduped through the exposure of a fraud: the child role.

The examples that follow are arranged in order of decreasing explicitness in terms of the way this idiom is used, thus demonstrating how the form of an idiom and its collocates affect its interpretability and the overall semantic complexity of the text.

(16) a. But it's *the emperor's new clothes*—they're seeing things that aren't there.
(*The Australian Magazine* 4 August 1990: 35)

b. My favourite review this year was one by Salman Rushdie, characterizing this year's hardest novel, Umberto Eco's *Foucault's Pendulum*, as "babble and gobbledygook" ... Altogether there were too many words of praise this year, far too many *emperor's new clothes* and not enough straight talk.
(*The Australian* 30 December 1989: 7)

c. Lies, damned lies and lovely motherhood ... The bloke who made the *emperor's new clothes* told me so. What followed was a nightmare ...
(*The Sydney Morning Herald* 1 May 1989: 15)

d. Professor John Talent's exposure of fraud by the Indian paleontologist V. J. Gupta is the subject of a new video produced by Film Australia in association with Channel 4 called *The Professor's New Clothes*.
(*Macquarie University Staff News* 3 May 1991: 2)

e. *The Emperor has lots of new clothes* (headline)
(*The Sydney Morning Herald* 28 October 1989: 31)

Of these examples, (16a.) is the most explicit since the immediate collocate of the *emperor's new clothes*, a clause, is a virtual paraphrase of the idiom's meaning. Example (16b.) requires more interpretative effort in order for the idiom's meaning and semantic scope to be grasped. While *the emperor's new clothes* is cited in this example, the complementary idiom is only implied in 'babble and gobbledygook':

the emperor's new clothes
words of praise   the self-deluded critics
not enough straight talk

babble and gobbledygook

the emperor has nothing on at all   the undeluded Salman Rushdie
                                       (the child role)

Example (16c.) is even more demanding than (16b.) in the required reading effort since the reader needs to associate *lies, damned lies* with *the bloke who made the emperor's new clothes told me, so* as well as respond to the contrast between the collocates *lovely mother-hood*, that is, believing the *lies*, the emperor role, and *nightmare*, the confrontation with the truth, the child role. The semantic relationship of these two collocational sets needs to be recognized and their relationship seen, deceived, then undeceived, for the irony of this text to be grasped. The irony is an important part of the meaning.

Example (16d.) requires the reader to identify *The Professor's New Clothes* with (1) *the emperor's new clothes*, the usual form of this idiom, (2) the *Professor with Gupta*, and (3) the novel version of the idiom with the collocate *exposure of fraud*, which is its paraphrase.

Example (16e.) is a heading; readers have to deduce for themselves what the *new clothes*, that is, the deceptions are, by reading through the text. The idiom can be seen as a form of thematization in the Hallidayan sense: it signals the global topic of the text that follows and in this function cues the reader to what the text is about.

The examples presented in (17) below focus on the complementary version of *the emperor's new clothes*, the idiom meaning 'undeceived', 'fraud exposed', the child role.

(17)   a. The story, based on interviews in 15 countries, began with a bold declaration that India's political *emperors are wearing no clothes*.
           (Reprinted from *The Washington Post* in *The Sydney Morning Herald* 26 October 1991: 20)

       b. ... as the mighty of the land made their precipitate departure, word of what happened will have been flashed on the bush telegraph to every household in Moscow. *The emperors have been revealed without clothes*.
           (*The Independent* (England) 2 May 1990: 19)

> c. ... quite unintentionally, I provoked the Great Literary
>   Debate with a modest little column which asserted that
>   *the Emperor was scantily clad* ... . I admitted that I found
>   a number of the most revered Australian authors, in
>   particular Patrick White and Peter Carey, just about
>   unreadable ...
>   (*The Australian* 13 January 1990: 20)

Examples (17a. and b.) are slight variations of the original form of
this saying and in each case convey the meaning 'exposure of empty
claims', such claims being fraudulent. The readers are left to make
the necessary links between the idiom and its textual referents, that
is, what these claims are as expressed in the longer discourse from
which these extracts have been taken. Example (17c.) provides the
greatest variation of *But the emperor has nothing on at all/the
emperor is wearing no clothes*, etc. and is intended as an ironic
understatement. The reader must link *scantily clad* with the contrasting collocates *revered Australian authors* and *just about unreadable*.
It is this contrast which makes the use of this idiom appropriate in
this context.

Examples (16) and (17) substantiate the claims made at the beginning of this discussion: that an idiom's variations and its collocates
foreground its meaning potential as well as adding to the overall
meaning and point of the whole text.

I have claimed that strategy is an important mode of behaviour in
Anglo-Celtic culture, as indeed it is in a number of other cultures.
Section 3.2.3 looks at another sort of strategy similar *to the
emperor's new clothes* in that they both share the same generalized
semantic component: 'sth which draws attention away from the
truth', yet differ in particularities: different situational contexts and
different collocates. Such differences are indicators that there are
many sorts of strategy recognized in the culture: they represent an
elaboration of the superordinate concept of winning in a battle of
wits, a game, a contest, etc. and are examples of the experiential
complexities of real life.

3.2.3 The politics of the Bloggs: red herrings

Red herring(s) may be glossed as 'sth which is used to deliberately
draw attention away from the truth or from what is important in a

situation', 'decoy', 'misleading diversion'. The clearest exemplification of *red herring* in terms of its origin (pickled herrings were once used to throw hounds off the scent in a fox hunt) and its present signification appears in the following examples:

(18)   a.   ... it was Mr Whitlam's campaign strategy that led the party **baying after** the constitutional **red herring**, instead of concentrating on the real issue on which the people finally voted.
(*The Australian* 16 December 1975)

   b.   There will be many alarums and excursions in the campaign now beginning—*false trails* and *red herrings* ... .
(*The Australian* 5 November 1975)

   c.   [radio interview]
No, we're pursuing a silly *red herring ... red herrings* that the leader of the opposition has been *trailing across the road*. [A]

Despite this type of explicit contextualization, the significance of the imagery will be most obvious only to those initiates who already know the origin and the meaning of this idiom. To such readers the imagery that makes (18a.) into a political fox-hunt (*baying after*) will correspond to the bits of information in the etymology of this idiom; for the uninitiated these images will be only picturesque embellishments with *red herring* being interpreted in a relatively limited way. The use of *red herring* in (18b.) is a conventional one, but false trails will evoke the fox-hunt, as well as *pursue* and *trail across the road* in (18c.), though, again, only for the initiated.

The use of *red herring* in examples (19) to (21) represents a continuum from the unmarked usual form of this idiom to strongly marked novel forms.

(19)   *Red herrings* and the Iraki breakfast (headline)
But Mr Whitlam has to talk about these things—any *red herring* will do—because as he showed us last week, he is unwilling to talk about the Iraki breakfast—he has to divert our attention from the uncomfortable fact: the Iraki breakfast happened ... For however some sections of the Labour Party allow themselves to be hypnotised by Mr Whitlam's *red*

herrings the rest of the world still grasps the salient point of
the affair—the Iraki breakfast happened.
(*The Australian* 4 March 1976: 6)

The usual form accompanied by predictable collocates like *divert*
or sometimes idiosyncratic ones like *breakfast*, as in (19), can be
used to evoke the real fish and so activate semantically related
terms like *fishy* in the associative networks readers hold in their
memories. In fact, one of the main points the writer of (19) wants
to make is that the Iraki breakfast is *fishy* 'dubious', and he/she
does this by the repetition of *red herring* and *breakfast*, the repetition itself being hypnotic in its effect on the reader. What emerges
again is that idioms, though conventionalized, are seldom used in
simple ways; nor is reading itself always simple despite the use of
commonplace vocabulary. In examples such as (19) the need for
semantic connections, only implicit on the surface, to be made is
very evident: the word *fish* or *fishy* is never once mentioned in this
text.

The examples of *red herring* looked at in (18b.) and (19) are
unmarked as far as form goes. The addition of an adjectival modifying *red herring* as in (18a.), *constitutional red herring*, and in
(20) below, is more than simply an idiosyncratic collocate like
Mr *Whitlam's red herrings* (19): such modifiers add further bits
of information to the already overspecified idiom's meaning
potential.

(20) a. He criticizes Mr Williams ... for ignoring the existence of
migrant children in the schools, *the most vermillion of red
herrings*.
(*The Australian*, Letters to the editor September 1975)

  b. But for myself, I cannot help feeling that however genuine,
the shroud can tell us nothing we do not already know ...
it may even prove an *idolatrous red herring* across the
painful path of Christian living. [BCET]

  c. The jury foreman, Mr Ivan Gogler, also said the verdict
was wrong. He said Wides 'escaped being found guilty on
a *legalistic red herring*'.
(*The Australian* 15 April 1989: 6)

117

A welter of red herrings referring to a particularly complicated whodunnit by the presenter of a television film (8 July 1977) is novel in the same way as *a shoal of red herrings* used to describe a similar film (*TV Guide* 1 January 1979) is.

The modified uses of *red herring* represent an elaboration of the signification of this idiom indicative of various additional context-specific meanings, the two most prominent in my corpus being (1) emphasis: *the most vermillion, a welter of, a shoal of*, all premodifying *red herrings*. (2) the nature of the *red herring*, the specification of domain: *constitutional, idolatrous*, and *legalistic*. Noteworthy, too, is how often the real fish (*vermillion*) and its original use in fox-hunts (*send the party baying, false trails, across the path of*, etc.) is invoked.

Even more marked than the modified *red herring* is *red herring* minus *red* or minus *herring*:

(21) a. *Herrings* supreme (headline)
There are enough *red herrings*, plots, twists and anti-climaxes in the first two hours of this drama to keep the keenest mind guessing.
(*TV Guide* 11–17 September 1978: 1)

  b. A seemingly solid case mounts against Wallace as the narrative darts like a fish through flash backs and time shifts. *Herrings, reddish* abound ... . The scent of doubt (or is it *herring*?) is pervasive in a classic piece of work.
(*TV Guide* 13–19 January 1992)

  c. Sir, Usually, I like *herrings*. This time I have to toss the *red one* fished up by Mr Patrick White olim Paddy back into the Skagarrack.
(*The Sydney Morning Herald*, Letters to the editor 25 May 1978: 6)

Red herring in the altered forms above gives us the most innovative use of this idiom. Discarding *red*, for instance, seems to free the language-user to vivify the dormant literal counterpart of *red herring* (the fish). However, these innovations are not without their point: they bring various evaluative meanings to the text ranging from ambivalent approval (21a. and b.) to contempt (21c.). Additionally, and more importantly they foreground the meaning of *red herring* as a misleading diversion by referring, albeit indirectly, to the original use of *red herring* as a diversion in fox-hunts. Example (21c.), on the other hand, locates the idiom in an idiosyncratic figurative context: angling.

3.2.4 Conclusions

Though idioms are often classed with clichés, because of their conventionality, such a classification is not altogether accurate. The idiom principle conventionalizes, but conventionality appears to challenge language-users, at least the more resourceful ones, to take liberties with established forms like idioms, confident that such variations will not prevent them from being understood. Those who take liberties with idioms appear to do so with a purpose: the variation is intended to add context-specific meanings to the idiom via elaboration of its signification by extending its literal image, as well as to foreground its usual meaning.

Apart from the issue of how individual idioms are used is that of idiom groupings. What is the significance of semantically related groupings such as that exemplified by 'strategy' (see Figure 3.1)? Idiom clusters such as this one indicate culturally significant meaning systems in the imagist mode. In the world of the speech community that produced the examples cited above, particular sorts of strategy are important for achieving one's ends. *The emperor's new clothes* and *red herring*, together with other idioms in the same cluster, denote forms of strategy intended to promote one's own interests, save face, and so on, indicating that such modes of behaviour are common, and even valid. What is of interest to the linguist is the number of idioms along with single words (*ploy, rort, lurk, misrepresent, fudge, delude*, etc.) that exist in English to signify the many forms strategy takes. Language has been seen as an analogue of reality, or alternately, to open a window onto the world. Only the examination of a range of examples, such as those presented above, can validate these claims.

3.3 Images of the world: inside Jane and Joe Bloggs

3.3.1 Introduction

In the foregoing discussion, I argued that the relative abstractness of a concept like 'strategy' is concretized in its many forms by being presented via scenarios with actors, actions, goals, and outcomes such as a deluded emperor who believes he is clothed when actually he is naked, and a fish used as a decoy in a fox-hunt. Such idioms are figurative: no emperor or red herring exists. These idioms are figurative without being metaphors, though being imagist they show one of the features of metaphor. The question that now arises is, what is metaphor?

The best starting point for a discussion of metaphor is by way of an example:

(22) a. If music be the food of love, play on;
          Give me excess of it, that, surfeiting,
          The appetite may sicken, and so die.
          (Shakespeare, *Twelfth Night* I.i.)

     b. The path of true love never runs smooth.
         (A proverb)

In both these examples, one *ad hoc* (22a.), the other an idiom (22b.), the ideas being conveyed are 'Love is an affliction' and 'Love is a journey' respectively. Decoding both texts is a process of 'understanding and experiencing one thing in terms of another' (Lakoff and Johnson 1980: 5). Lakoff and Johnson argue that 'our ordinary conceptual system, in terms of which we both think and act, is fundamentally metaphorical in nature' (ibid.: 3) and extrapolate from this claim to the further one that the way humans think is largely metaphorical. Ideational idioms add to the validation of this claim. Both *the emperor's new clothes* and its variants, and *red herring* and its variants, were probably once metaphorical in the broad sense explicated above: understanding and communicating one thing in terms of another. However, they are not now live metaphors, which lend themselves, because of their deep semantics, to being predicated in an x is y format where x is redefined in terms of y as with 'love is an affliction' and 'love is a journey'. Love is a complex experiential gestalt and so has a cluster of different metaphors standing for its different aspects, apart from those in (22) sometimes even contradicting other characteristics associated with the same emotion. Such clusters are useful for precisely this reason: established expressions like idioms allow the complexity of emotional experience to be conveyed in metaphorical language readily available to the user and readily accessed by the addressee.

The concern of section 3.3, as the heading indicates, is with internal states: emotion, cognition, and their conceptualization in language. One striking feature of emotional experiential gestalts like, for example, 'love' in contrast to those like 'strategy' is that a specific aspect of love can generate clusters of related metaphors: 'love is madness' is exemplified by several expressions such as *He's nuts/crazy/mad/wild about her*, etc., all of which convey the idea of insanity. Lakoff and Johnson (ibid.: 54) distinguish such clusters from

... idiosyncratic metaphorical expressions that stand alone and are not used systematically in our language or thought.

As examples of such isolated metaphors they cite *the head of a cabbage*, *the foot of a mountain*, and other similar expressions. Though belonging to the one experiential gestalt, namely 'strategy', *the emperor's new clothes, red herring, play cat and mouse with*, etc. are similarly isolated in that they cannot be seen as generated by a single, underlying metaphor like 'love is madness' where the surface words consistently reflect this meaning. From a linguistic point of view what this means is while certain experiential gestalts like 'strategy' tend to produce idiosyncratic figurative expressions, others like 'love' typically produce families of metaphors such as the different clusters comprising 'love is madness', 'love is an affliction', etc. The discussion that follows, particularly the reasons advanced in section 3.3.6, explain this difference.

We cannot help having emotions; they are part of the psychosomatic make-up of humans. However, while it is probable that emotions have transcultural physiological similarities—love and fear can both make the heart beat faster everywhere—such pan-human physical similarities are modified by what is socially acceptable both in terms of the body language and verbal responses associated with those emotions valorized in a culture. The socio-cultural features of emotion have been, predictably, most widely explored in cultural anthropology. In the anthropological view, emotions are not simply physiological phenomena within people; they are also the result of people's cultural interpretation of the world they inhabit. Consequently, the everyday language of emotion is seen as embodying culture-specific theories, sometimes with a long history, however naive these may seem to the contemporary professional psychologist. The vocabularies of emotions are in the view of some anthropologists 'essentially explanations and diagnoses of emotions rather than merely names for them' (Solomon 1984: 24). As such, they are part of the wider vocabulary of the 'psychology of self-description' (ibid.).

I have already stated, following Lakoff and Johnson (1980), that metaphor is central to emotion. The physical 'concretissima' of emotion appears in external expressive behaviours: blushing, trembling, changes in expression, eye contact or avoidance, etc. visible to others. Though others comment on the emotions of their fellows, only the experiencer can report on what is happening within with real authority. And what happens within, emotional states, are formless. In language, the formless is given form in imagery, a metaphorical mode already discussed in connection with *red herring* and *the emperor's new clothes*.

The English vocabulary of emotion, like the vocabulary in general, is of two sorts: single words (*bliss, ecstasy, rapture, delight, joy, happiness, pleased*, etc.) and idioms (*the (seventh) heaven, walk on air, over the moon, lighthearted*, etc.). These idioms delineate happy states through analogies present in their imagery and in this respect are different from the non-imagist single words listed. One of the imagist depictions of joy and happiness is 'happiness is up' (ibid.), a state that also goes with lightness (*light-hearted*). 'Grief is down' is a state that goes with weight (*a heavy heart*).

In getting at the beliefs that have given rise to emotion metaphors, the object of scrutiny is not so much the surface images of idioms like *walk on air* and *light hearted* or *down in the dumps* and *a heavy heart*, but rather the underlying metaphor common to these different surface images, in this case, being up or down. One likely source of such metaphors is the medieval theory of humours, which, though no longer current, remains in the Anglo-Celtic cultural memory, and possibly the European, as a form of folklore. Should we ask why 'joy' in one of its forms is in English heavenward ascent, and 'grief' earthward descent, the theory of humours offers an explanation of the metaphors implicit in these idioms, even though the theory itself has long been discarded.

The humours, choler, phlegm, blood, and melancholy, are linked, on the one hand, to planetary influences (Mars, Moon, Jupiter, Venus, and Saturn), and on the other to the natural elements, fire, water, air, and earth as shown in Table 3.2.

Humour	choler	phlegm	blood	melancholy
Element	fire	water	air	earth
Quality	hot, dry	cold, moist	hot, moist	cold, dry
Temperament	choleric	phlegmatic	sanguine	melancholic
Physiognomy	florid, red hair, bloodshot, yellow or green eyes	golden-yellow (salt-phlegm), white (natural phlegm)	either red or white complexion, tall, splendid, beautiful thick, curly hair	either swarthy, with black hair and eyes or red eyes with yellowish circles
Planetary influence	Mars	Moon	Jupiter or Venus	Saturn
Attributes	fiery, violent, martial, bloodthirsty, etc.	cool, moist, placid, sluggish, etc.	Jupiter: benign, noble, pacific, just, jovial Venus: playful, graceful, ardent, voluptuous, capricious, hot-blooded, etc.	malignant, saturnine, taciturn, heavy and slow, aged, etc.

*Note: The Sun and Mercury are not mentioned in connection with the humours though their influence is by no means absent in health and psychosomatic disorders.

Table 3.2: *The humours and the forces affecting them*
(based on *Chaucer and the Medieval Sciences*, Curry 1960)

The belief in humours as the causes of health and disease went with the belief in the influence of the planets as a factor affecting the proportion and combination of choler, phlegm, blood, and melancholy in the body. It is this variable proportion of any one humour that is relevant to the metaphors of emotion. In their imagery, idioms typically imply the superabundance of a particular emotion and by implication, at least to the knowledeable, the excess of a particular humour. The average language-user today, though unlikely to know anything about humours per se, draws on the resources of a language which still retains in its meaning system concepts traceable back to the Middle Ages and in some instances, such as distrust of the 'red man', even further back to the *Proverbs of Alfred* (Curry 1960: 82).

Current folklore models of emotion in the cultural ethos, traceable to a time when folklore was science, appear to be the source of emotion metaphors implicit in English idioms. Additionally, now as they did earlier on, people can feel the changes which certain psychosomatic states cause in the organs referred to in the idiom, for example, the heart, once believed to be the physical site of the soul and, therefore, also of these states. The heart, as opposed to the head, is the primary symbol of emotion in English equally dominating the imagination of the poets, and prose writers.

3.3.2 The heart and the head of the Bloggs

Choler, melancholy, passion, and sluggishness were thought to originate in the liver, the stomach, the heart, and the brain (ibid.: 10). The belief in such origins could be a possible reason for the preponderance of body-part idioms in English, a characteristic noted by Smith (1925) and also by many compilers of collections of idioms.

Dominating the imagery of the language of emotion in English are the heart and the head. The heart symbolizes the passions, the affections of the soul, itself identified with the 'physiological principle of vitality' (Curry 1960: 308), common to humans and animals alike, while the head symbolizes the spirit, the rational intellect identified with the 'psychological principle of creative energy' found only in humans (ibid.: 309). While the heart was generally accepted as the seat of the soul, there were many differences of opinion among medieval philosophers regarding the site of the rational spirit. Whatever the differences among philosophers might have been, English idioms favour the head and the brain as the seat of reason and the heart as the seat of emotion.

The affections vs. the intellect
His heart rules his head, etc.

Joy, love, sympathy, etc.
for one's heart to leap
steal sb's heart
lose one's heart to sb
leave one's heart behind (in + locative)
for sth or sb to tug at one's heart strings
for one's heart to bleed for sb
have one's heart in the right place
wear one's heart on one's sleeve
have a soft heart
be soft/kind/good hearted
a heart throb, etc.

Grief, depression, dismay, etc.
break sb's heart
broken-hearted/heart-broken
sob one's heart out
eat one's heart out
for one's heart to sink (into one's boots)
heart-ache
heartrending, etc.

Absence of the affections
a cold heart
cold-hearted
a hard heart/hard-hearted
heart of stone/stony-hearted, etc.

Fear
have one's heart in one's mouth
for one's heart to miss a beat
for one's heart to turn, etc.

Table 3.3: The heart: the affections

The metaphors implicit in the idioms shown in Table 3.3 show the heart in many different forms:

the heart as an object:	steal sb's heart lose/leave one's heart behind, etc.
the heart as mobile:	for one's heart to leap/sink/be in one's mouth/in one's boots/on one's sleeve/in the right place, etc.
the heart as a used-up resource:	eat one's heart out sob one's heart out, etc.

125

The intellect vs. the affections
Her head rules her heart, etc.

Reason dominates
have one's head screwed on the right way
keep one's head
a level head/level-headed
have a good head for something
a brainstrust
a brainwave
brainstorm (verb), etc.

Reason diminishes
scratch one's head
rack/cudgel one's brains
lose one's head
have one's head turned
have one's head in the clouds
feel one's head reel
a woolly head/woolly-headed
go off one's head
need to have one's head read
brainstorm (noun)
brainwash, etc.

Table 3.4: The head and the brain: reason

The metaphors implicit in idioms with the head as a symbol of reason are similar to those with the heart as a symbol of the affections:

the head as an object:	have one's head screwed on the right way
	lose one's head
	keep one's head, etc.
the head as mobile:	have one's head turned
	have one's head in the clouds, etc.

As befits its nature, the head is less prone to movement than the mobile heart, even though on occasion capable of an ascent into the clouds.

It is possible to see the brain, as it appears in idioms, as the ocean (*brainwave, brainstorm*), as an object (*brainwash*), or as a victim (*rack/cudgel one's brains*). However, it is the head that dominates in English as a key symbol of the intellect, not the brain.

Apart from idioms with the *heart* and the *head* as key words in their make-up, there are many others drawing on different images (see section 3.3). Like the *heart* idioms and the *head* idioms, these others, too, can be seen as referring to states believed at one time to originate in the humours.

3.3.3 The states of the heart: joy

Joy and its single-word synonyms (*ecstasy, bliss, euphoria, rapture, delight, happy, pleased,* etc.) are emotion terms whose signification also appears in comparable idioms: *in (the seventh heaven), walk on air, go mad/wild with joy, fall head over heels in love,* etc., all expressive of the playful, exuberant state associated with this emotion.

The definitions of *joy* most relevant to this study are both drawn from the *Oxford English Dictionary* (1989) listed senses 1 and 2:

1. A vivid emotion of pleasure arising from a sense of well-being or satisfaction; the feeling or state of being highly pleased or delighted; exultation of spirit; gladness, delight.
2. A pleasurable state or condition; a state of happiness or felicity, esp. the perfect bliss or beatitude of heaven; hence the place of bliss, paradise or heaven.

Reports of joy generally include the type of situation eliciting the emotion. Part of the experiential gestalt that is joy comprises giving and receiving affection, the intimacy and sociability associated with family life and friendship, achievement, recreations, etc., all connected with personal and social satisfactions. As examples (24) to (28) show, a sense of competence created by the absence of obstacles and opposition (a positive, pleasureable feeling), and energy are all important components of joy. In view of these features, it is not particularly surprising that one of the commonest metaphors for joy is 'joy is up':

(23)   My *heart leaps up* when I behold
       A rainbow in the sky
       ('My Heart Leaps Up' by William Wordsworth)

(24)   He is so sweet and tender, always wanting to please me ...
       I feel like I am in heaven.
       (*The New Hite Report* Vol. 3 by Shere Hite 1987: 357)

(25)   I was thrilled when I knew I was going to have my husband's child. I *was on cloud nine.*
       (ibid.: 478)

(26)   Our daughter had a very quick and easy delivery and a one hundred percent healthy baby and we were just *walking on air.*
       (ibid.: 361)

(27) The evening ended on a *high note* when my best friend from high school invited me to join him and his wife in their chauffeured Commonwealth car for the ride home. My *high heels* had hardly *touched the floor* for the past four hours and the luxury ride *topped off* my *euphoria*.
      (*The Sydney Morning Herald* 11 November 1991: 3)

(28) [prisoners on the occasion of their release, radio report]
      We are very happy and we are *over the moon*. [A]

A glance at Table 3.2 will show that Jupiter is always a happy influence (jovial) and so is Venus when she is not being volatile and capricious. Both planets are associated with blood (hot and moist) and its elemental counterpart, the air. In medieval belief the planetary influences controlled the proportion and combination of bodily humours resulting in their increase and decrease. Joy is characterized by sensations of upward movement, the corollary of lightness (23), resulting in the illusion of being airborne ('joy is up') evident in (24) to (28), and by those of warmth ('joy is heat') as in (29):

(29) [a personal letter]
      Your warm, enthusiastic & characteristically generous support for our project has *warmed the cockles of my heart*, if the spelling is right, so I felt I must reply. [A]

3.3.4 The states of the heart: grief

Grief and its single-word synonyms (*anguish*, *misery*, *suffering*, *despondency*, *distress*, *sadness*, *sorrow*, *pain*, *disappointment*, etc.) are emotion terms whose signification also appears in similar idioms in addition to those already quoted in Table 3.3: *be reduced to tears, dissolve in tears, a lump in the throat, in a black/blue mood, feel let down, sinking feeling, down in the dumps, feel low*, etc.

The definition of *grief* (sense 7) and of *sad* (sense 5) offered in the OED (1989), captures the main experiental components of these closely related states as they appear in (30) to (33) below:

Grief Mental pain, distress, or sorrow. In mod. use in a more limited sense: Deep or violent sorrow caused by loss or trouble; a keen or bitter feeling of regret for something lost, remorse for something done, or sorrow for mishap to oneself or others.

Sad   Of persons, their feelings or dispositions: Sorrowful, mourn-ful.

If joy makes people behave in a playful, exuberant head-over-heels way, especially at its height, grief produces' apathy, lethargy, and immobility.

(30)   [a personal letter]
       I am back again in my old state of partial pessimism and with-drawal ... . At the moment I feel *squeezed* out and *bereft*. [A]

Grief is a component of situations characterized by emptiness and barreness due to bereavement, the absence of those we love and other sorts of disappointment. Predictably, the metaphor implicit in many of the idioms signifying grief is the opposite of up: 'grief (sad) is down':

(31)   [a personal letter]
       It was the only job I could find and I suffered as never before ... . It was hell. [A]

(32)   [a personal letter]
       I slipped steadily *downhill* ... . I can't remember *being* so utterly *low before*. [A]

(33)   [a personal letter]
       Thanks a lot for all the support and encouragement when I was *down in the dumps*. [A]

(34)   After the exhilaration came the *let-down*.
       (*The Australian* 5 October 1991)

(35)   My *heart aches* and a drowsy numbness pains
       My sense as though of hemlock I had drunk
       Or emptied some dull opiate to the drains
       One minute past, and *Lethe-wards had sunk*.
       ('Ode to a Nightingale' by John Keats)

As mentioned above, in terms of the medieval theory of humours, joy is a state governed by the jovial Jupiter and Venus, delightful and playful. Swarthy Saturn presides over melancholy: those subjected to the saturnine influence suffer from depression and gloomy forebod-ings associated with an excess of black bile. Melancholy, cold and dry, has earth as its elemental counterpart in sharp contrast to air, the element associated with Jupiter and Venus. The ecstatic are airborne to heaven in transports of joy; the sorrowful plumb the depths of grief in hell (Fernando 1989).

Coldness, and sometimes dryness, the typical attributes of fear, also suggest the saturnine influence:

> Get/have cold feet, for sth to make one's blood run cold, feel a shiver run down one's spine, clammy hands, be in a cold sweat, for one's teeth to chatter, turn pale, for one's mouth to go dry, etc.

Disgust is another emotional state originating in the saturnine influence. In English, disgust is often associated with the stomach, an organ, according to medieval theory, especially susceptible to the machinations of Saturn:

> turn one's stomach, have no stomach for sth, feel like puking/retching/vomiting, fed up, sick of, etc.

In psychological terms, the action tendency aroused by joy is attraction, moving towards; that aroused by grief, fear, and disgust is repulsion, to move away from. The spatial metaphor favoured in psychological accounts of emotion is directionality (Davitz 1969; Collier 1985; Fridja 1986). These directional tendencies appear in some English idioms:

> run away from (fear), drawn to (love), go against the grain (repellent), fight against (oppose because hostile to), look up (improve), down-hearted (sadness), ups and downs (of life), etc.

The directionality of *up* and *down* creates a metaphorical parallelism between an emotional state and a physical direction. I have argued that such a parallelism can be traced to the relation between psycho-somatic states (the humours) and the planetary influences once believed to cause them: Jupiter and Venus governed the air (*up*), while Saturn held sway over the earth (*down*).

Every emotive expression in English, however, cannot be explained in terms of the theory of humours. The most vehement expressions of anger and disgust are the expletives directed against the self or another. These are the taboo words, profanities relating to religion (Christ's or God's name, Christ's blood and wounds, damnation, etc.) and obscenities relating to sex (body parts and intercourse), as well as to the eliminatory functions (excretion and

130

urination). In such expletives, there is direct reference or dysphemism to the taboo item: such references are non-literal without being metaphorical since there is no analogy at work here, e.g. *piss off*.

The body parts in idioms signifying disgust are typically those located in the lower part of the body: the stomach (belly), and the eliminatory and sexual organs. The heart symbolizes the soul productive of the affections, joy and love, grief and sympathy, and the head symbolizes the spirit productive of intelligence and reason. The lower organs, in contrast, symbolize coarser states like gluttony and lust. Consequently, they are just right for vehement expressions of disgust, anger, exasperation, frustation, etc.

Obscenities are often used to express strong emotions, generally negative, implicit in which are similarly negative evaluations. *Fuck* as an expletive or as one element in some multiword expressions, is selected as a vehicle for such emotions and attitudes for obvious reasons: it is one of the most offensive words in English. In *Bloggs has done the usual—fucked up* ('bungle') *the whole bloody works, the fucking bastard!* vehement feeling is unmistakable, especially in *fucking bastard* expressive, as it is here, of fury. However, this epithet can also be used between males to signal approval or intimacy: *A kilo of crack! So you've pulled it off, you beaut fucking bastard!* (*Bloody* used attributively as in *the whole bloody works* or or *her stupidity makes me bloody wild* can act as a vehicle of anger, exasperation, etc. as in the first instance or as an intensifier as in the second. In such uses *bloody* is not a profanity as an oath like *'sblood* is but, in terms of modern usage, an obscenity (*OED* 1989).) Other obscenities expressive of negative emotions, for instance, contempt, disgust, and exasperation, are *shit, pissed off*, etc. Examples (36) and (37) give additional support to these comments:

(36)   [quoted in a student essay]
       ... and I have to pass computers because there is *no fucking way* I will *bloody* do that again. [A]

(37)   [quoted in a student essay]
       Oh I'm so *pissed off* I got about 52% on my Maths 1 paper
       ... on the practical test the other week I just missed out on getting 80% *I'm so mad*. [A]

Be mad, a metaphorical idiom, is interesting because in form it coin-
cides in part with the idiom signifying intense love, *be mad about sb*.
Here it signifies intense anger. The common semantic component is
mental disorientation, a feature seen as being shared by both love
and anger.

3.3.5 The states of the heart: anger

Anger and its single-word synonyms, as in the case of the other
emotions discussed above, range from the intense (*explode, erupt,
enrage, infuriate*, etc.) through the moderate (*irascible, annoyance,
irritable*, etc.) to the mild (*cross, peevish, sulky, grumpy, ill-humour,*
etc.). Some comparable idioms are given below:

> for sb's blood to boil, burn with rage/anger, feel as though one
> would burst, blow one's top, flare up, fly off the handle, fly into a
> fury, lose one's cool, be mad at, tear strips off sb, go for sb
> hammer and tongs, tear sb apart, fight tooth and nail, jump down
> sb's throat, bite sb's head off, chew sb up, see red, etc.

According to the *Oxford English Dictionary* (1989) anger is 'The
active feeling provoked against the agent; passion, rage; wrath, ire,
hot displeasure'. (sense 2)

All the idioms cited above signify intense anger. Excess characterizes the metaphors implicit in some of the idioms of anger cited
below. In examples (38) and (41) extremes of 'hot displeasure' and
violence dominate.

(38) Australia Post is causing *blood to boil.*
      (*The Sydney Morning Herald* 1 February 1992: 22)

(39) *Hotheads* fail to break *the visitor's cool* (headline)
      The President, it is good to report, *kept a cool head.*
      (*The Australian* 4 January 1992: 1)

(40) [student's essay]
      All expressed the futility of attempting any discussion with an
      angry person and said they would stay calm and wait because
      eventually that person would cool *down*. [A]

Anger expresses the hot, dry humour of choler associated with fire.
The planetary power controlling choler is Mars with his florid

complexion, bloodshot eyes, red hair, and beard. Mars is fiery so the characterization of anger as heat and redness (*see red*, *go red*) is hardly surprising. Mars is the direct opposite of cold, moist, phlegmatic Lunar, expressing as she does, temperamental coolness or placidity. The contrast appears in (38) and (39), while (40) shows an anticipated transition from the choleric to the phlegmatic, that is, cooling down.

Besides heat, another common metaphor of anger is 'anger as violence'. Not only is Mars fiery, he is also bloodthirsty and vehement, unsurprising in a god of war.

(41) And there was Tom Hughes ..., who would show no mercy as he *tore* Warwick *apart*, limb by limb, during the court case
... .
(*Good Weekend* 2 November 1991: 24)

(42) Now you behave Mortimer you're too old to *be flying off the handle*.
(The screenplay of *Arsenic and Old Lace*)

(43) ... putting flowers or a vase in front of a photograph of a living person made him *tear his hair out*.
(*The Sydney Morning Herald* 3 February 1992: 3)

What marks these idioms is hyperactivity caused by some factor which leads to a loss of control. 'Anger as explosion' (*blow one's top*, *explode*, *fulminate*, etc.) also expresses a similar hyperactivity.

'Anger as explosion' is characterized by hyperactivity which contrasts with hypoactivity, expressive of the phlegmatic humour: *not bat an eyelid*, *not turn a hair*, etc.

Apart from heat and hyperactivity, idioms of anger also draw on colour for their metaphors. Mars is bloodthirsty, florid, and red-haired, so the angry *see red* or *go red*. His eyes are usually bloodshot, but they can sometimes be green as choler was believed to cause the liver to secrete green bile, a sign of being *green with envy*, envy being allied to anger, though, not of course, the same.

3.3.6 Conclusions

The theory of humours has long been discarded, but it has been preserved as a reasonably coherent system in English idioms of emotion making the metaphors implicit in emotion idioms also work as a coherent system. In this respect, such idioms are different from those associated with strategy: *the emperor's new clothes, play cat and mouse with, red herring,* etc. The idioms of emotion are unified by the theory they exemplify, which in turn generates clusters of metaphors characteristic of various aspects of an emotion such as joy or anger. The idioms signifying anger, caused by choler, exemplify the various characteristics of temperament and complexion of this humour and its governing planet, Mars: 'anger is heat/violence/ explosion'. Anger contrasts with placidity and self-possession, characteristic of the phlegmatic Lunar disposition: 'placidity/self-possession is cool'. A different sort of contrast exists between the saturnine ('melancholy/grief is down') and the jovial ('joy is up'). No theory of strategy governs the idioms associated with this experiential gestalt, so they remain isolated, each working on its own, though loosely unified as idioms of strategy as a conceptual domain. There is no cluster of fish metaphors along with *red herring,* for example, exemplifying 'misleading diversion' as one form of strategy.

I should mention that the humours, as far as their various manifestations go, do not contradict the nature of emotion in modern psychological theory (Davitz 1969; Collier 1985; Fridja 1986). Contemporary psychological theory has replaced the planetary influences with the subconcious drives and repressions of the mind. But modern accounts of what the emotions are as intrapsychic phenomena focus on more or less the same features as the theory of humours did: action tendencies expressed as spatial orientations, physiological sensations caused by changes in temperature (fear and grief are associated with cold; love and anger with heat) and different muscular reactions resulting in feelings of lightness (joy) or heaviness (grief). Each type of emotion is, in addition, associated with a characteristic expressive behaviour: jumping and gesticulating are expressive of anger; apathy and immobility of grief, and so on.

The major difference between the folklore view of emotion and that of current psychological theories lies in the dichotomy of emotion and reason appearing in the opposition of heart and head in popular thinking. According to recent psychological theory, emotional action tendencies are preceded by flashes of cognitive appraisal exemplified by such criteria as 'pleasant', 'unpleasant', 'safe', 'unsafe', etc.

> The positive consequence of this is that many theorists no longer see emotion and cognition as two extreme and incompatible poles. (Scherer 1988: 57–8)

My final point reiterates one of the major themes of this chapter: while emotion idioms are conventionalized, and like all other idioms exemplify the workings of the idiom principle, they are not automatized or formulaic in the way some idioms are, for example, *God save the Queen*. Idioms of emotion do not typically seem to show the elaboration of imagery or the novel variations that so often constitute the innovative element in other sorts of ideational idioms like the *emperor's new clothes*, *red herring*, etc. However, the occasional witty variation did occur in the corpus collected for this study:

(44)   I felt the most passionate when I '*fell in lust*' with a man I met in Paris, a brief interlude, a true Parisian coup de foudre.
(*The New Hite Report* Vol. 3, by Shere Hite 1987: 193)

Though the metaphors implicit in idioms of emotion are not elaborated upon, the fact that they appear as related clusters—for example, 'anger as violence' is expressed through a cluster of idioms characterized by images of attack—means that such metaphors capture the dramatic 'feel' of these experiential gestalts, their sensations, dynamics, and 'colour'. Emotions are internal and formless; language, in this case primarily idioms signifying internal states through images, gives emotions form and so empowers the language-user to concretize the amorphous by bringing two different experiential gestalts into analogical correspondence. A metaphor so produced ('joy is up/heaven/walk on air'), can then illuminate this gestalt, by symbolizing an apprehension of joy so intense that it can also evoke its opposite, through as many parallelisms as the imagination allows:

(45)   Elysium is as far as to
       The very nearest room,
       If in that room a friend await
       Felicity or doom.

135

What fortitude the soul contains
That it can so endure
The accent of a coming foot,
The opening of a door!
('Elysium is as far as to' by Emily Dickinson)

3.4 Men, women, manners, and morals: attitudinal appraisals

3.4.1 Introduction

Manners and morals are never neutral. Their usefulness to men and women lies in this fact for implicit in manners and morals are attitudinal appraisals. An attitude may be defined as a favourable, unfavourable, or ambivalent emotional bias on the part of a person to other persons, objects, happenings, etc. Though not an emotion like joy or anger, an attitude is closely allied to an emotion in that it too is expressive of intrapsychic action tendencies: moving towards ('good'), moving away from ('bad'), moving against either 'bad' or 'good' as the case may be. Like emotions, attitudes originate in cognitive appraisals and are, if anything, more strongly evaluative than emotions.

Since attitudes arise from beliefs and commitments, they can be implicit, as in the 'bad' of (46):

(46) The ABC (Australian Broadcasting Corporation) may not have become *a sacred cow*, but it is certainly a *fat cat*.
      (*The Sydney Morning Herald* 7 January 1977: 6)

Attitudes can also be explicit as in expletives like *Damn you*! or in inherently attitudinal vocabulary such as *cad/saint*, *nice/nasty*, *praise/censure*, etc. Whether explicit or implicit, attitudes arise from interaction (see Chapter 4): they are directed towards someone or something. I have already drawn attention to the attitudes carried by *fat cat* and *wear different hats* in section 3.1.4. However, despite attitudes being carried by all ideational idioms as part of their connotational meaning in discourse contexts, they are not *par excellence* realizations of the interpersonal function via the vocabulary. What I am calling interpersonal idioms are expressions like *There you go, (That's) a good question, You're kidding*, etc., which constitute possible turns in a dialogical exchange such as a conversation, or they are those idioms which are part of a turn explicitly marked for interaction, for example, *believe you me, mind you,* etc. By contrast, *sacred cow* and *fat cat* in (46) are interactionally neutral items.

Attitudinal appraisals can be systematized as I have attempted to do in employing the terms 'good', 'bad', and 'ambivalent', standing as they do for evaluative sub-components. The rationale for such a systematization is provided by semantic theories of a generative type complementary to functional ones in recognizing that meaning extends beyond language as a formal system to the social domains of language use. In addition to recognizing meaning components such as ± Animate, ± Human, ± Male, etc., some generative semanticists (Katz 1964) also recognize the semantic component 'evaluative' which I am calling attitudinal in this study. Attitudes comprise that component of meaning in which indirect (e.g. *fat cat*) or direct reference (e.g. *nasty*) is made to the appraisals of a community with regard to its aesthetic, social, or moral codes, in short, to its cultural value systems.

Attitudes have their origins in what is termed general or encyclopaedic knowledge of the world and how this knowledge is viewed in terms of the cultural values of a community. General knowledge is picked up much in the same way that the young child picks up his language: from hearing adults talk about men, women, manners, and morals, not from formal instruction. Such knowledge is not normally verified by its possessor as true or false. It is accepted at face value on the basis of widespread social belief and commonsense reasoning involving, as Downes (1984) points out

> ... not only a 'taken for granted' physics, geography etc, but a 'taken for granted' psychology, sociology, politics and so on.
> Downes (1984: 271)

If the belief turns out to be false, the attitude arising from it will not be justified and will have to be revised, or discarded altogether. Attitudes are based, therefore, on judgements resting on grounds insufficient to produce certainty. The absence of conclusiveness is what distinguishes opinion-based attitudes from appraisals arising from verification. Jaako Hintikka (1973) makes the distinction as follows:

'Games of exploring the world' are based on seeking and finding the existence of external objects...while indoor dialogical games are based on suitable sequences of logical symbols which may not always mirror the real world.
(Hintikka 1973: 81, 72)

What both philosophers and scientists concerned with exploring the world seek is objective verification of beliefs which can be proved to be true or false in the light of findings. The belief that all humans are mortal is easily verifiable as being true; the belief that all swans are white has had to be modified as black swans also exist.

Since there is no certainty attached to beliefs, our attitudes with their implicit appraisals can be the result of false beliefs open to revision in the light of new information. The difference between appraisals based on verified knowledge and those arising from commonly held beliefs is shown below:

scientific appraisals	—	non-scientific appraisals
true or false	—	'good', 'bad', or 'ambivalent'
objective intellectual	—	subjective appraisals in terms of
appraisals in terms of physical		social norms, i.e. point of
laws, i.e. verification		view or attitude

3.4.2 Attitudes in discourse

In theory, it may be possible to produce a totally neutral, non-committal text; in reality, such texts are not produced except in special circumstances, for example, short texts consisting of largely nonsense words: *All mimsy were the borogroves, And mane raths outgrabe.* (Lewis Carroll's *Alice in Wonderland*), etc. Apart from this kind of text, if non-committal texts occur, they are likely to conceal an unwillingness to take sides, to enter into debate and discussion. A habitually non-committal participant will eventually be seen as either a non-person or a 'sitter on the fence', who neither supports nor challenges other participants in the exchange.

Highly technical discourses, whether written or spoken, such as those belonging to the registers of mathematics or physics or symbolic logic may seem to be candidates for neutrality, but even these typically argue a thesis to prove or disprove a theory and therefore embody evaluations (Gilbert and Mulkay 1984). Appraisals in these types of discourse may emerge more strongly at the global text level, not at the micro-level of the individual sentence, unlike in conversational exchanges or in testimonials.

In non-technical, informal discourse such as conversation, discussion, or journalism, attitudinal appraisals of the topic of discourse and of the addressee are clearly present, sometimes markedly so. In responding to an informal questionnaire concerning the identification of attitudinal appraisals of the discourse topic, the majority of my respondents stated that their identification of the attitude implicit in a given text depended partly on learned conventions, such identifications being also strongly supported by the co-text of what seemed to them to be key attitudinally appraisive words. In other words, collocational patterns helped the emergence and subsequent identification of attitudes. Some of the respondents also recognized modifications to conventional attitudes created by word-play, etc.

The questionnaire referred to above can be found in the Appendix. The questionnaire was given to a group of twenty-six tertiary students, all of whom had a native or near-native control of English. The aim of this exercise was to get some informal feedback on the interpretation of the attitudinal evaluations conveyed by specific idioms.

The diagram below indicates the relationship of attitudes to what are normally socially valued and socially prohibited attributes in a speech community, though such attitudes will not always be clearcut, hence the evaluative sub-component 'ambivalent':

Item x, for example, *olive branch*, conveys 'good' because it implies:

    pacific
    open to negotiaton
    non-aggressive, etc.

Item y, for example, *red herring*, conveys 'bad' because it implies:

    dishonesty
    inaccuracy
    misrepresentation
    deviousness, etc.

Item z, for example, *red*
herring, conveys 'ambivalent'

because it implies:	that something can be exciting challenging, etc.
despite being:	misleading devious, etc.

For example, the twists of a plot in a whodunnit

A word now about the evaluative sub-components 'good' and 'bad'. They need to be seen not as absolutes, but rather as a gradation of more or less. Just as an emotion has to be seen as a continuum varying from *ecstasy*, *bliss*, *joy*, and *happiness*, to *feel fine/good*, *nice*, *comfortable*, etc. both in terms of intensity and quality, so the appraisal component ('good', 'bad', or 'ambivalent') of an attitude will also show a similar gradation in the set of words language-users can choose from to convey their attitudes. For example, if the target of an attitude is the interest factor of a film, the appraisal might be 'good', more precisely characterized by *riveting*, *gripping*, *thrilling*, *absorbing*, *entertaining*, *good fun*, *okay*, etc. The implication 'not good' that *okay* or *average* may carry does not mean 'bad'. When dealing with attitudes, we are not necessarily dealing with polarizations into clearcut 'good' and 'bad'.

In summary, attitudes and their implicit appraisals have the following functions:

They contribute to making the purpose of a text identifiable, constituting as they do part of the information package exchanged in any interaction. Though an individual item, for example, *red herring*, can generate different context-specific attitudes ('good' if suspenseful, 'bad' if a misleading ploy, etc.), in longer texts there are enough cues for one attitude to emerge and be identified by the addressee as being the preferred one. The identification of such a global attitude helps us read between the lines of a discourse to get at covert meanings.

Attitudes generate discourse by introducing a dynamic component into an interaction: participants respond to attitudes whether these generate conviviality or conflict.

It can be argued that absence of attitudes weakens the Co-operative Principle (Grice 1975), and the Interest Principle proposed by

Geoffrey Leech (1983) as part of interpersonal and textual rhetoric. Attitudes imply not only beliefs but also a point of view and this is crucial in an exchange.

3.4.3 Appraisals of manners and morals

An attitude has already been defined as an emotional bias on the part of the sender of a message to the content of that message or to the receiver or to both. The examples and analyses that follow are presented as exemplifications of this notion, focusing on attitudes to the topic of discourse. Some of these examples have already been discussed with reference to imagery as vehicles for experiential gestalts like 'strategy'.

(47)   Herrings supreme (headline)
       There are enough *red herrings, plots, twists and anticlimaxes* in the first two hours of this drama to *keep the keenest mind guessing*.
       (*TV Guide* 11 September 1978)

Example (47) refers to a whodunnit, a narrative mode in which suspense is an essential ingredient. The survey by questionnaire referred to above confirmed this impression. The majority of respondents identified the appraisal of the writer of the text as 'good' because the phrase *keep the keenest mind guessing* suggested the following:

   a challenge to the viewer; suspenseful; keeps up the mystery; promises the drama will be good, stimulating entertainment.

Other respondents identified the writer's appraisal as 'ambivalent' on the grounds that though suspense and excitement were present, *red herrings; plots, twists and anticlimaxes* indicated extra-complexity and distractions.

   A minority identified the writer's appraisal as 'bad' because the audience would be bored by not being able to follow the ramifications of the plot.

   All my respondents identified (47) as an appraisal, but in interpreting the writer's evaluation of the quality of the film they brought their own beliefs to bear on what constituted a good drama. The majority of my respondents interpreted the writer's attitude to the film's being intriguing as 'good', but some felt that he was also suggesting that being confused was not a fair price to pay for mystery.

(48)   ... and that is why I resigned but isn't Barbara a strewer of *red herrings* first of all rape and now my resignation.
Rape isn't a *red herring*. [BCET]

In (48), the appraisal 'bad' given to *red herring*, here a discoursal ploy, is recognized by Barbara, the addressee, and rejected as an accurate description of her contribution to the discussion.

Red herring is generally interpreted as carrying the appraisal 'bad' if used to describe a discourse strategy, a political, or social ploy. Consequently,

... Mr Whitlam's campaign strategy that led the party baying after the constitutional *red herring* ... (18a.) and
... false trails and *red herrings* ... (18b.)

for the majority of my respondents carried the appraisal 'bad' for the following reasons, which I have summarized as follows:

(18)   a. a strategy used by the unscrupulous to mislead people
       b. deliberate evasion of the key issue of concern to the people

In contrast to *red herring*, which generally carries a negative appraisal except in relation to the whodunnit, *olive branch* generally carries a positive appraisal:

(49)   Packer *waves olive twig* towards ABC (headline)
Mr Kerry Packer's World Series Cricket Organization offered a faint glimmer of hope yesterday of *a compromise* with establishment cricket. WSC's managing director, Mr Andrew Caro said, 'The situation is more conducive to *conciliation* than six months ago.'
(*The Sydney Morning Herald* 2 January 1979: 2)

The majority of my respondents identified the appraisal carried by the idiom as 'good' on the grounds that peace moves and conciliation are worthwhile processes in terms of social norms. Those who identified it as 'ambivalent' did so on the grounds that the usual *branch* of the idiom had been changed to *twig*. To them, this indicated half-hearted peace moves.

The texts below explicitly oppose peace (*olive branch*) and weapons (aggression), thereby foregrounding the appraisal carried by *olive branch*:

(50)　a.　[radio news report]
　　　　When the Palestinians arrived in Madrid *carrying olive branches* they presented a different image ... they presented a different picture from Yasser Arafat *pistol on hip*. [A]

　　　b.　[radio news report]
　　　　People call us terrorists but we have come with *the olive branch* we have not come with *guns*. [A]

There have been some instances in the examples already cited of idioms being used as titles of news reports in newspapers. Such a use foregrounds idioms as succinct appraisals of the way of the world, which place the topic of the text that follows in relation to the value system, the cultural ethos of its readers, and by extension to the society they belong to.

Those ideational idioms which are proverbs serve as vehicles of the conventional wisdom. As such they may seem to straitjacket the language-user both linguistically and intellectually. However, resourceful language-users resort to 'inventive imitation' to express new meanings through variations of conventional expressions as so many of the idioms already cited show. As for the intellectual side, conventional wisdom ensures cultural continuity: *let sleeping dogs lie*, for example, goes back to Chaucer:

(51)　It is *nought good a slepying hound to wake*
　　　It is Ne yeve a wight a cause to devyne, ...
　　　(*Troilus and Criseyde*, III, c.1374: 764–5)

To the language-user, idioms offer familiar, succinct ways of getting across complex information packages, not only in terms of referential function, but also in terms of the attitudinal, evaluative one. Language-users fulfil many roles: that of reporter, persuader, apologist, and so on. But whatever the role, it never brings forth discourse that is neutral in context. To be able to rely on standard, well-established viewpoints is an asset when addressing Jane and Joe Bloggs; it is they who are the backbone of society. Provocative, individualistic ideologies are all very well for philosophers and poets, but Jane and

Joe Bloggs, together with every Tom, Dick, and Harry, feel most comfortable with the conventional.

The idioms in the examples that follow are all used as headings in news reports and feature articles in newspapers. Their function is to be a pointer to the content of the discourse, to serve as a point of departure for its global message in the way that, on a smaller scale, the left-most element of a clause, 'the theme' in the Hallidayan sense (1985), serves as 'the peg on which the message is hung', both in referential and attitudinal terms.

(52)   ALP plans to *tighten* govt *fat cats' belts* (headline)

Example (52) is especially interesting because it contains two idioms: *fat cat* and *tighten one's/sb's belt* 'economize'. The text that follows gives an approximate paraphrase of the expression in the opening paragraph, a typical positioning for this type of explication:

> More than 500 senior NSW *public servants*—all of whom are en-
> titled to salary packages of at least $70,000 a year—*(fat cat)* will
> be demoted or have their wages *cut substantially* if the NSW
> Labor Party is elected to office ... (*tighten sb's belt*)
> (*The Sydney Morning Herald* 13 May 1991: 5)

Since threats of war always bedevil attempts to keep the interna-
tional peace, the frequency of *olive branch* and other semantically related idioms as parts of headlines is unsurprising:

(53)   a. Israel *offers an olive branch* to Palestinians (headline)
            (*The Australian* 28 January 1989: 11)

        b. US may *offer olive branch* to Managua (headline)
            Washington: The administration of President Bush is
            considering *resumption of normalised relations* with
            Managua ... .
            (*The Australian* 4 March 1989: 16)

        c. Two Koreas sign accord to *bury the hatchet* (headline)
            Seoul: North and South Korea stepped back from four
            decades of *Cold War confrontation* today and signed a
            nonaggression pact to open a new chapter in their *fratici-
            dal relations*.
            (*The Sydney Morning Herald* 14 December 1991: 15)

Two of these examples (53a. and b.) are especially interesting in that the *image* evoked by *olive branch* versus *hatchet* appears to attract different, but in each case, compatible collocations: *bury the hatchet* is accompanied by phrases implying a much greater degree of violence than *olive branch*. This impression of the typical collocates of *olive branch* is reinforced by examples such as (53d.):

> d. [TV serial: family drama]
> come on mum *kiss and make up* ... he's *holding out the olive branch* ... Robert *make peace* [A]

As I have already noted in discussing (50a. and b.), if reference to violence and weapons occurs in texts employing *olive branch*, it is in explicit contrast to *olive branch*, a symbol of peace. The contrast between *olive branch* and *bury the hatchet* suggests the semantic differences between these two partially synonymous idioms: *offer/hold out/wave the olive branch* signifies a conciliatory overture; *bury the hatchet* the termination of a conflict.

It seems appropriate to end this discussion of attitudinal appraisal with an example of 'inventive imitation':

(54)   A bird *in the pot* is worth two in a bush
       (*The Sydney Morning Herald* 3 July 1989: 3)

heads a feature article on promoting emu meat.

3.4.4 Conclusions

What has been emphasized in the foregoing sections is the pervasiveness of attitudinal appraisals, and hence the nonneutrality of all contextualized discourse. Even ideational and interpersonal idioms as citation (see Chapter 4 for the latter) items may carry appraisals for language-users arising from the past contexts in which they have encountered these idioms. For example, *red herring* may carry only the appraisal 'bad' as part of its meaning profile for those language-users who have encountered it in political contexts like (18a., b., and c.) and (19), or like (48) where it is presented as a misleading ploy. For others who have also encountered it with reference to detective films or stories, it could have the appraisal 'good' when used with reference to an intriguing whodunnit as in (47).

Whatever the appraisal, what is important is that this appraisal is part of the meaning of a discourse carried by its vocabulary. We are continually judging our fellows, their actions, their manners, their morals in one way or another and such appraisals appear in our verbal reports. The action tendencies, moving towards, away from, and against, that arise as a component of emotions appear in our judgements as well. 'Good' relates to joy, 'bad' to grief, fear, disgust, and anger. Mixed emotions exist and are referred to in conventionalized expressions like *love-hate* or *ad hoc* ones as in Emily Dickinson's *Elysium* of *felicity or doom*. They correspond to the appraisal 'ambivalent'.

Language-users are continually evaluating the world and everything in it. The objective speaker, like the ideal one in a homogeneous speech community, is a convenient myth.

3.5 The world, language, and language-users

Ideational idioms, conversational and written, in the corpora drawn on in this study occurred in newspapers, in academic discussions, and in answers to a questionnaire (in Hite 1987) as well as in the correspondence of people with a tertiary education. Though there is no evidence that these idioms are confined to the members of such highly literate milieux, it is very likely that such allusions such as *the emperor's new clothes*, *the Trojan horse*, *where angels fear to tread*, etc., and even *red herring* and *olive branch* are much more frequent in the language of these milieux than in others. It is not simply the choice of such idioms that marks the language of the highly literate, but also the manner of their use.

As far as the choice of ideational idioms go, there appear to be two major factors influencing language-users. First, there are the attitudinal appraisals they wish to convey to their addressees regarding the topic of their discourse. Such attitudinal appraisals typically constitute part of the stable expressive meaning of vocabulary items, single or multiword (see section 3.4), and arise from their informational content, the imagery conveying this content, habitual collocates, and habitual contexts of use over time and space. Atypical appraisals arise from appropriate management of the co-text accompanying the idiom.

The second factor influencing the choice of ideational idioms rather than similar single words is the sort and quantity of information language-users wish to convey. The ideational function of language embodies the organization of experience in terms of both semantic elements (participants, actions, attributes, and circumstances) and grammatical elements (subjects, objects, predicate complements, together with modifying adjectivals and qualifying adverbials) as these appear in clauses realizing transitivity. When speaking or writing, language-users will choose lexical items in accordance with the degree of specificity the context and the discourse type demand in communicating real-life experience. Ideational idioms will be chosen in accordance with the level of impressionistic delineation of the world language-users wish to achieve, in terms of participants, actions, processes, attributes, and circumstances, as well as the degree of succinctness they are aiming at.

Ideational idioms can be used in conventional ways or in ways which demonstrate 'inventive imitation'. The way ideational idioms are used stylistically depends primarily on the type of discourse. In informal spoken discourse and in written discourse of varying degrees of informality, language-users employ ideational idioms in novel ways in order to enliven their texts. In so doing they realize what Halliday (1973) terms the imaginative use of language in order 'to excel in meaning'.

Some language-users are more adept at rhetoric than others. Generally, they are the ones that need such skills professionally: literary artists, journalists, politicians and entertainers, who depend on verbal art, are some obvious instances that come to mind. A large number of the idioms cited above came from journalists determined to 'excel in meaning' by means of 'inventive imitation', in other words, a partial variation of the original (see also sections 2.3.2 to 2.3.4). The literary artist seeking to mimic truth and novelty born of imagination comes up with

(55)   He sees everything in the Universe
       Is a track of numbers racing towards an answer
       (*Crow's Account of St George* by Ted Hughes, 1972)

a daring image of the mechanistic, mathematical view of the universe.

The journalist, tends to concentrate on what is newsworthy in a mundane world concerned, at least ostensibly, with facts rather than with fictions. Generally, the closest he or she comes to turning the prosaic into the poetic is through the skilful employment of idioms. Such skill in its more flamboyant expressions takes the form of transforming the conventionalized by permuting or deleting words within the idiom, adding to them or substituting a new word for the old to dramatize an otherwise tame description. Despite their conventionality, the mind is not anesthetized by idioms but rather activated into 'imitative invention' (see the examples with *the emperor's new clothes* and *red herring* in sections 3.2.2 and 3.2.3). In less poetic, but still graphic presentations of events, the speaker or writer will simply choose to use idioms in preference to non-idioms to get the message across as in the already cited (32):

> I slipped steadily downhill ... I can't remember being so utterly low before.

instead of

> I got steadily worse/I declined steadily ... I can't remember being so depressed before.

Media persons habitually use lexicogrammar more poetically than other speakers and writers, barring literary artists and copywriters, because that is one of the things they are employed to do. Their language must foreground the protagonists engaged in creating history on the global or local stage and the high points of such history in the making. Consequently, ideational idioms with their imagery or implicit metaphors are relatively more common in journalism than they are in academic discourse or letters.

As a final example of how the members of milieux for whom language skills are also bread and butter use language—but, even more importantly, as an example of how language choice relating to the four dimensions presented in the introduction to this chapter work together—I shall now analyse example (1) in this chapter, concentrating on its vocabulary. I shall look specifically at its idioms—in this example they are all pure idioms, with the exception of *fail to deliver (the goods)*, which is a semi-idiom:

> For Gorbachev, Yeltsin was a convenient *red rag* to wave at the *hardliners*. Gorbachev would *give an inch*, Yeltsin would take *a mile* and Gorbachev would *claw back*, secretly glad of the excuse to yield 100 yards.

148

But it was Yeltsin with his bluff, charismatic demagoguery, who *stole the people's hearts*. Gorbachev had become *the darling* of the liberals from East Berlin to West Side Manhattan but at home he was the man who had *failed to deliver (the goods)*.

In this text, we have what is external to language-users: the world; we also have what language-users bring to their messages: their specific perceptions of the world from which their attitudes and appraisals derive and their experience in using the lexicogrammatical resources the language offers them. The actors of the drama in (1) and their actions have elicited certain vocabulary choices determined primarily by the attitude of the writer towards his subject: two men locked in a power struggle while another power élite (the hardliners) waits in the wings to take over. What is foregrounded is strategy in the form of provocation, concession, and an expedient courtship of the public or of power elites.

I have already categorized attitudinal appraisals in terms of their semantic subcomponents:

good

vs.   ambivalent

bad

The attitudinal appraisal of the writer of (1), as far as it is deducible from the text, is 'ambivalent'. The view that politics is a dirty game emerges in a *convenient red rag* implying as it does clever opportunism as well as the predatoriness of *claw* and *give an inch, ... take a mile*. Gorbachev and Yeltsin are recognized as charismatic: Yeltsin *stole the people's hearts*, Gorbachev *had become the darling* of the liberals. Admiration for the charisma of the two men is mixed with a distaste for the powerplay in their strategies.

There are many language registers, some of which, like the sciences and social sciences, favour a preponderance of terms of varying degrees of generality such as *phenomena, entities, organisms, humans, mankind, society*, etc., and *exist, become, evolve, progress*, etc. By contrast, other registers like journalism, fiction, and letters are concerned primarily with individuals—the heroes and villains of extraordinary or ordinary life, rarely the faceless collective, the anonymous mass. Ideational idioms can be useful for characterizing such foregounded personalitites in media reports as (1) shows.

Proper names as opposed to common nouns are void, which is why they are not listed in dictionaries. But once a name has been given to a person, that name, Mikhail Gorbachev or Boris Yeltsin, is the ultimate in specificity. The dramatis personae in this text can be ranked from the general to the specific as follows:

people's
hardliners
liberals from East Berlin to West Side Manhattan

Yeltsin ... who stole the people's hearts
Gorbachev had become the darling of the liberals
he was the man who had failed to deliver

As in a drama, the two protagonists are foregrounded against the relatively anonymous masses of the crowd scenes.

Every type of strategy used in this power struggle is presented via an idiom:
Provocation: For Gorbachev, Yeltsin was *a convenient red rag to wave at the hardliners*

Implicit here is the image of Gorbachev, the picador, using Yeltsin, the red rag, to excite and inflame the hardliners, the bulls.
The idiom captures the triangular power struggle graphically and concisely.

Concession and greed: Gorbachev would *give an inch*, Yeltsin would *take a mile*.

This is the strategy of taking advantage of a small concession to gain a larger one, but in this case a machiavellian ploy which in this text is part of the larger, superordinate one of provocation. In real-life such a move encompasses several events; here a complex scenario is transformed into an idiom figuring the appropriation of space suggested by *give an inch* and *take a mile*.

Courtship: *stole the people's hearts* had become *the darling* of the liberals

Courtship is an affective matter, so courtship is conveyed by two emotion idioms signifying 'the heart as an object' and 'the favourite'. Since home is where the heart should be, and the power certainly is, Yeltsin wins.

150

When analysed in this way, the quantity and type of information this text contains, and the manner in which the writer has chosen to convey it, is much clearer. Translated into literal English, it reads:

Gorbachev used Yeltsin to anger and provoke the hardliners. When Gorbachev made small concessions, Yeltsin took ten times more than was intended. However, this is exactly what Gorbachev wanted. Despite this policy, Yeltsin was loved by the people at home, while Gorbachev became a favourite among the liberals from East Berlin to West Side Manhattan. But at home he was a failure.

The impact of strategy, which is salient in the original as a result of the idioms used is attentuated with courtship virtually disappearing. Consequently, the force of the attitudinal appraisal also weakens.

3.6 Conclusions

In this chapter, I have attempted to draw attention to the characteristic features of what I am calling ideational idioms, as well as to show how they are used in a wide range of texts. The main issues presented in the foregoing pages can be summarized as follows:

1   Language-users choose vocabulary, both idioms and non-idioms, to construct meanings in keeping with their attitudes and assessments of people and events.

2   The information carried by ideational idioms, if these idioms are transformable, may be modified by various transformational operations: addition, permutation, substitution, and deletion. In each case, the conventional meaning is varied adding to the interpretative effort on the part of the addressee. Elaboration of the imagery or other figurative features of an idiom also modifies the idiom's meaning and may add to its information load.

3   Imagery pervades language reflecting the role of the imagination and the intellect as mediator between the concretissma-filled world out there and the generalizing tendencies in language. The image reflects the compromise effected by language-users to gain the advantages of the general without sacrificing those of the particular: *fat cat* represents a type, but a very specific type among humans.

That meaning resides in components other than steady-state dictionary definitions is well established in semantic studies but what these
components within the semantic spectrum of a word are, and how
they function to add to and modify or even to change a conventional
stable signification, is less well established.

The main purpose of the discussion and examples of discourse in
this chapter has been to demonstrate how conventional and stable as
well as variable, context-specific meanings are conveyed via the lexical resources of English, particularly idioms; additionally, I have also
tried to show how fluent speakers and writers of English use their
verbal skills to reinforce and even extend the meaning profile of
ideational idioms through modification of their form and their habitual collocates. Such skills, in their turn, show the natural complementarity of the conventional and the novel, the idiom, and the
open-choice principles.

4
Interpersonal idiomatic expressions: conviviality and conflict in verbal interactions

The polished conversationalist is a familiar figure. He breaks smoothly into conversations, picks up the thread effortlessly, holds his listeners enthralled as he develops his point, and then elegantly bows out of the conversation.
(Eric Keller, *Gambits: Conversational Strategy Signals* 1979)

McAlmon asks: 'Is Eliot afraid of the interchange of relationships, with their attractions and antagonisms and experiences?'
(Humphrey Carpenter, *Geniuses Together* 1989)

4.1 Interpersonal idiomatic expressions: vehicles of participation and exchange

4.1.1 Introduction

If ideational idiomatic expressions of various types provide language-users with a resource for communicating information about the world in an impressionistic way, interpersonal ones provide them with the following:

1 A resource for signposting verbal interactions so that their beginnings (greetings), middles (the development of the exchange), and endings (farewells) are clear.

2 A resource for expressing through different interpersonal functions, the two great forces of social life: conviviality and conflict.

Ideational idioms were seen as realizing the various clausal elements of transitivity in the semantic roles of participants, processes and circumstances, thereby enabling language-users to talk about the world not only in an impressionistic way, but also in imagist, metaphorical terms.

Interpersonal idioms are very different from ideational ones in several of their characteristics, understandable in view of their different functions. Chapter 3 listed those characteristics of ideational idioms which make them especially appropriate for how they are used in discourse. A similar profile can be drawn for interpersonal idiomatic expressions, whether these are pure, semi-, or literal idioms. Also serving as vehicles for the interpersonal function are restricted collocations and common locutions:

1 Interpersonal idiomatic expressions are overtly or covertly marked for interaction, most commonly in terms of *you, I,* and *me,* e.g. *Believe (you) me, Let me tell you, I wouldn't worry* (literal idioms), *You're kidding/joking, mind you, Are you deaf?* (semi-idioms), *Has the cat got your tongue?* (a pure idiom), etc.

2 They are discourse-oriented expressions as they imply preceding co-text even as citation items, e.g. *the question is ..., a good question* (semi-idioms), *That's true, as I said before, thank you/thanks a lot* (literal idioms), etc.

3 They contribute to structuring talk so that a coherent organization is discernible in different sorts of talk, e.g. *Hi, how are you?, Who's next?* (beginning), *Have you heard this one?, To change the subject, by the way* (body of discourse), *See you later* (end). These expressions are all literal idioms, except for the rhetorical question, *Have you heard this one?* (a semi-idiom), and *by the way* (a pure idiom).

4 While some interpersonal expressions such as *How are you?* (literal), *What have you been up to?* (semi-literal), etc. are fixed and lexically invariant idioms, others appear embedded in variant forms such as *Wishing you a happy birthday* (literal), *Have a very happy birthday,* etc. in which *Happy Birthday* exemplifies idiomaticity on its own as well as by collocating with items from a restricted set; or the expressions could be common locutions (*This way, please; To your right/left,* etc.) which also show habitual co-occurrence of a restricted set of lexical constituents.

5 Though there are many interpersonal idioms that are non-literal pure idioms, e.g. *come off it,* or variant semi-literal, semi-idioms

154

such as *There/Here you go*, *There/Here you are*, etc., they are not at the same time imagist and metaphorical in the way typical ideational idioms are.

Interpersonal idiomatic expressions provide a resource for the language-user to be, at the very least, a coherent conversationalist, sometimes even a polished one depending on individual aptitude. Equally importantly, they determine the emotional key of a discourse as one of attraction or antagonism.

4.1.2 Interpersonal idiomatic expressions as markers of conviviality: politeness routines

Convivial can be defined for the purpose of this chapter as 'sociability resulting in amity'. Amity, however, does not normally arise involuntarily. With regard to verbal behaviour, what produces amity is conformity to the social mores governing who says what to whom, when and where (Fishman 1968).

The model of a dramatic performance, such as a play, lends itself very well to bringing out the salient characteristics of convivial verbal behaviour. Firth (1957) implied such a model when he characterized speakers as bundles of social personae saying what their fellows expect them to say in appropriate settings. A similar view is also put forward by Halliday (1978). In this respect, most interpersonal idiomatic expressions are very different from ideational ones, which though conventionalized, are not formulaic in their uses. However, it is precisely their formulaic use which results in interpersonal expressions promoting conviviality. Any deviation from such formulaic use could be regarded as a tactless joke or a *faux pas* such as saying *Happy birthday* when it is not someone's birthday, or *My deepest sympathy* when there has been no bereavement. Joke or *faux pas*, the impression created is one of discourtesy, hardly conducive to amity. Amity requires adherence to regulative politeness routines, these routines being at the very heart of social life.

Leech (1983) characterizes the nature of such routines as a kind of constructive self-effacement by each interlocutor so that given such a mutually congenial state, a specific outcome, productive, not destructive, will result. The formula for such constructive self-effacement, the one which in effect underlies all of the six maxims (Tact, Generosity, Approbation, Modesty, Agreement, and Sympathy) which make up Leech's Politeness Principle, takes the form:

minimize cost to other: maximize cost to self
maximize benefit to other: minimize benefit to self

where the benefits to the other take the form of praise, agreement, approbation, or sympathy and the cost to self a particular form of self-effacement.

Conventionalized as they are to the point of being formulaic, interpersonal idiomatic expressions expressive of Leech's politeness maxims exemplify powerfully the workings of the idiom principle within situational contexts of conviviality or conflict.

The key strategy apparent in polite verbal behaviour is mutual alignment (Stubbs 1983: 186ff) as evidenced by the use of such familiar expressions to promote amity. The assumption that mutual alignment will occur in the course of talk is implicit in Leech's politeness maxims:

request—compliance (Generosity)—thanks (Approbation)
apology—acceptance (Sympathy)
assertion—endorsement (Agreement), etc.

Failure to observe the Politeness Principle results in non-productive situations as, for instance, when a speaker resorts to irony (Leech 1983: 142). Irony may be intended as 'insincere politeness', but, like mockery, it is a better weapon to outwit an opponent than unconcealed antagonism if an interation takes the form of a verbal contest (see section 4.4.2).

Grice's Co-operative Principle, as Leech points out (ibid.: 40), complements and so works together with the Politeness Principle to prevent 'uncooperative and impolite behaviour'. Four categories, each with its maxims and sub-maxims, comprise the Co-operative Principle (Grice 1975: 45–6). These can be summarized as follows:

1 QUANTITY relates to the amount of information 'as is required (for the current purposes of the exchange)'. In other words, do not say too much or too little.

2 QUALITY relates to truth value, i.e. 'Be truthful', and provide adequate evidence for what you say.

3 RELATION concerns relevance, especially with regard to the subject matter of talk and also to shifts in topic.

4   MANNER enjoins avoidance of obscurity, ambiguity, prolixity, and incoherence (disorderliness). In other words, 'Be perspicuous'.

The discourses in the following section show how the workings of the Politeness Principle and the Co-operative Principle ensure productive talk. Non-productive talk, generally conflictive, often arises from covert or overt power struggles. Hierarchy is a fact of social life giving people at the top ascendancy over those below. The Politeness Principle, in particular, requires that power be mitigated in appropriate ways. That a stock of interpersonal idiomatic expressions already exists in the English vocabulary makes it so much easier for speakers to do this. The principle of least effort is very evident in the use of these interpersonal expressions.

4.1.3 Service encounters

Service encounters, like medical and legal consultations or job interviews, have specific purposes prescribed by social convention: the exchange of goods and services. That is, their *raison d'être*. Of all these types of verbal exchange, the service encounter is the most explicit in terms of what is being exchanged: the goods and services are visible and the money, cheque, or credit card payment immediate. The verbal interaction itself embodies a relatively easily recognizable structure which, if reduced to its typical form, appears as an obligatory *request–compliance–sale–purchase–closure* sequence (Halliday and Hasan 1985). In reality, most service encounters generally show optional elements arising from contextual variables and, consequently, have a more extended structure than the obligatory one given above. There could, for example, be a repetition of this sequence, a kind of loopback as in example (1). Other optional elements are also possible: 'repairs' such as a request for clarification, and 'foils', for example, a sales request which elicits a rejection due to the unavailability of an item, resulting in a modification of the original request (ibid.). The sheer commonness of service encounters has made almost every speaker's turn in the progression of the interaction into either an idiom or a restricted collocation.

Many such expressions suggest the dominance of the customer, especially with regard to terms of address, for example, Sir/Madam vs. waiter as in (1) below. The customer also decides if a sale is to take place, and, if so, when it is completed as in (1).

However, the waiter and the vendor have the power to keep customers waiting by passing them over in favour of other customers. A vendor can refuse a customer service as, for instance, a chemist, if the customer has no prescription for sales-restricted drugs. A vendor can reserve the right to check customers' bags and even charge them with shoplifting. In the case of the shoplifting charge, customers, of course, can countersue if wrongly prosecuted.

Examples (1) to (3) illustrate the way in which both vendors of various sorts and customers preserve the *status quo* in the conventionally prescribed manner:

(1) [at a delicatessen]
Vendor: *'Morning. Something I can get for you?*
Customer: Oh, yeah. Is that Australian or Greek fetta? The one over there?
V: That one's Greek.
C: Great. Um, just give me that little piece at the back. Tah.
V: *Anything else?*
C: Nah, that's great.
V: *Rightie oh.* That'll be two fifty-three.
C: *Here we go. Thanks a lot.*
V: *Bye now.*
C: By ... Oh, ah, actually d'ya reckon I could have a ... oh, about two-fifty grams of black olives as well? *Sorry!*
V: Sure, *no problem.* Two-fifty, was it?
C: Yep, thanks.
V: *There ya go.* One forty-three, love. Thanks.
C: *Tah, bye.*
V: *See you later.* [A]

(2) [at the butcher's]
Vendor: *Who's next?* (Indication by customer) *Good morning. What can I do for you?*
Customer: *Good morning. I'd like a kilo* of mince, please.
V: *Will there be anything else,* Madam?
C: *How much* is your leg-ham?

158

V:	Eighteen dollars fifty a kilo.

V: Eighteen dollars fifty a kilo.
C: No, *thanks, that'll be all.*
V: That's three ninety-three thanks.
C: (Hands money)
V: *There's your change.*
C: *Thank you. Bye.*
V: *Bye. Have a nice day.* [A]

(3) [Gilbert's (à la carte) Manly Pacific Hotel]
Waiter: *Good evening,* sir.
Customer: *Good evening. I have a table booked in the name of Griffiths.*
W: Yes, Mr Griffiths for two.
C: *Thank you.*
W: *This way,* please.
   (After meal)
C: Waiter, *could I have the bill,* please?
W: Certainly, sir.
   (On the way out)
C: *Thank you,* dinner was excellent.
W: *Thank you.* Good night, sir, *good night,* madam.
C: *Good night.* [A]

Some of the idiomatic expressions occurring in the service encounter, for example, those functioning as initiators and terminators, are not confined to this type of verbal interaction:

Initiators: *(Good) morning; Good evening*
Terminators: *See you later; Have a nice day; Good night; Bye (for) now*

Others are typical of the service encounter, and, consequently, act as identificatory markers of this type of interaction:

Initiators: *Something I can get (for) you? (1); Who's next?; What can I do for you? (2),* and from a similar exchange elsewhere in my corpus, *Can I help you?; Are you ready to order?* varied in a similar exchange to *Would you like to order now?*
Terminators: *Here we go* or *There you go (1); Could I have the bill, please? (3); Thanks a lot (1)* or *Thank you (2)*

These initiators and terminators comprise invariant literal idioms (e.g. Who's next?), variant semi-literal, semi-idioms (e.g. *Here we go, There you go, There/Here you are*), variant literal idioms (e.g. *Thank you, Thanks a lot*), and common locutions (*Are you ready to order?, Would you like to order now?*, etc.). Typical expressions associated with the body of the service-encounter script are: *(Will there be) anything else?* (1), (2); *That'll be all, No, thanks* (2); *Thanks a lot* (1) *(Just) give me (that)* ... (1); *I'd like a/some ..., How much is ...?, There's your change* (2); *I have a table booked in the name of ..., A table for ... (two, five, etc.), This way, please* (3).

These expressions all exemplify idiomaticity by virtue of the habitual co-occurrence of a set of lexical constituents. Common locutions such as *Anything else?* and literal idioms such as *That'll be all*, etc. are marked for cohesion with their preceding co-text by virtue of their semantic content: they indicate prior requests and compliances or imminent compliance as in *No problem* (1). The common literal idiom *No worries* is also a possibility in a situation of compliance. *Thanks a lot*, like *thank you*, may also occur in the body of a discourse.

The conviviality of (1) to (3), consistently maintained throughout, arises from close adherence to what is expected. Consequently, no power struggles arise.

The expected, for example, *Who's next?*, is commonplace, and therefore relatively low in information value. In (1) to (3) the words highest in information value are the variables in common locutions such as *I'd like some ..., How much is ...?, A table for ...*, etc., as well as the response to an idiom like *Who's next?* also high in information value as it indicates who is next in the queue.

In the matter of information, interpersonal idiomatic expressions, it is worth mentioning, are very different from ideational ones. Not only are all ideational idioms high in information content, especially when subjected to novel variation, but additionally, the discourses they occur in do not have the quality of a script whose lines are familiar to the speakers as in the routinized type of verbal interactions presented above.

4.1.4 Small talk

At certain points in service encounters, the interlocutors in the course of talking, give each other facts high in information value elicited as responses to questions in the form of expressions low in information value themselves because of their predictability in this type of interaction:

What can I do for you?   I'd like *a kilo of mince.*
(Who's) next, please?/Who's next? *I am.*

The essence of small talk is that it is low in the kind of factual information that *a kilo of mince*, and *I am*, etc. represent. However, though low in the kind of factual information crucial to the progression of a verbal interaction such as a service encounter, small talk conveys other sorts of information as a result of:

1 checking on the physical and emotional state of the other;

2 expressing opinions conveying evaluations of the sort presented in Chapter 3: good, bad, and ambivalent

even though such information may sometimes be inaccurate, that is, a white lie. On the other hand, it could also be accurate. Facial expressions, eye-contact, and tone of voice are probably the best guides to the veracity of *I'm fine* or *it's really great* in discourses like (4).

(4) [a conversation between neighbours at the Whyte's house]
    Alison: Hello, Mr Whyte.
    Mr Whyte: Oh, hello, Alison, *how are you?*
    A: Oh, *I'm fine*, thanks. I just came over to thank you for the T-shirt you brought back from France. *It's really great.*
    Mr W: Oh, I'm glad you like it. Does it fit you alright?
    A: Yeah, *it's fine.*
    Mr W: Well, we wanted to bring you back something to thank you for feeding Pippa (a cat).
                (Mrs Whyte appears)
    Mrs W: Hello, Alison.
    A: Hello, Mrs Whyte.
    Mrs W: *How are you?* Do you like the T-shirt?

A:	Yeah, *it's really nice*, thanks. Actually, I had it on this morning.
Mrs W:	Yes, I thought you might like it.
A:	How was your trip?
Mrs W:	Oh, *it was lovely*. We had a wonderful time, didn't we, Bill? [A]

As with (1) to (3), there is here an exchange of goods and services, the key difference being that the exchange has already taken place: the gift of a T-shirt in return for feeding a cat. This exchange is not a commercial one, so the emphasis is on the sort of conviviality created by much more personal responses than those in the service encounters above. Idioms of polite inquiry, for example, *How are you?* and restricted collocations expressive of appreciation such as *It's really great/nice/fine/lovely*, etc. are frequent. In (4), the latter function as compliments to the donors of the gift. Compliments whether sincere or not, are also implicit evaluations and those in (4) take one of the forms (Wolfson 1981) commonly used in making such evaluations:

Subject–Verb (Copula)   (Intensifier)–Adjective

Self-evaluations (*I'm fine, thanks*) and other types of evaluations (*It was lovely*), have the same form though they are not compliments. While *I'm fine/good/okay/not bad/alright* as a response to *How are you?* is a collocation with a restricted set of variants, *It is/was lovely* as an evaluation of something has no such restrictions: *It is/was lovely/fantastic/wonderful/incredible/great/nasty/awful/frightful*, etc. The latter is a relatively unrestricted collocation but sufficiently conventionalized to exemplify idiomaticity in the language.

Evaluations of various sorts ('good', 'bad', and 'ambivalent') many of which take the form of different types of idioms or exemplify idiomaticity in the form of restricted collocations, characterize small-talk. Example (4), one specific example of such talk, abounds in the kinds of information identified by:

1   checking on Alison' s pleasure at the gift of the T-shirt;

2   Alison's expressions of pleasure.

The latter, expressed via familiar collocations are exactly suited to the situation. The gift is a modest one and unusual or elaborate expressions of appreciation could violate the Maxim of Quantity ('Give only the right amount of information') and that of Quality ('Be sincere'). Alison strikes the right note by keeping to predictable conventionalized expressions in applying the Approbation Maxim, i.e. maximize praise of the other.

The turn-taking structure of (5) provides the basis for the consistent maintenance of the Sympathy Maxim: maximize sympathy between self and the other. Mutual checking on each other's well-being by means of formulaic expressions of inquiry elicit appropriate restricted collocations of self-evaluation or satisfaction (e.g. *That's good*):

(5) [a conversation between two friends at a social gathering]
    A: *How are you?*
    B: *All right, thanks.*
    A: *That's good.*
    B: Yeah. *How are you?*
    A: *I'm good.*

The conversation continues with mutual inquiries and responses, regarding the current preoccupations of the two friends:

    A: *What are you up to?*
    B: Oh ... *essays.*
    A: *How's it going?*
    B: Busy. *How about you?*
    A: Mm ... *much the same* ... assignments. [A]

Idioms of greeting and farewell have occurred in many of the discourses above, but have not been commented on. *How are you?*, sometimes preceded by *Hi* and *Hello*, is the commonest greeting in my corpus and everyday experience. Farewells show greater diversity. *See you later* (4) is very common; so is *see you sometime* and, if the occasion demands it, *see you soon* may occur. Another increasingly common idiom of farewell is *Take care. Look after yourself* and *I hope you are keeping well* (the latter used either at the beginning or end of a letter) are also possibilities. All three express concern as well as informality and middling or minimal social distance. *It's been nice talking to you* and *Nice to have met you*, being more formal, signify maximal social distance.

The conviviality of (4) and (5) is unbroken because the interlocutors know their 'lines' perfectly and so come in effortlessly on cue.

4.2 Institutionalized good wishes and sympathy

4.2.1 Introduction

The view of culture as a system of meanings appears in statements such as:

> ... culture represents a consensus on a wide variety of meanings among members of an interacting community approximating that of the consensus on language among members of a speech community. (LeVine 1984: 68)

Personal experiences vary greatly from individual to individual, but such idiosyncratic differences are off-set by communal, institutionalized events invested with shared meanings and a conventionalized set of expressions conveying these meanings (Appadurai 1990). Those events that are institutionalized are universal, for example, birth, illness and death, marriage, travel, and professional success.

In Anglo-Celtic societies, the greetings card industry has arisen to cater for the different sorts of emotions associated with various institutionalized events. The communal nature of these events means that the emotions they arouse, though private in origin, assume a social aspect. Consequently, verbalization is obligatory to such 'social' emotions, the intention behind such expressions like that of small talk, being the creation of social solidarity. Though related to private emotions, 'social' emotions are very different in that convention permits them to be expressed by proxy: the language of the card is not the sender's. The expression of private emotions may draw on idioms, for example, *walk on air*, but though conventionalized, such idioms are not formulaic; nor is the expression of private emotions confined to idioms. The sentiments expressed in cards, in contrast, are genre-oriented and must conform to the distinctive formulaic idioms and restricted collocations of each genre: the language of Christmas greetings, though sharing some similarities, is different from that of birthdays. However, cards can also be novel, but they still work by proxy.

The 'borrowed' idioms and restricted collocations used by the sender because of their formulaic or semi-formulaic nature are easily interpreted in a culturally informed way by the receiver. The sender adopts a persona created by the card industry: humorous, sentimental, sympathetic, genial, etc. The act of sending a card indicates attraction on the sender's part for the intended recipient. The intention is to maintain and enhance a current relationship.

4.2.2 Christmas and New Year greetings

In Anglo-Celtic cultures Christmas and New Year are typically linked together in greetings cards as Christmas begins and New Year concludes the festive season. Of the two, Christmas has stronger symbolic associations linked implicitly or explicitly to other times, places, and events, not simply to the present. However, the original strength of the early associations expressive of a joyful reverence for the Christ Child have dwindled with the secularization of society and the advent of science and technology. In contemporary Anglo-Celtic cultures, Christmas is much more a social than a religious event. The conviviality of Christmas festivities strengthen personal ties, not ties with God, the focus of the greetings being you, not Him.

The Christmas–New Year message is built on the following restricted collocations:

Happy Christmas/New Year; Merry Christmas; Christmas Wishes/Greetings; Season's/New Year Greetings

Such expressions normally occur on the front page of the card. Elaborations of these appear within the card and constitute the language of this type of greeting:

(6) [Christmas/New Year greetings cards]
    a. Wishing you a very Merry Christmas
        and a very Happy New Year [A]
    b. With All Good Wishes
        For Christmas
        And the New Year [A]

Both the restricted vocabulary and the grammar of Christmas and New Year cards (6) are analysed below:

1 Various grammatical forms of *wish*: *wish/wishes*; *wishing*

2 Christmas and New Year with or without adjectives, *merry* and *happy* being the commonest, though a constraint operates on *A*

happy New Year, merry being unacceptable: *A merry New Year*

3 Quantifiers: *all, every*
4 An *I/you* polarity, with *I* being always implicit and *you* sometimes.

4.2.3 Birthday greetings

The birthday as a social institution arises only in cultures where ages are known and constitute transitional points in one's life. In Anglo-Celtic culture such points occur at:

18/21: the age of majority
30:     the beginning of middle age
60/65: retirement and the later years
70:     the accepted average life-span

Normally, 18/21 and 70 elicit congratulatory messages while 30 and 60/65 elicit humorous ones.

The commonest type of birthday card contains near formulaic expressions classifiable as literal idioms or literal restricted collocations:

(7) [birthday greetings cards]
  a. A Birthday Wish
      (Just For You) (For Every Happiness)
  b. A (Warm) Happy Birthday to A Very Special Person/
      Someone Special/Someone Nice/My Very Special Friend,
      etc.
  c. Wishing you
      A Wonderful Birthday
  d. For Your Birthday
      With Warmest Wishes
  e. With Warmest Wishes
      For Your Birthday
  f. A Special Birthday Thought
  g. Happy Birthday
  h. Birthday Greetings [A]

As with Christmas and New Year cards, the idiom of the birthday card rests on a very restricted vocabulary combined in limited and, therefore, conventionalized ways:

1   An implicit *I* and explicit *you* polarity
2   Different evaluative adjectives, for example, *special* or *nice*, preceding or following *person* or *someone*
3   Different variations and elaborations of the key phrase *Happy Birthday*, the commonest oral greeting:
    a. with a form of *wish*: *wish/wishes*; *wishing*
    b. an evaluative adjective, for example, *wonderful* or *warm* preceding *birthday*, the one lexical constant in written greetings.

A common theme of the birthday message is the specialness of the recipient or the wishes, though in what way remains undefined. The humorous birthday card, apart from the formulaic *Happy Birthday*, has to be novel to make its point. A typical gag takes the form of:

(8)   Turning 39/40/45, etc. isn't so bad, let's see …

followed by a number of variables such as a *broad smile/your lovely hair*, etc. with a drawing of a toothless grin/a balding head, or some other sign of aging, generally exaggerated. These examples are modelled on gags from greetings cards.

   Humorous birthday cards are designed for the ageing in a society where youth is celebrated and consequently, age is something of an embarrassment with humour being one way of coming to terms with it.

4.2.4 Condolence, sympathy, and congratulations

My examination of the idiomatic expressions of Christmas, New Year, and birthday greetings shows the way near-formulaic language functions in order to communicate certain key cultural meanings inhering in widespread cultural practices in a particular society. This section looks at other events which also have cultural significance and evoke conventionalized responses. Each has its own formulaic expression composed of the following:

1   A nominal phrase or semi-clause with or without evaluative adjectives

2   A form of the pronoun *you* with *I* being implicit.

Death, like ageing, is something we can really be certain of. When certitude becomes reality, moral support is necessary which, unlike in the case of ageing, appears not as humour, but as sympathy:

(9)   [sympathy cards]

    a.   Extending/With Deepest/Sincere Sympathy

    b.   Sending you a special message of Sympathy

    c.   With Sympathy in Your Sorrow [A]

The key phrase in condolences is *With (deepest/sincere)sympathy.*

Though illness, like ageing is related to death, like ageing it is generally treated humorously. The key literal idiom (restricted) here is *Get well (soon).*

Novel elaborations appear in (10):

(10)   [sympathy card]
    Get well soon followed by an injunction to do it *quickly/at once*, etc.[A]

Congratulations represent the recognition of personal and professional success. The key collocation here is *Congratulations on your ...*, though, as with other restricted collocations, this has its variations:

(11)   [congratulations cards]
    a.   Congratulations on your engagement
    b.   A New Baby—Congratulations
    c.   Congratulations—Well done [A]

A *new baby* is itself a semi-idiom meaning that there is a new member of the family. *Well done*, a literal idiom, is a synonym of *congratulations* and acts here as an intensifier.

From engagements and babies, it seems logical to proceed to anniversaries. Anniversaries are celebrated on the widely held cultural assumption that time enriches marriage. Thus, we have a progression from a paper anniversary (one year), through silver (twenty-five years) and golden (fifty years), to the grand culmination of a diamond one (sixty years). The key literal idiom on anniversary cards is *Happy Anniversary*, which is obligatory. Some common elaborations are:

(12) [derived from anniversary greetings cards]
   a. To Two Wonderful/Marvellous People/Persons, etc.
   b. I love you more/more than ever, etc. [A]

I love you, like *Will you marry me?*, is a conventionalized expression with idiom status, any variants being unusual enough to qualify as novel.

As with private emotions expressed through ideational idioms in personal self-reports, the 'social' emotions of the interpersonal expressions discussed above also convey affection and sympathy for family and friends. The social, in the final analysis, is rooted in the individual and reflects, as in the case of greeting cards, the individual's desire for solidarity and moral support through interaction with others. Despite people using prefabricated messages in choosing greeting cards, such messages express goodwill as well as attraction, and so promote a high degree of conviviality.

4.3 Forums: information-oriented talk

4.3.1 Introduction

The essence of information-oriented talk is factual content in varying degrees. Consequently, the subject matter of such exchanges cannot be assimilated with least effort as that of small talk or greetings cards can. Talk-back radio is one instance of such information-oriented talk providing a forum for the discussion of topical subjects between host and caller(s) with the listeners as the unseen audience. Since talk-back radio gives the public an opportunity to air their opinions, share their expertise or seek advice, a specific topic is a *sine qua non*. Such a topic can elicit agreement or opposition resulting in conflict or conviviality. The examples and analyses below focus on various markers of amity in convivial forums.

4.3.2 Endorsements

The basis of convivial forums, like all other convivial interactions, is alignment (Stubbs 1983). Alignment in this situation can be regarded as expressing the Agreement Maxim of the Politeness Principle: maximize agreement between self and the other. In forums, such alignments assume various forms: acceptance, acknowledgement, and endorsement (ibid.). However, the forms of alignment that are of most relevance to conviviality are idioms and restricted collocations of endorsement. As Stubbs (ibid.: 189) points out, such strong agreement functions as indicators:

1   of being on the same wavelength;
2   of utterances having been accepted into the ongoing discourse;
3   of mini-topics being established and sustained by ratifying the other's point of view.

Examples (13 to (15) show how endorsement expresses the speaker's enthusiasm at being *en rapport* with the addressee. Example (13) is part of an exchange between a host (A) and a caller (B) who is annoyed by an Australian TV commentator not distinguishing between kayaking and canoeing in his commentary on the Seoul Olympics:

(13)   **A:** So you insist that kayaking is a genuine and tough Olympic event and it should be properly described.
       B: *That's right. That's exactly right.* [A]

In example (14) the caller wants to know the difference between hamsters and guinea pigs. The host (B) who confesses his ignorance of the topic, and the caller (A) try to work out the difference:

(14)   **A:** Yes, about half the size of a guinea pig.
       B: Yeah.
       A: And doesn't have the same teeth arrangement but I'm not exactly sure what the difference is.
       B: Ah, *thank you very much.*
       A: *A pleasure.*
       B: But it's a Greek animal.
       A: Yes, *it is indeed.* But yes, *you're right.* [A]

(15)   ... Mind you I was travelling in August (yes) which is the most crowded season of the year.
       Yes, *that's true.* [BCET]

All these speakers accept (*Yeah, yes*), acknowledge (*thank you very much*) and endorse (*that's (exactly) right, you're right, it is indeed, that's true*) each other's point of view, supported by similar expressions of appreciation (*it's a pleasure*). The exchanges proceed smoothly with either endorsements or appreciation occurring at regular intervals, so that a pattern of supportive feedback is established.

Another type of endorsement appears in (16):

(16)   … In the opinion of the team, what would they consider to be absolutely necessary?
       Good question, Janet Goodacre. [BCET]

Good question here means: 'your contribution is relevant though we hadn't thought of it'. This semi-idiom is a way of endorsing the introduction of a possible new topic into a discussion. It must be distinguished from another almost similar in form, but with a different stress pattern (*'good question vs. a good 'question*) signalling a difference in function.

(17)   [a conversation between friends at A's house]
       a. **A:** The French Government has made it illegal for anything but unbleached flour to be used.
          B: How do you bleach flour?
          A: *A good question.* I don't know. [A]
       b. [part of a conversation in a shop]
          A: How much does this cost?
          B: *A good question.*
          (Looks up price list) [A]

A good question indicates topicality, but also implies the inability of the addressee to satisfy the interlocutor's query. As with other types of endorsements, *A good question* demonstrates conviviality.

4.3.3 Mitigation

Between peers there is the assumption of equal status and power. Mitigatory expressions strengthen the solidarity and goodwill between peers.

Interactions between non-peers may demonstrate inequality. In such exchanges the more powerful participants have the option of either heightening or mitigating their ascendancy by appropriate verbal behaviour and by this means saving the 'face' of the other(s).

The need for mitigation may arise even between peers, especially to counter disappointment: no relationship exists indefinitely on the same level and the same affective key. Appropriate idioms exist for such needs and help maintain the conviviality of the exchange. Some of the situations in which mitigatory strategies are used, along with appropriate idiomatic expressions are listed below:

A negative circumstance: someone or something that should be there is not.

(18)   a. *I'm afraid* I can't come. [BCET]
       b. *I'm afraid* I don't have a brochure. [BCET]
       c. *I'm sorry to say* that Terry Wogan is unable to be with us. [BCET]

Softening an implicit reproach or criticism

(19)   a. *I'm sorry to say* that we didn't have Edward's vote in favour of it when we carried it through. [BCET]
       b. Michael Foot *I'm sorry to say* hasn't got it quite right. The fact is … . [BCET]
       c. *I'm afraid* he carries no credibility. [BCET]
       d. That's probably a gross overstatement and *I daresay* there are some old Summerhill students who now would be very offended by what I'm saying. [BCET]

Mitigating power

(20)   a. *I'm afraid* I have to stop you there. [BCET]
       b. … You're a member I believe of the Royal Commission currently investigating the Health Service. Is that right? *I'm afraid so.* [BCET]

The preferred behaviour according to the Politeness Principle is to fulfil the needs of others as dictated by both the Tact and the Generosity Maxims. Hence the apologetic mitigation in (18).

Example (19) also reflects the Tact Maxim: minimize cost to other; maximize benefit to other. If approbation is impossible, then speakers show awareness of the dangers of dispraise (cost to the other): they imply regret as in *I'm afraid* (a semi-idiom), *I'm sorry to say* (a literal idiom), or suggest the possibility of being wrong as in *I dare say* in order to both minimize dispraise and cost to the other.

172

Tact also operates in relation to (20): it is the appropriate consideration to take into account in forums which aim at convivial discussion and which, therefore, require a mitigation of power.

4.3.4 Generosity

One of the key features of casual conversation is disorganized, self-directed turn-taking. In contrast, the turn typically taken at the invitation of another identifies forum-style discussions such as seminars, media debates, etc. *How do you feel about …?*, *What do you think of …?*, where *feel* and *think* have the specialized subsense 'opinion' are interpersonal semi-idioms with two functions:

1 they give participants a chance to take a turn in the discussion;
2 they allow for opinions which maintain the discussion by permitting endorsements or challenge a point of view.

These observations are borne out by (21) and (22):

(21) **M:** And I'm sure often unions find power in their hands they don't particularly want.
  D.J: *How do you feel about* it, Antonia?
  A.F: Yes, I agree with Miles on his last point. [BCET]

(22) **P.V:** *What did you think of* Ron Daniel's last production?
  A.S: I thought it was very slick. [BCET]

Both the good conversationalist and the good chairperson acknowledge the presence of others by taking positive measures to allow them to take a turn. However, idiomatic expressions of the kind given above are normally used not only in the interests of politeness, but also to promote informed discussion.

4.3.5 Informing strategies

Information-oriented talk has a specific subject-matter which requires, unlike that of small talk, sustained concentration. A set of conventionalized expressions exist in the language to mark given segments in such discourses so that what is relatively important and what is less so are both clear, thereby enhancing both understanding and conviviality. Some of these expressions are presented below.

What, you may ask ('you don't know all the facts'), and its variants, like *Guess what?*, is a rhetorical question by means of which speakers foreground information they consider newsworthy because of some unusual circumstance:

(23) a. *What, you may ask*, was Bobby Gould doing ...? [BCET]

     b. *What, I hear you ask*, a hockey player being mobbed? [BCET]

     c. *What, you ask*, if Napoleon had conquered? Or Hitler? Well, they didn't? [BCET]

What, you may ask, and its variants implies superior knowledge on the part of the questioner (I) since he/she does not really expect an answer from the addressee (you) who has, actually, asked no question. In fact, the questioner usually supplies the answer as in (23c.). This type of rhetorical question, which can be considered a semi-idiom, appears in written or formal types of spoken discourse, like a lecture, and contrasts with the colloquial *Guess what?*, which also performs a similar function. Both expressions indicate information still to come.

Another expression which also foregrounds what the speaker considers to be significant information is *(This/That is/was) what I'm/am saying*, a semi-idiom. In using *what I'm saying* (*saying* here has the specialized subsense 'claiming') the speaker affirms something already said and which he/she considers sufficiently important to emphasize in case the others have not got the point. Example (24) illustrates this kind of signposting in discourse:

(24) a. **H:** Do you really think he had that much honour?
       T: No, I don't think he did in practice—*this is what I was saying*—but in theory ... . [BCET]

     b. **C:** Yes, but obviously—somebody who's, you know, a native speaker has got an advantage over a over an ...
       I: *That's what I'm saying*—what advantage has he got—or she got? [BCET]

     c. So *what you're saying* is that the temptation is very strong indeed just because we happen to have supplies of oil and natural gas to use them straightaway. [BCET]

This type of reaffirmation is not the same as ordinary checking as in

Are you sure you don't have any difficulty in following what I am saying? Reaffirmation has an anaphoric function in that it points backwards to some prior portion of the discourse. In this respect, *what I'm saying* contrasts with *what, you ask,* etc. and *Guess what?,* both of which have an anticipatory or cataphoric function.

Two semi-idioms, both containing *a question,* which in these expressions carry the subsense 'issue', are frequently used in information-oriented talk as a way of emphasizing an important point:

(25)   a.   And *it's a question* of going to the right schools ... . *It's* not so much *a question* of going to university. [BCET]

       b.   I think *the question is* partly a political and partly a legal question. [BCET]

A less direct way of emphasizing significant information is to contrast it with what is not, for instance, by the use of a restricted collocation such as *It doesn't (really) matter/count/doesn't mean a thing/anything, etc.,* giving what is significant end-focus:

(26)   a.   So whether she's in a big house or a small house, *it doesn't really matter.* She's not going to cook. (end-focus clause) [BCET]

       b.   *It doesn't (really) matter* whether your name is Maude or Tindall or Halsey or Redhead—they have you, if you can do the job. (end-focus clause) [BCET]

Moving from one topic to another in discussions is often accomplished by means of *another question,* in this expression *question* meaning 'topic'. Such expressions are also a means of drawing every participant into the discussion:

(27)   a.   Let's move on if we may to *another question* please. Do you think ...? [BCET]

       b.   Let's have *another question* please Sue. What do you think ...? [BCET]

Speakers foreground information they consider significant in order to facilitate understanding and ensure co-operation; they may also foreground the non-significant features of a situation for the same reasons. Intended as reassurances, the function of a literal idiom like *Not to worry* and its variants *Don't worry/I wouldn't worry* is to indicate what is non-significant in a given context of situation. Such expressions refer to ongoing activity out there, not to a prior segment of the discourse as with *what I'm saying* or what follows as with *what, you ask*.

(28) a. Don't worry Andrew, you can do it in whatever order you like ... [BCET]

   b. Some of their towels are soaking wet, but *never mind. Not to worry.* [BCET]

The semi-idiom *never mind* overlaps in its pragmatic function, though different in form, with *Don't/Not to worry* and is typically interchangeable with it, though if both forms occur in the same conversational turn as in (28b.) for *never mind* to follow *Not to worry* would be non-idiomatic. The interchangeability of these expressions appears below.

(29) a. Can't quite work that one out but *never mind* we'll find another questionnaire. [BCET]

   b. *Don't/Not to worry*, we'll find another questionnaire. [I]

Idioms foregrounding irrelevance also belong with those that foreground non-significance:

(30) a. After my operation for gallstones I can't bend but *that's another story*. [A]

   b. **A:** How is Yolanta's brother?
      B: Yolanta's brother? *That's another story*. [A]

Example (30) contains a semi-idiom indicative of non-topicality in terms of the overall discourse. *That's another story* can be glossed as: 'Let's postpone the subject for a more opportune moment' or 'I don't want to talk about the subject'. The speakers using the idiom know that the subject in question raises side-issues and so could be a waste of time with the addressee probably being bored if given the whole story, or they may wish to avoid the subject altogether. Accordingly, even though the preferred norm is to answer questions, the addressee in (30b.) in replying is thinking ahead to the undesirable consequences of being accommodating. *That's another story, it'll keep*, etc. are related to both Grice's Quantity Maxim ('Be brief') and Relation Maxim ('Be relevant').

When Grice formulated his Maxim of Quality 'Be truthful', he was pinpointing a typical expectation among participants in a verbal interaction. Truthfulness and the allied virtue of sincerity are prized in most societies, though the Tact Maxim of the Politeness Principle permits the white lie, especially in small talk, in order to save either one's own social face or the social face of the other. With this one exception, falsehoods and insincerities will commonly diminish conviviality.

In cases where there is the possibility of disbelief, speakers may affirm their sincerity:

(31)   a.   Only in Britain would eminent highly educated people ... think it was worth mocking modern art. Please *believe me*, this is absolutely true. [BCET]

      b.   ... and I felt like saying ugh—I felt like saying some achievement *believe you me*. [BCET]

A more common practice is to affirm that adequate evidence exists for the validity of some statement. Such affirmations range from the relatively mild *in fact, as a matter of fact* (literal idioms), to the stronger *it's true/evident/obvious*, etc. *that* (restricted collocations), *it's certainly/clearly/absolutely true*, etc. *that* (restricted collocations) and the literal expressions *the mere fact that, the fact of the matter is, by virtue of the fact that*, etc., all idioms by virtue of their invariance:

(32)   *It's certainly true that* a lot of people are teaching the subject without ... really understanding the internal refinements. [BCET]

(33)   ... *the fact of the matter is* if they weren't spent on a moon-shuttle—I'm afraid I don't believe given the sort of culture that produced the moon-shuttle—they'd be spent on feeding. [BCET]

(34)   ... our sovereign right to legislate has been eroded away *by virtue of the fact* that individuals can now claim the benefits of essentially a foreign system of law in our own states. [BCET]

In all these text fragments, there is a commitment to the validity of the proposition introduced by the clause following the idiom.

Example (33) is specially interesting because *I don't believe*, a common locution, is used to support *the fact of the matter*. Such a combination shows that truth value can be supported both positively (e.g. *it's true*) as well as negatively (e.g. *it isn't true*).

Truth value is also expressed by caveats: by implying some qualifying circumstance, the speaker protects his commitment to asserting only what he really believes is accurate. What emerges in such instances is that the truth is not always clear cut:

(35) a. I think though that its audience is now so accustomed to seeing pictures, but *mind you* seeing pictures is to be misled perhaps. [BCET]

b. She (i.e. June Barry) usually is wonderful and in this case she was absolutely first rate. *Mind you*, we were dying for somebody ... to show up this spoilt brat of a poet for what he was. [BCET]

In (35b.), for example, it is clear that an external circumstance, which had nothing to do with June Barry's intrinsic talents, also assisted in enhancing her performance. Circumstances of this sort, which modify the situation as originally specified, are introduced by *mind you*.

Other common caveats are the semi-idioms *I wouldn't go so far as to say*; *so far, so good*; etc.

Information-oriented talk presents a significant contrast to service encounters, small talk, and institutionalized good wishes, all of which have been discussed above. One of the bases of this contrast is the functionally different expressions in each of these types of discourse. Another is that in information-oriented talk speakers rely less on a conventionalized 'script'. The focus of interest in the service encounter is the exchange of goods and services (e.g. *Can I help you?*), in small talk and good wishes the welfare and activities of the other (e.g. *How are you? Get well soon*). In information-oriented talk, interest centres primarily on content (e.g. *What I'm saying is ...*, *The fact of the matter is ...*). The expressions used in the last type of discourse ease the understanding of content. However, whatever the type of discourse, the conventionalized expressions I have discussed in the foregoing sections indicate alignments of one sort or another: personal alignment in the service encounter, small talk and good wishes, sometimes even emotional alignment as in the last case, with intellectual alignment being the norm in the case of information-oriented talk.

4.3.6 Conclusions

The foregoing discussion has focused on interpersonal idiomatic expressions whose use produces conviviality. Such conviviality arises through the politeness evident in greetings, farewells, thanks, etc., as well as through the display of affection, goodwill, sympathy, and support evident in good wishes. Also productive of conviviality are endorsements, generosity, and mitigatory strategies, and the affirmation of truth value and sincerity when these are required in a discourse. All the verbal activities listed above express alignment testifying to the importance of making alignments of various sorts verbally explicit in Anglo-Celtic culture. In some cultures (Sri Lankan, both Sinhala and Tamil, for example), such alignments may be traditionally expressed through smiles, gestures, and other forms of body language. The result is a relative sparseness in the sort of conventionalized interpersonal expressions so abundant in English.

4.4 Interpersonal idiomatic expressions as markers of conflict

4.4.1 Introduction

Conviviality was defined as 'sociability resulting in amity' (4.1.2). In convivial interactions, mutual alignment, the strategy adopted to achieve compatible goals, creates goodwill, and above all, the preservation of the other's 'face', or social persona.

In conflictive interactions, the participants are at variance with or in open opposition to one another. Consequently, instead of accord, there is discord arising from opposed goals.

I used the model of a play, a dramatic performance, to bring out the salient characteristics of convivial verbal behaviour more clearly. Such a model focuses on the co-operation arising from mutual alignment with the participants generally saying what the other person expects them to say. Mutual alignment is absent in conflictive interactions since the dynamics of such interchanges arises from opposed goals. Hence, the model most appropriate for such exchange is one in which opposed goals constitute an essential element as in a game with two or more contestants each playing to win within the constraints of a set of rules.

There are, of course, several sorts of games, language-games being just one sort. Wittgenstein's language-games (1953: 11e, 12e), where words used in a particular way are inseparable from the activities in which they are embedded as, for example, *Ring-a-ring of roses*, are of a non-contest type. By contrast, Halliday's 'settings' (Halliday 1973) exemplified by card-games like pontoon and contract-bridge are contests where there are winners and losers.

If winning is a goal, then winning requires a choice of options from a set of options, i.e. a strategy (Rapoport 1960). Each player strives via his/her chosen strategy for the winning pay-off, i.e. outwitting the opponent.

Competitive language-games exemplifying as they do incompatible goals include arguments, the genre selected for illustrating conflict in relation to interpersonal idioms.

4.4.2 Conflicts

The purpose of an argument is to validate your reasons for holding a particular opinion and by this means refute that of your interlocutor.

(36) [part of a discussion on industrial relations in Australia]
    A: Forget about the old days Joe, they're over with.
    B: But ...
    A: This is Australia 1991!
    B: I know, *but let me tell you*—I've got to tell you ...
    A: Yeah, but Joe we don't ...
    B: 9,000 men in 1950, 900 men today, 90% of the workforce is gone ... .
    A: Okay Joe *let me* just *say* this, we'll finish the debate right now ... in eh ... Hong Kong and Tokyo it takes them one day to turn ... eh ... a container ship around ... .
    B: You don't *know what you're talking about*, ... mate.
    A: Mate, I *do know what I'm talking about* ... [A]

The male participants, in this segment from a talk-back radio session, treat each other as peers equal in status and power, a fact underpinned by their using the same restricted collocation (*let me tell you/say sth*) and terms of address to make a point and to dismiss the other's argument: *don't/do know what you/I'm talking about.*

Example (37), also from talk-back radio, is a request for advice, but the host (A), despite the light-heartedness of his initial comments, violates the Agreement Maxim in an attempt to provoke a conflict:

(37)   [part of an exchange containing a caller's (B) request for information and advice]
    A: Well, *come on*, what ya gotta say, woman?
    B: Can you help me with my ballot for my NRMA elections?
    A: *Ohhh God!* Yes, *my dear*, the NRMA elections, *go ahead.*
    B: It's important.
    A: It's not important ... *go ahead.* [A]

The mixture of condescension (*woman, my dear, Ohhh God!*) and, going on the accompanying idioms, mock imperiousness (*come on* 'be quick', 'make an effort', pure idiom, and the twice-repeated *go ahead*, 'proceed', a literal idiom) may be felt by the caller as challenging her 'face' and so could weaken conviviality. This caller, unlike the one in (36), wants help, not conflictive argument. However, the host in an attempt to turn the exchange into a debate, contradicts her assessment of the NRMA elections, then orders her to continue in a kind of cat-and-mouse game.

In contrast to (37), (38) begins with a challenge from the caller suggesting a kind of coquettish playfulness beneath the seeming antagonism. The caller (A) charges the host (B) with an unfavourable bias in his comments on one particular Australian politican in relation to another:

(38) a. **A:** Hello, Jay.
       B: Yes, Lou.
       A: I'd like to have a go at you, if I may.
       B: Oh, no!
       A: Oh, yes.
       B: Oh, no.
       A: Yes, I will. [A]

The host takes up the challenge, but does not choose to engage in the other kind of play the caller indirectly offers and ends up abusing her:

b. **B:** Darling *let me tell you*, you are a sad indictment of the problems that beset this country ... *I'm sorry to say* that to you ... but one of the great problems with this country is that there are too many ill-informed people and unfortunately you are one of them.

   A: Yeah, *I'm afraid* I am.

   B: *I'm afraid* you are. [A]

In order to win this verbal duel, the host's strategy, apart from abuse, is:

1   to employ an excluding imperative form: *let me tell you*;

2   to employ what is obviously mock commiseration in the overall context of the discourse: *I'm sorry to say, I'm afraid*.

In convivial exchanges these are genuine mitigatory strategies; here they function as vehicles of 'ironic ... truthfulness' (Leech 1983: 83) in that they only serve to highlight the host's total lack of sympathy or respect for the caller. The caller appears to use *I'm afraid* as a mitigatory strategy to mollify the host, judging by his complacent response. However, there may have been an ironical edge to her tone not deducible from the transcript, though in terms of her initial overtures she is likelier to be crestfallen rather than ironic.

Example (39) exemplifies a different sort of dismissal:

(39)   **A:** Well, presumably they'll have beds of er um scrap iron or something that they'll be allowed to mess about with.

   B: Like kindergarten?

   A: Yes.

   B: *You're kidding*! [BCET]

You're kidding (a semi-idiom used to express disbelief) violates the Agreement Maxim just as *not know what you are talking about, come off it, go tell it to the Marines, I wasn't born yesterday*, etc. do. These are all idioms which challenge the credibility of the speaker who is then called upon to justify whatever claim has been made.

4.4.3 Conclusions

Idiomatic expressions appropriate for use in conflict situations are far fewer than those indicative of conviviality in the corpora consulted. This disparity could be attributed to conviviality being much more valued as a social norm than conflict. In the process of being socialized, speakers are normally schooled in the 'scripts' exemplifying politeness; conflictive expressions are not normally taught. Both Leech's Politeness Principle and Grice's Co-operative Principle are from a social point of view regulative principles functioning to control anti-social behaviour by the use of appropriate expressions, interpersonal ones being very common among these.

The verbal strategies for worsting one's opponents, for example, challenge, irony, etc., are generally acquired as a result of painful experience. The expressions embodying such strategies are then also learnt should the violation of the Politeness Principle and the Co-operative Principle be called for by the exigencies of a particular situation.

4.5 General conclusions

The profile given of interpersonal idiomatic expressions in section 4.1 detailed their salient attributes:

1 Form: many interpersonal idiomatic expressions are, overtly or covertly, marked for interaction by their pronouns, for example, *let me tell you, (you're) not to worry.*

2 Function: (i) these expressions constitute forms of social behaviour realizing as they do various pragmatic functions such as greeting, thanking, challenging, etc. As such they show a far wider contextual distribution than ideational idioms, appearing in discourses as different as service encounters, casual conversation, and talk-back radio. (ii) Additionally, they structure verbal interactions marking openings (greetings), topic and topic changes, and closures (farewells).

Novel variations on the form of interpersonal idiomatic expressions were absent in the corpora consulted, though they appeared unaltered in novel variations of the generic language of various types of greeting card, for example, the humorous birthday card. Neither their composition, typically literal and non-imagist, or their function, pragmatic rather than propositional or poetic, result in their attracting novel variations in the way ideational idioms do. Consequently, the workings of the idiom principle emerge even more strongly in the interpersonal component of language than they do in the ideational one. Many interpersonal idiomatic expressions are virtually formulaic. Such conventionalization in no way diminishes their efficacy in promoting conviviality or in generating conflict.

5
Relational idiomatic expressions in exposition and narrative

Everyone reasons in ordinary life as well as in the schoolroom and the laboratory.
(G. H. Bird, *A Student's Guide to Intellectual Methods* 1969)

When man places himself in relation to actual events in time, he performs three, and only three acts: he experiences, he recalls, he anticipates.
(William E. Bull, *Time, Tense and the English Verb* 1968)

5.1 Relational idiomatic expressions: vehicles of logical and temporal coherence

5.1.1 Introduction

Ideational idioms of various types convey packages of information about participants, actions, and events, as well as about their attributes and circumstances in the world of the senders and receivers of such information. Idioms of this type contribute to the content of a discourse.

Language-users employ interpersonal idioms, semi-idioms, and collocations of various types in a variety of interactional functions, greetings and farewells being among the most common. Such idioms also enable their users to signpost verbal interactions so that their organizational structure, the beginning, the body, and the conclusion, is clear.

The primary function of relational idioms of various types, though not their only one, is to make explicit the semantic unity of a discourse. Even the conceptually appropriate juxtaposition of utterances in speech or sentences in writing may be insufficient to enable the addressee to comprehend the implicit connections arising from X

185

preceding Y with Z following. Explicit connectives need to be used at various points in a discourse depending on its length and subject-matter in order to make complex semantic connections clear.

A semantic relation such as Adversative signalling 'contrary to claims, expectations, etc.' can be conveyed by juxtaposition alone, as (1) below demonstrates:

(1) 1 Mr Medley further suggests that the exhibition is narrow in its scope. .
    2 As inspection of the catalogue will confirm,
    3 there is hardly an aspect of British art of the period that is not represented ... . [BCET]

On the contrary initiates clause 2 in the original of this extract from The Birmingham Collection of English Text. That the second clause discounts the claim of narrowness made in 1 is clear without the cohesive *on the contrary* omitted in example (1) in order to demonstrate that juxtaposition is sometimes sufficient for inferences to be correctly drawn from the information presented in a discourse or a portion thereof. In the case of (1), clause 3 performs that function. In other contexts, however, connectives are needed for comprehension, as (2) and (3) show.

(2) You are so clever, Peter. (Reason) *No wonder* he's an Ambassador, Paddy. (Result)
     *You are so clever, Peter. ( ) he's an Ambassador, Paddy. [BCET]

No wonder signals a deduction based on connecting a specific Result to its Reason and by this means arriving at an explanation. In other words, *no wonder* conveys the meaning, 'it's obvious why'.

Example (3) also illustrates the need for connectives in some texts in the interest of clarity:

(3) Specialist books by women are particularly under-represented (Result) presumably *on the grounds* that the authoritative voice is male. (Reason)
     ?*Specialist books by women are particularly under-represented. Presumably the authoritative voice is male.
     (*Australian Campus Review Weekly* 13–19 August 1992: 14)

The right inference would probably be drawn by a highly literate reader, but it is likely that the less advanced will be grateful for a connective unambiguously indicating Reason and Result.

The comparison offered of ideational, interpersonal, and relational expressions at the beginning of this section focused on their respective functions. In their formal aspects, these expressions favour different types of constituents in their syntactic make-up, differences corresponding to their different functions: phrasal verbs, noun phrases, especially those of the Adj + N types, and semi-clauses of various types abound among ideational idioms; appropriate pronouns mark interpersonal idioms, overtly or covertly; the relational group is distinguished from the other two either by conjunctive or sequencing idioms and by expressions signalling the location in time of an event or of its duration, long or short. The formal differences characterizing ideational, interpersonal, and relational idioms are illustrated by some examples in the following summary:

Ideational expressions	Interpersonal expressions	Relational expressions
make up	(I wish you) Good morning	the more Y ... the more X
make off with	Happy Birthday (to you)	X ... no wonder Y
the emperor's	I'm afraid (that) ...	not only X ... but also Y
new clothes	You're kidding/joking	in order that
red herring	Has the cat got your tongue?	at that time, at the same
blue film/joke, etc.	etc.	time as
bury the hatchet		in the small/wee hours
spill the beans		in a jiffy
walk on air		round the clock
be down in the		etc.
dumps		
etc.		

Table 5.1: Examples of ideational, interpersonal, and relational idioms

Up to the 1970s, ideational idioms formed the staple of scholarly work on idioms. The notion of idiomaticity as a related but distinct concept from that of idioms, together with its most typical exemplars, habitual collocations, not regarded as proper idioms, received little attention. The acceptance of conventionalized interpersonal and relational multiword expressions as idiomatic shows an extension of the idiom principle, and, consequently, an advance in idiomatology itself. To regard conjunctive and temporal connectives and other time indicators invariant in form or with restricted variants as idiomatic expressions is in keeping with current scholarly opinion (see section 2.7.2).

Table 5.1 shows certain formal differences between the three groups of idiomatic expressions, i.e. ideational, interpersonal, and relational, discussed in this book. What of the functional differences? Below I give a synopsis of the major functions of conventionalized expressions:

Ideational expressions	Interpersonal expressions	Relational expressions
contribute to the subject matter of a discourse by functioning as impressionistic packages of information.	organize the flow of verbal exchanges and facilitate interaction between language-users, especially in promoting conviviality.	at the microlevel they relate phrases or clauses within sentences (intra-sentential) or relate sentences within a discourse (inter-sentential); indicate a point in time, or temporal duration.
		At the macrolevel they relate portions of a discourse, for example, paragraphs introducing new topics (meta-discoural). Macro relational expressions also indicate a global temporal frame.

Table 5.2: The major functions of conventionalized expressions

The discussion that follows looks at what idiomatic relational expressions, both conjunctive and temporal, do in a general way before going on to a more detailed examination of each.

Intra-sentential connectors work primarily to integrate the information presented in the various clauses making up the discourse in a cohesive and coherent way (Pawley and Syder 1983). For example:

(4)   ... the beneficiaries would include *not only* husbands and wives ... *but* any children they might have ... .
(*The Sydney Morning Herald* 9 January 1993: 17)

The relational idiom, *not only ...but (also)*, establishes an intra-sentential semantic connection between two clauses, in this case, one of Bonding (Crombie 1985). The outcome of such Bonding, more specifically the sub-type, Coupling, is a longer unit, a multi-clausal sentence whose parts encompass different aspects of the same situation, and in so doing emphasize it: protection of the rights of all the members of a family.

Not only ... but also is incremental to what precedes it: the second sentence develops the content of the previous one.

Meta-discoursal organizers of information work globally to make the semantic unity of a discourse explicit through a set of relational expressions, but of a different sort from those cited above (Crismore and Farnsworth 1990; Nattinger and DeCarrico 1992).

(5) *On the subject of communication* ... . *On the subject of networking* ... . *Lastly, but* I hope *not least* ... .
    (*Sirius*, Summer 1992: 2)

While the meta-discoursal expressions in (5) qualify as unrestricted collocations, for example, *on the subject/topic/theme of communication/networking*, etc. functioning as topic-introducers signposting the unfolding discourse, *last(ly) but not least* (a literal idiom), signals concluding item in an enumerative list such as topics, individuals, objects, etc. There is here an implicit interaction between writer and reader: the writer orientates the reader, as it were, in the direction of his/her thinking, making comprehension of expository discourse much easier. This, in fact, is the primary function of meta-discoursal expressions: to index the structure of a discourse rather than to add to its informational content.

I have so far talked mainly about conjunctive and meta-discoursal connectives. However, as the epigraphs at the beginning indicate, this chapter also covers temporal expressions, one of whose functions, like that of conjunctive and meta-discoursal connectives, is to knit portions of a discourse together. Apart from this cohesive function, temporal expressions also locate a discourse in time thereby giving it a time-frame: we need to know the 'when' of events.

I have argued above that relational idiomatic expressions are very different from ideational ones in that their primary function is to make explicit the way a discourse hangs together, not to add new information. Idiomatic expressions referring to time are, however, closer in function to ideational idioms than to conjunctive ones as they do add to the content of a discourse, barring formulae such as *Once upon a time*. But this is only a very general functional similarity. At a more delicate level of analysis, temporal expressions are different. Ideational idioms function as very specific packages of information about participants, events, and actions, their attributes and circumstances; temporal expressions add information to a discourse, but this information works to indicate either the number of time units (e.g. *three years*) or the happening order of a series of smaller events, which then appear as constituting a larger one, the way the sequence in which a ship calls at various ports constitutes a voyage from one country to another. This is precisely what (6) illustrates:

(6) a. *In the spring of 1978* ... 'Sir William Hardy' was transformed into Greenpeace's first European campaign ship.

  b. *By the summer of 1981*, the Warrior was in need of extensive repairs.

  c. *During the first half of 1983*, the Warrior sailed northwards
      ... .

  d. *In July 1987*, Greenpeace sent the Rainbow Warrior to the Atlantic ...
      (*The Rainbow Warrior* 1978–1988, information sheet)

Example (6) is a good example of culturally institutionalized time classifiable into calendar time (Bull 1968). The characteristic features of institutionalized time are:

1 The names of the seasons: *spring, summer, autumn,* and *winter.* These are usually embedded in prepositional phrases with reference to specific years as in (6a. and b.). References to the seasons can stand on their own without prepositions as in Winter *dragged on*, but even here temporal implications are hard to suppress as evidenced by *drag*.

2 The names of the days of the week, e.g. *on Monday next week.*

3 The names of the twelve months: *January, February*, etc. These, like the names of the seasons, usually appear embedded in prepositional phrases plus optional time-indicators as in (6d.). Like the names of the seasons, these too can be free-standing: *European Decembers are icy-cold.* Such free-standing occurrences, however, do not qualify as restricted temporal collocations: though months have only a restricted set of names, their possible attributive collocates show no such restrictions:

  Asian/Arctic/Antarctic/Antipodean, etc. December(s).
  Freezing/icy/broiling/sizzling, etc. December(s).

In such uses, *December* frees itself from a set of temporal collocates. However, there are constraints on the way clock- and calendar-time units collocate, which makes it possible to speak of restricted collocations in this area: *five minutes ago* is usual, but *half an hour ago*, rather than *thirty minutes ago* is the preferred form in colloquial discourse; similarly, *I'll see you the day after tomorrow/on Wednesday/next month/in December* are the usual expressions, not *I'll see you two days from now* or *in fourteen days' time*, etc. (see section 5.2.2).

4 References to centuries or decades as wholes (see (6b.) *of 1981*), or as segments (6c.), (*the first half of 1983*). Once again, prepositions figure as part of the collocation.

5 Units of clock-time, obviously different from those of calendar-time: seconds, minutes, and hours.

Terms denoting clock- and calendar-time units and the four seasons function with various predictable collocates which specify the desired number of temporal units the language-user has in mind (*three seconds/centuries, four summers*, etc.), as well as appropriate time phases (*early/late in the day, at the beginning/end of the year, before/after Christmas*, etc.). The latter also denote the order in which events occur. The key words in temporal collocations are restricted to a small set and so are their possible collocates. In this respect, temporal collocations resemble those used in greeting cards. Though more numerous and varied than those in cards as with the idiomatic 'vocabulary of greetings', we have a distinctive idiomatic 'vocabulary of temporality' in English. In fact, the two overlap to some extent: *Good morning/night*, etc., *The Season's Greetings/ Happy Christmas/New Year*, etc.

Temporal expressions of the sort identified above will be discussed in more detail in section 5.2.

This introductory section to Chapter 5 has identified two major types of relational expressions:

1 Expressions which establish conjunctive connections (Addition, Concession, Condition, Reason, and Result, etc.) within or between sentences, as well as connections between portions of a discourse directing the addressee to its structural organization, that is, its beginning, body, and conclusion.

2 Expressions which sequence events in ways that are chronologi-
cally appropriate to the situation presented via the discourse.
Such expressions may also signal, at the same time, the time-
frame in which events take place.

The relational expressions falling into Group 1 are used to make the
'logic' of exposition explicit. Exposition is a component of a wide
variety of discourse types ranging from conversation, narratives,
letters, etc. to the scholarly lecture and academic paper. Since academic discourse, whether spoken (a discussion or lecture), or written
(the scholarly paper) is the best exemplar of exposition, I shall use it
to illustrate the way conjunctives work.

Group 2 consists of temporal expressions. While these appear in
expository modes of discourse, they come into their own in narratives of various sorts. I shall, therefore, take narrative as being the
par excellence exemplar of the way temporal expressions of various
sorts work.

Being part of the non-specialist vocabulary of English, conventionalized conjunctive and temporal expressions appear in a wide
range of discourse types working together as in (7) below:

(7)   *Once upon a time* (temporal) there lived in Berlin, Germany, a
      man called Albinus. He was rich, respectable, happy; *one day*
      (temporal) he abandoned his wife *for the sake of* (conjunctive)
      a youthful mistress; he loved; was not loved; *and* (conjunctive)
      his life ended in disaster.
      (Vladimir Nabokov, *Laughter in the Dark* 1961: 1)

Nabokov explains the *why* and the *how* (conjunctive relations) of a
particular phenomenon (Albinus's misfortune), and the *when*
(temporal relations) of this event (non-historical and deictic, hence
vague in time reference).

Exposition being a form of argumentation relies more on conjunctives (*X so that Y; if X ... then Y; in case of Y; on the one hand X,
on the other Y; no matter what; not only X, but also Y;* etc.) for
creating appropriate connections between statements than on
temporal ones (*one day, some weeks later, in a jiffy, in the spring of
1993,* etc.).

In narratives (personal, historical, fictional, etc.), where chronology is crucial, temporal connectives, not logical ones, provide the

semantic support structure at the story, or 'what-happened-next', level. Chronological expressions provide a time-map essential for guiding the addressee through the sequence of narrated events. There are, of course, other components in a narrative apart from chronology, but chronology is the principal organizing device in storytelling.

Sections 5.1.2 to 5.2.2 deal with the typical functions of conjunctive and temporal expressions in greater detail, but with each type being presented separately for analytical convenience, though as indicated above they work together in many discourses.

5.1.2 Anaphoric and conjunctive idiomatic expressions in action

This section begins with a profile of anaphoric and conjunctive idiomatic expressions that function relationally to connect various portions of a discourse. Such a profile parallels those drawn for ideational and interpersonal idioms in Chapters 3 and 4. As in those profiles, the focus will be on those features of relational idioms and restricted collocations which contribute most to their functional efficacy in discourse:

1 Idiomatic relational expressions, like their ideational and interpersonal cousins, are more specific in terms of their semantics than their approximate single-word counterparts. *And*, for example, is the general factotum of the relational family. Its functions range from Coupling two clauses on the same topic (e.g. *London is Britain's capital and Moscow Russia's*), through Chronological Sequencing (e.g. *Nureyev died and was buried in Paris*), to Causality (e.g. *Khomeni returned to Iran and the once-happy Shah was very unhappy*), as well as other semantic relations such as Conditionality, etc. In contrast, the functionally similar but much more specific *not only … but also*, because of its specificity, is confined to Coupling. Being uni-functional, it can emphasize and highlight the Coupling of two statements much more strongly than *and*.

2 In addition to exemplifying semantic relations such as Causality, Addition, Concession, etc., multiword relational expressions, often by virtue of the words used in their make-up, fulfil certain speech act functions, for example, discounting: *on the contrary, quite the reverse, no matter what*, etc. (Fogelin 1978).

3   Several multiword relational expressions are dead metaphors of a spatial or visual kind (Lakoff and Johnson 1980): *as far as, the extent to which, in so far as, far from, in view of, seeing that*, etc. A few like the contrastive *on the one hand ... on the other (hand)* show body part imagery. These images reinforce the specificity of relational idioms and conventionalized relational collocations.

4   Some relational idioms with a conjunctive as well as an anaphoric function show cohesive functions in the words that are used in their make-up: *in addition, furthermore, on the contrary, quite the reverse*, etc. They are obviously text, not system sentence markers, and as such refer backwards to earlier parts of the discourse. Other relational idioms, for example, *as a result of, in order to, on the grounds of*, etc. make the coherence or logical consistency of a discourse explicit and in this way strengthen its explanatory adequacy.

I have already explained my reasons for choosing academic discourse as the best examplar of how anaphoric and conjunctive multiword expressions work and elaborate further on these reasons below.

Academic discourse is primarily factual dealing selectively with the world's physical, social, and verbal phenomena. Some academic discourse goes beyond reportage to offer explanations for these sorts of phenomena (Fogelin 1978), why the world and its inhabitants are as they are, they were, or they will be. Such discourse qualifies as exposition. Exposition typically offers an explanation for a state of affairs formulated as a thesis (Martin 1985). The type of explanation in exposition shows the workings of informal logic, of everyday reasoning, which then turns expository explanations into arguments leading to conclusions.

(8)   Reviewers participate in a genre which has *no terms of praise* for women's products. *Quite the reverse*: indicators of femininity are commonly used to describe the weakness or failure of a text. The highest praise a woman producer can receive from these reviewers is that *she 'thinks like a man'*.
How do women participate in a reviewing practice which describes a powerful text as 'having balls'? *How do they deal with patronising evaluations of their work as being*, (as Spender

and Connie Burns and Marygai McNamara have been described) '*in silent and unsororial competition*'—in the certain knowledge that scholarly texts by men in similar areas are never described as being 'in silent and unfraternal competition'? It simply does not happen. The men writing these books are professional writers and scholars. To suggest that they should not write a particular book *in case another man was also writing a book on that topic*; or to suggest that any man writing a book about another man (or men) should first contact all other male scholars and writers to make sure that he is not proposing a topic which another man is attempting, *is patently ridiculous. Furthermore, it is professionally degrading since it identifies all these male authors on the basis of their gender, not in terms of professional skills or competence. Worse, work by women often does not get reviewed and so is not brought to the attention of the public.*

When they are reviewed, works by women are lumped together (for example, as 'women's fiction') so that valuable column space can be reserved for writing by men.

Specialist books by women are particularly under-represented, *not only in production but also in reviews, presumably on the grounds that the authoritative voice is male. In addition, the reviewers themselves are mostly male*, with the attendant problems of patriarchal positioning and experiential blindness.

Furthermore, the review pages as a whole construct femininity as passive and women as objects through the use of illustrations, headlines, inset quotations and the unequal allocation of space for reviews of men's and women's books.

As a result, readers are positioned not to regard women as authoritative, serious or worth reading.

(Anne Cranny-Francis, *Engendered Fictions*, 1992)

A statement of the thesis of example (8) 'Sexism in book reviewing' is offered as a nub of this expository text analysed below. The wider implication of male sexism in intellectual life, not simply book reviewing, is left to be inferred by the reader of this extract.

1   Reviewers participate in a genre which has *no terms of praise for women's products.*

2 *Quite the reverse … .*

3 The highest praise a woman can receive from these reviewers is
   that she *'thinks like a man'*.

The emphatic *Quite the reverse/contrary* (point 2), a variant literal
idiom, here applies only to part of (point 1) (*terms of praise for
women's products*), and is used to discount completely the existence of such a vocabulary resource, in case some people assumed
it did exist. *Quite the reverse* carries here the semantic relationship
of Concession–Contraexpectation and is used for the purpose of
discounting a putative claim of equality. In this context, *Quite the
reverse* points anaphorically backwards to 1 and forwards to 3. In
other words, what the writer asserts is: 'There may be an assumption that women's works and men's are treated by reviewers
equally (Concession), but in actual fact they cannot be due to
terminological deficiencies, exemplified by "*she* thinks like a *man*",
being a term of praise, in the language of reviewing' (Contra-
expectation). *Quite the reverse*, as a citation item, has only the
meaning of Contra-expectation, but here carries an additional
context-specific meaning, Concession, as the writer is *conceding*
popular assumptions, but simultaneously discounting these by
contrary assertions. The idiom, by virtue of its lexical make-up,
allows strong foregrounding of the claim of sexist bias important
to the argument.

4 How do they deal with patronizing evaluations of their work as
   being … 'in silent and unsororial competition' …?

Points 3 and 4 develop the claim of tendentious reviewing by juxtaposition alone.

5 a. To suggest that they (i.e. men) should not write a particular
      book *in case*
   b. another man was also writing a book on that topic … is
      patently ridiculous.

Point 5a conveying a possible consequence and 5b a possible prior
condition are welded together by *in case*, a relational semi-idiom of
condition. The idiom performs a function akin to *if … then*, for
example, *In case/if he doesn't come, (then) you can take the bus*, but
with an emphasis on possibility. In 5a its placement in the sentence

196

signals that the suggestion referred to here is unlikely, which, once again, supports this writer's line of argumentation.

6 *Furthermore,*
   a. it is professionally degrading since
   b. it identifies all these male authors on the basis of their gender, not in terms of professional skills or competence.

The assertions presented in points 6a and b are introduced by the single word *furthermore*, a choice that emphasizes the addition of *more* new information to the argument of point 5, and so signals both an elaboration and validation (*further*) of that argument. *Furthermore* is discussed here in order to facilitate comprehension of the argument of this text, even though it is not an idiom (see section 2.7.2).

7 *(Even) Worse,*
   a. *work* by women often does not get reviewed
   b. *and* so is not brought to the attention of the public.

The abbreviated idiom *(even) worse* works anaphorically and so reaffirms the evaluations carried by the nonce phrases *patently ridiculous* (point 5b) and *professionally degrading* in point 6. Cohesive ties of this sort show how evaluations run through the whole of language acting as indicators of what situations call for protection and defence and what can be safely enjoyed.

And so in point 7b is marked for Result with point 7a conveying Reason.

8 a. When they are reviewed, works by women are lumped together (*for example*, as 'women's fiction')
   b. *so that* valuable column space can be reserved for writing by men.

Points 8 a and b together constitute a Reason–Result pairing with *so that* marked for conveying Result, but with the additional semantic component 'purpose'. The Result is not fortuitous. Other semantically similar idiomatic expressions are *in order to/that, for the purpose of*, etc.

The normal function of *for example* in point 8a is to make the general particular through specific illustrations, which is its role in point 8. Its composition is lexically transparent: it is, like *on foot, by hand*, etc., a literal idiom.

9 a. Specialist books by women are particularly under-repre-
      sented, *not only* in production *but also* in reviews, presum-
      ably *on the grounds*
   b. that the authoritative voice is male.

Not only ... but also is used in 9a to bond two phrases, *under-repre-sentation in reviews*, and *in production*. This idiom, because of its compositional specificity (Neg. + adverb ... adversative conjunction + adverb), is strongly emphatic, the reason why it is used in prefer-ence to the functionally similar *and*.

On the grounds in 9a, like so many other multiword expressions discussed in this section, is distinguished by its specificity in contrast to its nearest synonym, *because*. Both signal Reason.

10 *In addition*, the reviewers themselves are mostly male ... .

11 *Furthermore*, the review pages as a whole construct femininity
    as passive ... .

Both 10 and 11 exemplify points already made above: the composi-tional specificity of these expressions stress their incremental and developmental function over the general *and*.

12 *As a result*, readers are positioned not to regard women as
    authoritative, serious or worth reading.

The literal *as a result* in 12 converts points 1–11 into a series of inter-connected Reasons with 12 as the overall Result explainable by all these Reasons. Point 12, therefore, functions as the conclusion to the argument presented in this extract from a larger discourse by Anne Cranny-Francis (1992). The connectives this writer uses continually work to make explicit the reasoning which is part and parcel of her argument. These fall into five groups (see Table 5.2), 1–3 of which are modelled on relationships identified by Crombie (1985).

The thesis of example (8) was formulated as 'Sexism in book reviewing'. The principal relational devices used to validate this claim are Causative and Bonding ones, which in different ways simultaneously present a state of affairs and explain why it exists.

5.1.3 Conclusions

The focus of the foregoing section (5.1.2) has been the role of multi-word connectives in contributing to the coherence and cohesion of a

Causative (1)	
Reason–Result:	*and so, so that, as a result, on the grounds (that/of)*
	Other similar items: the more ... the more, in order that/to, etc.
Condition–	*in case*
Consequence:	Other similar items: on condition that, come what may, be that as it may, in that case, etc.
Coupling (2)	
Coupling:	*not only ... but also*
	Other similar items: as well as, together/along with, neg. ... let alone, etc.
Addition:	*in addition*
Adversative (3)	
Concession–	
Contraexpectation:	*quite the reverse*
	Other similar items: quite the contrary, on the contrary, at the same time, no matter what, in spite of, etc.
Evaluative (4)	
Unfavourable:	*(even) worse*
	Other similar items: as if that weren't/wasn't enough, after all, etc.
Favourable:	better still, etc.
Exemplification (5)	*for example*
	Other similar items: for instance, that is, in other words, etc.
Scope (6)	on the whole, to some extent, the extent to which, so far, in so far as, all in all, by and large, etc.
Signposting (7)	Micro: as I, etc. said before, as we shall see, in the first place, etc.
	Macro: from beginning to end, from start to finish, as a whole, etc.

Table 5.2

discourse. Martin (1985) points out that connectives do not create logical relations, they simply reflect the inferences that can be drawn from the juxtaposition of clauses and sentences. Sapir's (1921) claim for juxtaposition as being one of the most powerful syntactic devices available to the language-user has already been cited as one of the epigraphs in Chapter 2. However, the communication of large and complex bodies of information require that:

1   Implicit inferential relationships be made explicit via conjunctives in order to avoid ambiguity, perplexity, or the possibility of choosing one of many likely, but not necessarily intended, inferences.

2   Stylistic options need to be offered for foregrounding different pieces of information, for example, the option of presenting Result before Reason as in example (8) points 6 and 9, or vice versa as in example (8) point 7, that is, Reason–Result. Both options require conjunctives.

The analysis offered of example (8), together with Table 5.2, show that connectives realizing Causal relations of various types appear to be at the heart of explanation, providing as they do, relatively speaking, the strongest rationale for any claims put forward. This view is supported by Crombie's (1985) categorization of what I term connectives in which the sub-divisions under 'General Causative' are among the most numerous. The Adversative category is also significant, but it seems to be relatively less powerful in uncovering the *whys* of the world around us. A similar assessment holds for Bonding, Evaluation, and meta-discoursal Signposting devices. They contribute to coherent exposition, but unlike Causality, do not appear to constitute the keystone of such discourse.

5.2 Temporal idiomatic expressions in action

Time is a physical phenomenon intimately bound up with the nature of the universe, being, as it is, one of its natural laws. However, though all people, as far as we know, see time as a feature of the cosmos, whether associated with nature or a Deity, these perceptions of time are culture-specific and appear as such in the grammar and vocabulary of their languages. How time is perceived by a European people, and how such perceptions are realized in English, a Germanic language, is as good a place to start as any in this discussion of the part played by conventionalized multiword temporal expressions in establishing chronological order, and by such means coherence and cohesion within narrative discourse in English.

The scientific concept of time as the fourth dimension complementing three-dimensional space is encapsulated in the term *space-time* (Whitrow 1972; Hawking 1988). Another multiword expression, the metaphor *arrow of time*, also identifies a key attribute of time: its directionality, more specifically its uni-directionality (Whitrow 1972; Hawking 1988). Time moves into the future, hence the image of the arrow which only goes forward. It does not have the bi-directionality of the boomerang which goes forward, and then returns.

The concepts associated with *space-time* and the *arrow of time*, are fully accessible only to physicists. However, the concept of time, even when understood only in terms of everyday experience, yield a number of insights which can be used to construct a profile for the conventionalized multiword expressions used to order different types of narrative discourse in English.

1   Whereas time is one of the natural laws of the cosmos, tense is a grammatical category. In English, tense when morphologically realized appears in the changes to the composition of the verb, for example, in various forms of the present (*runs/running*) and the past (*ran*); when tense is syntactically realized, it appears in complex verb forms like the future (*will run, is going to*), etc.

2   Tense alone, as the linguistic expression of physical time, is insufficient to convey people's perceptions of time as it works for them. In fact, verb forms are frequently supported by restricted collocations signifying precise clock times, minutes, hours, etc., or calendar times by way of reference to a specific day, week, month, or year (see example 6). Apart from such indicators of time, the number of other sorts of temporal expressions in English indicate that for most language-users there exists not a single time, some homogeneous cosmic time which is the fourth dimension, but a plurality of times determined by socio-cultural and psychological factors.

3   Events located in time are very frequently talked of in English, and some other Indo-European languages, as if they were located in space. The locative prepositions, *in, at, by, on, within*, etc. are used to place events in their temporal location within a discourse as in X *happened at the beginning of May.*

4   The *arrow of time* is a scientific metaphor which, defined simply, signifies the uni-directionality of time as a result of which we move continually into the future, leaving the present behind as the past: '...what happens now was once the future and will be the past' (Whitrow 1972: 166).

5   There are only three possible chronological orders in which

events occur for language–users when they speak (Bull 1968: 9):

before the event	simultaneous with the event	after the event
past	present	future

6   Chronological order refers to the sequence in which events occur in time and in which they are reported. This sequence is determined by any given event the language-user chooses to use as 'an axis of orientation' (ibid.). This axis may be implicit as in *It was lunch-time* (present-in-past) *when he arrived*, which indicates in the schema of meals that breakfast is in the past as it is *before lunch*, and *tea* and *dinner* future as both take place *after lunch*, or explicit as in *The Great War of 1914–1918* (distant past) *preceded the World War of 1939–45* (less distant past).

7   Temporal overlap occurs when two events happen in the same time-interval, whether this time-interval is located in the present, past, or future. In other words, these events occur at the same time. Such co-occurrences, or coincidences, are common in narratives of one sort or another.

8   All events have duration, however fleeting. Duration is directly measurable by clocks; mathematical calculations relating to astronomy produce calendars, which can also be used to measure duration, though in a relatively less direct way than clocks. This perception of duration is also expressible in terms outside the clock and calendar systems. The clock time-unit, second, for example, is replaceable in some forms of narrative discourse with *in a jiffy or in the twinkling of an eye*, etc.

The profile above pinpoints several attributes of time as it is experienced in everyday language. While all these attributes are relevant to an analysis of temporal expressions in discourse, and will indeed be taken up in the discussion that follows, I have chosen the notions of public and personal time together with clock- and calendar-time, (ibid.) as being the most appropriate for showing how time is understood and temporal expressions used by people in a range of narrative discourse types.

5.2.1 Introduction: public and personal time

In some types of discourse, for example, casual conversations, narratives, oral and written, personal letters, etc., references to public and personal time may both be present. In other types, such as historical discourse, the predominance of public time is more apparent largely due to the subject-matter of such discourses: history deals with public events. In the sections that follow, I will be looking at the use of temporal expressions in fictional and historical narratives.

5.2.2 Public time

Clock-time
Small time units, like *two or three seconds, half a minute*, etc., associated with clock-time function as restricted collocations. Anything from a second to sixty seconds sounds unmarked because coming within the time-span of a minute:

(9)   Doing what took two and a half days in *40 seconds*
      (*Australian Campus Review Weekly* Vol. 3, 7, 1993: 6)

Anything over 60 seconds appears as marked, as for example, seventy seconds, likeliest in the context of stopwatches and sporting events. A minute can be segmented into a quarter, half and, three-quarters. Though such time units qualify as parts of restricted collocations they are, outside the sporting register, of little interest. My reason for presenting them here is to contrast such minuscule units with those much more interesting time units resulting from the division of a day into a.m. and p.m.

   The division of a day into two halves, of twelve hours each, is tied to the earth's daily rotation on its axis, so that clock-time also signals, though indirectly, a class of natural events, for example, sunrise (dawn), the sun at its zenith (midday), and sunset (evening and night). As a.m. and p.m. together add up to twenty-four hours and twenty-four hours add up to a day, clock-time connects up with calendar-time, the bridging unit between the two being provided by a day.

   Examples (10 to (16) show combinations of clock- and calendar-time and come from John Wyndham's novel, *The Kraken Awakes* (Penguin 1953/1958):

(10)   One time it was three of the things by night; the other it was
       half a dozen of them *by daylight*. [p.14]

(11)   It went on the air *the same evening* ... . [p.15]

(12) The real descent was announced for *the morning of the fourth day*. [p.28]

(13) *Soon after sunrise* we were clustering round the bathyscope where it rested on its cradle. [p.28]

(14) '... we shall conduct the operation *tomorrow morning*, commencing *as soon* after dawn *as possible*.' [p.33]

(15) 'You'll hear it *on the 9 o'clock news tonight* ... .' [p.36]

(16) A night or two before the Whittiers left we had a late party where some one *in the small hours* had tuned in a New York transmitter. [p.223]

With the exception of *in the small hours* (a semi-idiom) and *as soon as possible* (a literal idiom), all the other temporal expressions in the extracts above are restricted collocations, manifestations of idiomaticity, or the co-occurrence tendencies of the vocabulary. The possibility of lexical variants in (10 to (15) (12, for example, can be transformed into *the evening of the second day*) in no way diminishes the importance of studying such habitual, though not invariant collocations. Such variable expressions predominate in language over those that are invariant and reflect that interweaving of the *ad hoc* and the habitual in language referred to in Chapters 1 and 2.

Also linked to clock-time, though indirectly, are meal-times: *breakfast, lunch (time), tea (time), dinner (time)*, and *supper (time)*. These events are associated with specific or approximate clock-times and can be expected to show cross-cultural variations:

(17) ... he went down there himself *one evening after dinner*. (M.R. James, *More Ghost Stories*, Penguin 1959: 23)

In some cultures, dinner or its equivalent is eaten after the sun has set and so will be associated with early night rather than the evening.

The temporal expressions used in examples (10) to (17) indicate:

1 The chronological order of events through the use of habitual or predictable restricted collocations such as *three ... by night*; ... *half a dozen of them by daylight* (10); *soon after sunrise* (13), etc. Expressions such as *early in the morning, late at night, the end of the day*, etc. also indicate the happening order of events, habitual or incidental, as do other sequential markers: *the beginning (early), the end (late)*.

2   The passage of time: past, present, and future. A good example of *when* events occur is the restricted collocation *on the 9 o'clock news tonight* (15), which presents a future event from an axis of orientation *before 9 o'clock. Tonight* falls within *today* and to that extent is 'present'. Examples of temporal idioms referring to past and future are *the day before yesterday* and *the day after tomorrow.*

Calendar-time

Some typical temporal expressions referring to the units of calendar-time are exemplified in examples (18) to (22) from Wyndham's *The Kraken Awakes,* and (21b.) from The Birmingham Collection of English Text.

(18)   a.   But *the days passed* and nobody squealed. [p.21]
       b.   *The first day passed* safely. [p.24]

(19)   a.   For *a couple of weeks* reports of sightings [...] continued to pour in. (p.20)
       b.   *In the course of the following week*, two more fireballs ... were exploded by a ship ... . [p.21]

(20)   An uneasy situation ... drew out *over months.* [p.22]

(21)   a. I've heard of two instances ... *in the last year.* [p.14]
       b. I would have said as I say *20 years ago* that virtually no undergraduate was married. [BCET]

(22)   I started this account *at the beginning of November.* It is *now the end of January.* The water continued to rise slightly, but since about *Christmastime* there has been no increase ... . [p.235]

The names of the days and months, with the year identified by a numeral and the weeks implicit in the names of the days, form the core of calendar-time expressions and are of varied syntactic composition:

1   Adverbial phrases of time headed by prepositions: *over months* (20); *in the last year* (21a.).

2   Noun phrases signifying time intervals: *20 years ago* (21b.).

3   Clauses signifying the passage of time: *the days passed* (18a.).

The specificity of a temporal expression is increased if its exact duration can be given: *20 years ago* is more specific than *several/some/many/a few years ago*. But while the time span for years is indefinite, ranging from one to trillions, with the possibility of expansions such as a trillion light years, conceptually different from a trillion years, the collocation numeral + day(s)/week(s)/month(s) is restricted by usage.

One day as in

(23)   He had been caught only *one day* after entering Afghanistan. [BCET]

signifies the digit 1 and simply as a co-occurrence of *one* + *day* showed up as having 31 occurrences in the (BCET) at the time of consultation: April to June 1990. However, the majority of homonymous counterparts in the (BCET) of *one day* have the indefinite meaning of 'some time in the future' as in example (24), and not *one* as a cardinal number as in the set *one/two/three days*, etc.:

(24)   Even the Pyramids might *one day* disappear. [BCET]

signals 'precise time unknown or not significant' as in

(25)   *One day* ... I climbed the 199 steps to the Abbey. [BCET]

Two days as in

(26)   After *two days* the Army declared itself neutral. [BCET]

had 72 occurrences and *three days* 85 occurrences. The number of occurrences for this type of collocation dwindled as the cardinal number increased with *four days* showing 38 occurrences and *ten days* only 2 occurrences. These figures may have been dictated by the newsworthiness of the reported events: news that is more than three days old is old hat.

Idiomatically speaking, though, to say *She arrived fourteen days ago* is a relatively marked expression compared with the more usual *two weeks ago*. Similarly, *six months* is more idiomatic in normal discourse than *twenty-four weeks*, an exception being the medical register, and two years more usual than *twenty-four* months. The same constraints, however, do not apply to years, as I have already noted above:

(27) a. ... he came to Sussex about *two and a half years ago* from
         Oxford. [BCET]
      b. I could envisage *2,000 years ago* guys sitting on this same
         site as we sit now. [BCET]

Temporal expressions with *years* open the way to a large-scale
picture of time which goes beyond days, weeks, months, and a
specific year. The time-units of the calendar suit daily life. Historical
and evolutionary events need other sorts of temporal units identified
by suitable restricted collocations appropriate to these time scales:

(28) The Indus Valley civilization declined in *the second millen-
     nium B.C.* and had almost completely disintegrated when (by
     1500 B.C.) the Aryans entered north-west India.
     (Romila Thapar's *A History of India* 1979: 29)

(29) But now we must go back *three centuries* in our story to tell
     of a great teacher ... . This was Gautama Buddha ... .
     (H. G. Wells, *A Short History of the World* 1987: 100)

(30) ... but these people of *the Middle Ages* ... were passionately
     convinced of the wisdom, the completeness and finality of
     their beliefs ... .
     (H.G. Wells, *A Short History of the World* 1987: 205)

Examples (28) to (30) record the history of human events. Restricted
collocations such as *the Iron/Bronze Age, the Middle/Dark Ages, the
Classical/Modern Period, the Elizabethan/Victorian Age*, etc. are
associated with the perception of historical time. We also have the
history of the earth (geology) and the history of the cosmos
(cosmogony) each with its own specialist set of terms. Historical
time reinforces the notion of linear time, which, being forward-
moving, is irreversible: neither the conquests of Genghis Khan nor
the dinosaurs will ever recur. History is reconstructed recollection,
not re-living.
   Examples (31) and (32) show how temporal expressions of public
time function in longer texts than those looked at so far.

(31) *At first* the newspapers stated that the king was gaining great
     victories over the insolent rebels. *A little while later* it was said
     that the army of the infamous Duke Padella was in full flight.
     A day or two afterwards it was said that the Royal Army

would soon come up with the enemy; *and then—then* news came that King Cavolfiore was vanquished ... .
(W. M. Thackeray's *The Rose and the Ring* 1969: 12–13)

(32)   *Years before the time* when this story *begins*, Valoroso's brother, Savio, had been King of Paflogonia. When he died he left his brother Regent ... . But *no sooner* was Savio dead than the faithless fellow caused himself to be proclaimed King ... .
(W. M. Thackeray's *The Rose and the Ring* 1969: 5–6)

What the temporal expressions in (31) and (32) do is:

1   To order events in a sequence.

2   To embed smaller events, for example, battles, in temporal phases (beginning, middle, and end) indicative of the stages of a larger event (a war) of which they are a part.

The rationale of narratives, whether personal, fictional or historical, is 'what happened next'; hence, sequencing events in their proper order is crucial to narrative coherence. Such a sequencing can be achieved either by making the telling order and the happening order of events coincide, as in (31), or by using suitable temporal expressions, such as *years before* (32), to compensate for a disruption of such an order.

In (31) the emphasis is on a number of events (battles) which belong to various temporal phases signalling the progression of a war:

Phase 1   Initiating: *at first ... victories over the insolent rebels*
Phase 2   Medial: *a little while later, a day or two afterwards*
Phase 3   Terminating: *and then–then*

Expressions which use words such as *first*, *the beginning*, *early*, *the onset*, etc. are typically initiating. *Later* and *afterwards*, obviously non-initiating, could either signal a middle or terminating phase depending on context. *The end*, *last of all*, *lastly* are clearly terminating. *And then* is probably the most common discoursal indicator that events are being narrated in their happening order. In (31), the co-text, *news came that King Cavolfiore was vanquished* makes it clear that *and then* signals the end of the war in this context. It need not necessarily have this function in others.

Example (32) begins with a flashback, always a disruption of chronology, signalled here by *years before the time when this story begins*. The key phrase, *before the time*, indicates a more distant past than the past of the story.

No sooner (32), *as soon as, the moment that, in a jiffy/a tick*, etc. are idioms paralleling *instantly, immediately*, and other similar single words. All these convey instantiality. Longer intervals of time are catered for by *all day/night, in due course, in the course of time, in the fullness of time*, etc.

Clock- and calendar-time expressions, as they occur in the texts presented above, clearly indicate institutionalized ways of perceiving and referring to time. Prepositions, especially locative ones, for example, *in, at, on, by*, etc., have the function of locating events within institutionalized time intervals as in *This book was written in seven years, though at times it seemed never-ending*. Others, such as *before* and *after*, sequence events in chronological order. The idiomatic expressions that appear in the discourses above also show that certain words, apart from prepositions and clock/calendar time-units, keep recurring. *Time* itself is probably the most frequent of such words (Moon 1986). Others that are common in temporal expressions are forms of *long* and *short* and *ago*.

5.2.3 Personal time

Windisch (1990) argues that time is perceived differently by various groups of people because it functions differently in their lives. Farmers, for instance, are most aware of time through seasonal changes, not represented in clock-time and only indirectly in calendars, though both clock- and calendar-time play a part in their lives.

Businessmen, obsessed by clock-time, see time as a commodity determining profit and loss: *time is money, a waste of time, thanks for your time*, etc. are idioms which, in varying degrees, represent the business ethos.

However, it is not only socio-economic groups, such as those referred to above, but also individuals who perceive the duration and passage of time differently as (33) shows:

(33)   a.   What did you think of the Fresher's Conference *a long time ago last October*? [BCET]

b. ... but of course it was *a long time ago about* fifteen years I think ... . [BCET]

c. Dear me it's all such *a very long time ago—thirty years ago.* [BCET]

What is perceived as a long period of duration varies from *last October* to *thirty years ago.* What is perceived as a short time ago could also vary similarly.

A relatively large stock of conventionalized multiword expressions exist in English for talking about time from the individual's point of view, rather than from institutionalized clock or calendar orientation. Some of these personalized ways of perceiving time will be looked at in the sections below in terms of various temporal attributes such as duration, deixis, and temporal overlap.

Duration

Personal time, as both Bull (1968) and Windisch (1990) observe, is not always accurately measured and for this reason typically expressed in vague, imprecise terms: 'lived time is not clock time' (Windisch 1990: 176). Such imprecision appears in the language of temporality in examples (34) to (36):

(34) **A:** Hi John. You're up early.
B: Good morning. So are you?
A: As *the clock ticks past forty* there's *no time* to stay in bed.
B: So how are things?
A: Fine ... . And what about you? Haven't seen you *for ages.*
[A]

(35) The lions made a dash at the open gate, gobbled up the six beefeaters *in a jiffy* and away they went.
(W. M. Thackeray's *The Rose and the Ring* Edward Arnold 1969: 80)

(36) [telephone conversation]
I must get a pen to write this down—*just a tick.* [A]

Example (34) has a reference to age, a crucial indicator of temporality in human life as the birthday card industry discussed in Chapter 4 shows. The conventional way of referring to age in English is to insert an appropriate numeral into the first word slot of the restricted collocation *X years old/of age. Of age* is restricted to humans, whereas *X years old* can be used to refer to virtually anything with the numeral ranging from a day to billions, as when talking of the age of the universe.

As the clock ticks past forty is an unusual way of referring to a person's age, one of the few non-habitual ones in my corpus. The unconventionality of this expression draws attention to the feeling, common with increasing age, that the passage of time is swifter and swifter. This sense of 'Time's winged chariot hurrying near' is carried over to *no time*, 'no leisure'. Expressions such as these contrast with their opposites in durational span, but all these perceptions of time, as being durationally brief or prolonged, are idiosyncratic.

Table 5.3 illustrates the different perceptions of the duration of time intervals and their passage:

Personal time: brief	Personal time: prolonged
in a jiffy/trice	for ages
in the twinkling of an eye	all day/night long
before sb could say Jack Robinson/knife	around the clock
in (next to) no time	a long time/some time ago
time's running out	for hours/days/weeks
time flies	quite a while
wait a minute/a bit	for donkey's years
hang on for a sec/a tick	since the year dot
just a minute/a tick	all the time in the world
won't be long	in due course
no sooner	in the fullness of time
as soon as	at a snail's pace
at very short notice	etc.
a short while	
etc.	

Table 5.3

Deictic time

Deictic expressions of the temporal sort locate an event in time, but with that time unspecified in terms of the clock or calendar systems. The occurrence of the event in time has to be deduced by reference to the overall situational context, and is therefore only approximate. Some common temporal idioms in this deictic function are given below:

(37) The people who did were under twenty-five and couldn't get insured and *by the time* they got old enough to be insured they didn't want to. [BCET]

(38)   … we did start a little experiment on the Cambridge line, not incidentally with Cambridge University, who *at that time* were not very interested … . [BCET]

(39)   … the buyer who paid three million dollars for the piece known *up to now* as the Calibre 49 wishes to remain anonymous. [BCET]

(40)   *It is time* Messrs Waddingtons brought Monopoly up to date. [BCET]

Temporal overlap

Two events if they occur simultaneously coincide in time and so show temporal overlap. Such overlaps are especially common in narratives where they may be invested with different sorts of significance. In personal narratives temporal overlaps may be regarded as representing intriguing coincidences or simply portraying an incidental happening of two or more events at the same time (41). In fiction, they usually constitute part of the plot, especially in detective stories. In history, they may be taken as signifying general trends in spiritual or intellectual evolution (42), or as signifying social and political trends.

(41)   Alec crawled to the phone and *in the meantime* the fiancée of the young man had got hysterical … . [BCET]

(42)   This was Gautama Buddha, who taught his disciples at Benares in India *about the same time* that Isaiah was prophesying … .
       (H. G. Wells, *A Short History of the World* 1987: 100)

The approximate overlap in (42) signalled by *about* can be expressed as *at the same time*, if the situation warrants it.

   Temporal connectives and other time expressions have the function of locating events in specific time-intervals, corresponding to the units of clock- or calendar-time, so that the chronological sequence of events (past, present, and future) and the time-span of events (duration) are clear to the addressee. Precise reference to the time at which events occur places a discourse within the domain of public time. Using expressions in English which do not make such precise reference to clock- or calendar-time make it possible to locate a discourse in context-specific personal time.

5.3 General conclusions

The language-user always produces discourse in some context or another. The linguist, interested in naturally-occurring discourse, looks for the contextual variables that make one discourse different from another. The most common of these variables are different composers resulting in no two discourses being identical, the different addressees to whom such discourses are directed and the different content of such discourses. Even the same person speaking or writing to the same addressee will never do so in the identical context as time is irreversible. Consequently, barring formulaic discourse, normal discourse is unlikely to be repeated in an identical lexicogrammatical form because of the presence of significant contextual variables. In Hallidayan terms (1985) these variables, mentioned above, correspond to different participants and different fields of discourse, and different modes, spoken and written.

Relational idiomatic expressions, conjunctive ones such as *no matter what, on the grounds of, providing that*, etc. or temporal ones such as *no sooner/later than, in the fullness of time, for ages*, etc. are marked as occurring in mature discourse. Mature discourse is not necessarily associated with the age of the composer, but rather with literacy skills. *And, but, because, X years old, 1 o'clock, once upon a time*, etc. are neutral and may occur in both mature and immature discourse in the sense I have defined mature. Any significant differences in the use of these neutral words lies in their repetition and distribution.

Single and multiword relational expressions, conjunctive and temporal, aid cohesion and thus aid coherence in discourses that go beyond a few sentences. These expressions may be broadly classified as:

1 conjoining in semantic terms and integrative in discoursal terms;

2 temporal in semantic terms and sequential in discoursal terms;

3 meta-discoursal in semantic terms and organizational in discoursal terms.

As with ideational and interpersonal idiomatic expressions, conventionalized relational expressions of various types provide language-users with a ready-made resource for introducing the habitual along with the non-habitual, and also provides them with a means of presenting semantic relationships between phrases, clauses, and sentences with varying degrees of generality and specificity.

In all the discourses so far cited we do not find any two that are identical despite the use of familiar expressions in all of them. Different vocabulary selections and different combinations of these show a nice balance of the idiom and open-choice principles.

6

Idiomatic expressions as vocabulary resource: interdependencies, interconnections, and practicalities

The balance of routine and creativity in language is an empirical question which has long been neglected and only recently have researchers begun to explore the issues carefully.
(J. R. Nattinger and J. S. DeCarrico, *Lexical Phrases and Language Teaching* 1992)

6.1 What this chapter is about

The three foregoing chapters show how various types of conventionalized multiword expressions work in discourse: ideational expressions contribute to the content of a discourse as well as lend themselves more readily than other types do to word play; interpersonal expressions are high in evaluative and attitudinal information, and, consequently, one of their most common functions is the phatic one; relational expressions strengthen the cohesion and coherence of a discourse, arguments and narratives being especially good examples of discourse types using them. Each of these kinds of multiword expression makes its distinctive contribution to a discourse, but at the same time, all work together to convey a specific message.

The interdependency of the open-choice principle governing the ad hoc creation of phrases and clauses, that is casual collocations, and the idiom principle governing the use of prefabricated multiword expressions, is the central thesis of this book, linking all its six chapters and reiterated in the epigraph above.

215

Apart from the issue the epigraph to this chapter raises, two others are also taken up here.

What status can we assign to prefabricated multiword expressions in relation to the rest of the vocabulary? Especially relevant to this question are the notions of core and non-core vocabulary, and the allied issues they throw up of distribution and currency. Just as the conventional interweaves with the *ad hoc* or novel so that no discourse of reasonable length consists wholly of conventionalized expressions unless formulaic, like a Mass, or wholly of ad hoc novel ones, unless it is a poem, but is a mixture of both the conventional and the ad hoc, so no naturally-occurring discourse consists completely of core vocabulary but is a mixture of core and non-core items.

I have already drawn attention to the referential function of the vocabulary: words are packages of information (see Chapter 3). Vocabulary, accordingly, is the most obvious pointer to the content of a discourse. The third issue taken up in this chapter is the extent to which content, for example conflict, in a register like media reportage will elicit clusters of predictable topic-related collocations. Collocations are at the lower end of the idiomaticity scale being only weak realizations of the idiom principle (see Table 2.1). However, the restricted type of collocation is partially prefabricated, as greetings (Chapter 4) show; sometimes even unrestricted collocations are similar as, for example, *catch a bus/train/plane*, etc.

This chapter is concerned with idioms and collocations, both being types of word combination which lend themselves to repetition by virtue of being wholly or, as in the case of some collocations, partially prefabricated. Prefabrication and repetition are key features of language use: both facilitate comprehension, and, consequently, language learning (sections 6.5 and 6.6).

I conclude this chapter with some suggestions for further research into the role of multiword expressions in language learning and into the stylistic effects possible through their variation.

6.2 The general and the specific reconsidered

The specificity of most idioms relative to vocabulary showing under-specification, that is, general words, has already been discussed (sections 3.1.2 to 3.1.4). Vocabulary defined as 'core' shares some of the features of underspecified general words such as *animal, human,* and *man*: core vocabulary is, therefore, typically general, unmarked and neutral. Carter's (1987: 41) example illustrates the point: *kitchen, left,* and *right* (general and core) vs. *galley, port,* and *starboard* (specific to the nautical register, non-core). In other words, core vocabulary has a wider privilege of occurrence and so can function in a variety of discourse types, unlike specialist terminology, which is context-restricted.

Fire (noun) as illustrated in Table 6.1, is a good example of what the features of a core word are and how it behaves. This collection comprising idiomatic expressions, almost all containing the word *fire*, was collected from news broadcasts on Radio National (Australia) and TV (Channel 2) between 31 December 1993 and 7 January 1994. Also appearing in Figure 6.1 are other vocabulary items habitually associated with *fire*, for example, *arson, back burn, flames*, etc.

1   A total fire ban has been declared indefinitely.
2   About 90 fires are burning out of control.
3   We caught up with the fire fighters just as they were about to attend to another fire.
4   Not half an hour later they are out there fighting fires.
5   the fire fighting effort
6   Mark Manning had never come face to face with a wild fire.
7   a few confirmed reports of arson
8   Some of the fires were deliberately lit.
9   About a third of the bush fires are started by arsonists.
10   new blazes starting
11   as scrub land caught fire
12   New South Wales remains in the grip of fire.
13   The flames were in retreat.
14   the advancing lines of flames
15   as the fire storm gathers pace
16   back burned in that area
17   bush fire emergency
18   the bush fire hot spots
19   as it faces another day under threat from fierce bush fires
20   particularly fire-prone

Table 6.1: Natural disaster: fire

Core vocabulary has been characterized above as being general, unmarked and neutral. As the least specific of its co-synonyms, *fire* acts as a superordinate, the most general term among these. A general term like *fire* is unmarked for referential information like size, intensity, and so on, as well as for attitudinal overtones unlike its co-synonyms (*blaze, conflagration, holocaust, inferno*, etc.) and, therefore, is also neutral, its neutrality leading to its use in a wider range of discoursal contexts than *blaze, conflagration,* etc. Additionally, *fire* shows a capacity for 'extension', a capacity for entering into new, complex word forms of which it is one element, a further property of core words (Carter 1987: 37). *Fire* functions as a premodifying element in compound and phrasal idioms (*fireman, fire-prone* (20), *fire ball, fire brigade, fire fighter* (3), *fire storm* (15), etc.) or as the head (*bush fire* (9, 17, 18, 19), *wild fire* (6), etc.). In functioning as a word element, *fire* increases its frequency. However, neither generality nor frequency make a word indisputably core. Research into the validity of tests for identifying core vocabulary show that there is no one unitary and discrete core vocabulary (ibid.: 33 and 39). What we have are several core vocabularies associated with different registers. Thus, *galley, port,* and *starboard* will be core words in the nautical register of English, but not in its general main-stream vocabulary. 'Coreness' is a relative concept.

The idiomatic expressions displayed in Table 6.1 are non-techni-cal, hence the number of common, familiar words they contain. Considering the extent of the damage (600,000 hectares of bush land) the use of *conflagration, holocaust,* or *inferno* would not have been inappropriate. Instead, the news reports choose phrasal idioms like *wild fire* (6) and *bush fire* (9, 17–19), one instance of which is modified by *fierce*, a predictable collocation, but not part of the idiom. The intensity of the fire is also indicated through lexical elab-oration, in this case pre-modification, *the grip of fire* (12) and in pre- and post-modifying metaphors of advancing and retreating armies (*the advancing lines of flames* (14), *the flames were in retreat* (13)). The likeliest reason for this kind of vocabulary choice is that national news reports are for everybody, unlike special interest features which may target particular groups, for example, cricket fans, environmentalists, etc. Additionally, news broadcasts are rela-tively short making 'words of broad referential scope' likely to be chosen (Downing 1980: 90). However, even national news broad-casts use specialist expressions, including some that qualify as idioms as they are invariant and non- or semi-literal, for example, *green-back,* 'US banknote', *fringe benefits* 'benefits not included in one's wages', etc. These are not core items, but their frequency makes them part of mainstream vocabulary and so accessible to the majority. Others like the collocation *off-shore borrowing/banking*, etc. are somewhat more technical in meaning and may be understood only by the initiated. In short, news broadcasts, like most other 'everyday' discourses, show a judicious use of core and non-core vocabulary, idioms being in the latter category and functioning as packages of very specific kinds of information, in contrast to relatively under-specified core words.

6.3 Currency reconsidered

The currency of various sorts of idioms has been already looked at in section 2.6.2. It will be taken up again here but from a different perspective. Obviously, a core word like *fire* has a wide currency adding to its frequency and a high functional value. What is the functional value of non-core items of limited currency, especially if they are idioms?

Smell a rat and *raining cats and dogs* are good examples of functionally significant idioms in restricted fields of discourse. The uses they are being put to in these fields show how their 'idiom-ness' has been exploited to serve different purposes.

Smell a rat occurred once in The Birmingham Collection of English Text at the time of consultation (April to June 1990) and twice in my own corpus of idioms with no special contextual connotations. However, I was informed by a student of lexicography at a seminar I conducted (6 April 1993) that *smell a rat* occurs frequently in the crime/science-fiction Batman TV series, with Batman, a cartoon hero, who perennially thwarts the machinations of several evil adversaries. In this context, *smell a rat*, by virtue of its meaning 'become suspicious' and its form, a multiword expression, functions as a suitable formula for signalling that 'sth is not as it should be'.

Though current, the rarity of *raining cats and dogs* (it appears once in my corpus) in general use has been noted by Moon (1990: 500), an observation she qualifies by drawing attention to its new uses:

As an active item in the English lexicon, the idiom is disappearing, yet it is nonetheless widely known. A recent catalogue of novelties and souvenirs in Britain includes an umbrella decorated with running cats and dogs; a recent British TV commercial showed someone standing in the rain and catching a falling cat ... . The image has become institutionalized in a different semiotic system. The frequency or currency of an item is not the only reason for entering it in the inventory that is the headword list of a dictionary.

In the case of *raining cats and dogs* its literal meaning has been converted into the visual, but interpretation of its graphics depends on knowledge of the idiom both in its literal and non-literal senses.

The moral of all this is that the functional value of an idiom cannot necessarily be judged by its rarity in general use as it could have assumed new uses elsewhere.

Kick the bucket 'die' and *shoot the breeze* 'chat idly' are also idioms which, like *raining cats and dogs*, are rare, though current. These have a functional value as highly marked items and, therefore, are not attitudinally neutral:

(1)   Even James McClelland, an old friend who'd become Kerr's ardent enemy, felt grief when Kerr *kicked the bucket*.
      (*The Australian* 8 June 1991: Review Section 2)

(2)   Mostly people who work in solitude, writers rarely get together to *shoot the breeze*.
      (*The Sydney Morning Herald* 10 April 1993: 93)

Sinclair (1991: 17) observes that one of the principal uses of a corpus is to identify what is central and typical in the language. Presumably, what is central and typical would also qualify as being the core vocabulary of a language. The conclusions arrived at by Sinclair (ibid.: 20) on this issue appear to suggest that while individual lexical items recur, their co-occurrence with other items in recurrent patterns, that is, the recurrence of idioms and habitual collocations, is outnumbered by huge amounts of *ad hoc* or casual collocations. Consequently, examples of typical patterns are difficult to find (ibid.: 101). In other words, idiomaticity in the sense of the co-occurrence of words in accordance with usage preponderates in English, not idioms. The frequency of any given idiom or habitual collocation is relatively low in comparison with that of novel expressions in the sense of being ad hoc and non-institutionalized. However, the *ad hoc* collocations associated with specific topics, though not identical, show similarity to one another. Identically repeated patterns may be hard to find, but partially repeated ones are easier to locate (see section 6.4).

What most discourses are likely to show in the domain of vocabulary is a suitable distribution of:

1   core vocabulary;
2   vocabulary, single and multiword, typical of that register. For example, *who is next?*, *how much is* ...? typifies sale-purchase service encounters;
3   *ad hoc* collocations;
4   idioms and habitual collocations.

Using the vocabulary of a language requires awareness of the general and the specific, the marked and the neutral, as well as the wholly or partly conventionalized and the wholly or partly novel in relation to specific topics. What this means in practical terms will be looked at in the following sections.

6.4 Topic-related collocations

This section has the following aims:

1   To show how vocabulary on the same topic is used in related discourses, which occur at different times. In other words, what is analysed is repetition, a discoursal feature also observed by other scholars (Tannen 1989; Hoey 1991), though the analysis offered here is not as delicate as theirs.
2   To show the way in which *ad hoc* and conventionalized expressions interweave and complement each other as a normal feature of vocabulary choice.

News reports, whether relayed via the broadcast or print media, yield good examples of identically repeated single words and partial repetitions such as provided by variations in word forms (complex repetition, Hoey 1991). One-off collocations generally composed of the habitual and the *ad hoc* also represent a form of partial repetition, but at the phrasal and clausal level. The consequences of repetition, identical or partial, specially relevant to idiomaticity are:

1 Identical repetition in different discourses over time results in initially casual collocations turning into conventionalized multi-word expressions of various sorts.

2 Repetition in different discourses increases the frequency of a given item.

Sinclair (1991) observes that the huge amounts of casual collocations in the illustrative texts that constitute a corpus make the recurrent, and, hence the typical, difficult to isolate and to define. In other words, the repetition of given expressions in mammoth corpora, built on excerpts from longer discourses, is difficult to find. The relative infrequency of items such as idioms or habitual collocations in these corpora could also be partly due to their not being topic-centred, partly due, possibly, to partial repetition being discounted. Even collections of the sort presented in this chapter, despite their being topic-centred, yield many more partial repetitions than identical ones. Because of their being generated by the same topic, these partial repetitions occur in similar contexts and could, therefore, be used for vocabulary reinforcement.

I will now go on to look at the vocabulary generated by 'conflict' and 'conflict resolution'. The collocational clusters collected from news reports in the broadcast media—Radio National and two TV channels (the Australian Broadcasting Corporation (ABC) and the Special Broadcasting Service (SBS), Australia)—between 31 December 1993 and 8 February 1994, and the print medium (The Sydney Morning Herald 7 January 1994: 1 and 9) yielded these two contrasting topics among others.

Similar and partially similar collocations showing some form of repetition drawn from Table 6.2 appear in Table 6.3 in a classification which owes much to Hoey (1991). Repeated words like *violence* exemplify identical, or simple, repetition; grammatical variations altering word forms, for example, *bloody/bloodiest*, exemplify complex repetition. Where I differ from Hoey (1991) is in focusing on collocations in order to illustrate the interweaving of the ad hoc and the habitual. Column 1, of Table 6.3, for example, illustrates the different patternings in which *violence*, *flee*, etc. occur in forms abstracted from Table 6.2 to which the reader is referred for a fuller understanding of how the *ad hoc* and the habitual combine in the register of news reports. Identical repetition of a collocation is rare here, though single words are repeated often. Despite showing differences, the collocations in Table 6.2 are closely related as they all belong the same semantic field: 'conflict'. Thus, *bloody fighting* (5) and *bloody confrontation* (6) signify types of aggressive behaviour. Similarly, *bombs, shells, explosions, carnage,* and *massacre* are likely vocabulary items in 'conflict'.

1   Ten people were killed when a mortar round slammed into a line of people waiting for flour.
2   a denial that it had fired the shell
3   A row erupts as the race draws to a close.
4   The attack, which transformed the market-place into carnage and chaos was the bloodiest ...
5   After several days of bloody fighting a family feud has led to bloodshed.
6   It turned into a bloody confrontation.
7   At least 10,000 people were forced to flee their homes.
8   He was forced to flee the capital, Tiblisi.
9   a large array of weapons
10 Russia is developing a new nerve gas.
11 A mass grave uncovered yesterday in Croatia ...
12 the mass grave in Vukovar
13 the war crimes tribunal
14 one of General Dustan's strongholds
15 A whole family was wiped out.
16 Gunmen sprayed the bar ...
17 A sniper opened fire.
18 A bomb has exploded.
19 ... tit for tat killings.
20 a serious escalation of the conflict threatening the prospect of peace
21 had to give up its violent campaign
22 unless it renounces violence
23 end violence
24 renounces violence for good
25 The IRA must give up its violent campaign.
26 a violent end to one of South Africa's bloodiest years
27 fears of a violent backlash after an attack on a bar
28 campaign of violence
29 Sarajevo bombing: a heinous act of violence.
30 the opening of fire from Bosnian Serb positions
31 A mortar shell exploded ...
32 A mortar bomb killed ten people.
33 A mortar attack killed sixteen people queuing for bread.
34 fired the mortar bomb
35 A bomb explosion narrowly escaped killing ten civilians in Baodoa.
36 a horrific massacre in a crowded market place
37 the new shelling of Sarajevo
38 The carnage, the killings exist, were possible.
39 a game of brinkmanship

Table 6.2: Conflict: war, terrorism, disputes, etc.

Identical repetition of a word, similar phrasal grammar, related contexts	Similar repetition of a word, different phrasal grammar, related contexts	Similar repetition of a word, different phrasal grammar but similar meaning, related contexts
bloody fighting (5) bloody confrontation (6)	led to bloodshed (5) bloodiest years (26)	violent campaign (25) campaign of violence (28)
campaign of violence (25) act of violence (29)	end violence (23) violent campaign (21)	opened fire (17) the opening of fire (30)
violent campaign (21) violent end (26) violent backlash (27)	tit for tat killings (19) killed ten people (33)	
end violence (23) renounce violence (24)	Sarajevo bombing (29) a bomb explosion (35) a bomb has exploded (18) fired the shell (2) the new shelling of Sarajevo (37)	
mortar barrage (32) mortar attack (33)		
a bomb has exploded (18) a mortar shell exploded (31)		
fired the shell (2) fired the mortar bomb (34)		
to flee their homes (7) to flee the capital (8)		

Table 6.3: Some of the related collocations in Table 6.2

The expressions presented above are intended as illustrations of topic-related collocations. Collocations not only act as an interface between vocabulary and grammar, but when elicited by specific topics they can also realize types of sense relations such as synonymy, antonymy, and hyponymy, albeit in a looser form than single words do. Thus, *renounce/end violence* (column 1, Table 6.3) repeat *violence*, and are also synonymous. Additionally, the two phrases are grammatically identical. *Violent campaign* and *campaign of violence* (column 3), on the other hand, are semantically identical but grammatically different. Similar examples are *open fire/the opening of fire* (column 3) and *fired the shell/the new shelling of Sarajevo* (column 2). These two examples show a nominalization transform.

The different collocates of fire (Table 6.1, natural disaster) and those of fire (Table 6.2, conflict) illustrate homonymy in different collocational clusters. There is a conceptual difference between *bush/wild fire* and *gun fire*, though both can cause holocausts, havoc, and death, a conceptual difference evident in the very different collocational patterns of the two figures.

Conflict is either accompanied or followed by conflict resolution, also generating its own sets of topic-related expressions such as the one presented in Table 6.4.

1	one of the stumbling blocks in the way of ...
2	thrown up stumbling blocks
3	stalemate
4	will not accept violent solutions
5	resolve the issue of Palestine
6	Israel wants to resume negotiations but not at any price.
7	stepping up efforts to present itself as a credible negotiator
8	overcome the deadlock
9	defusing the situation
10	It (the Khmer Rouge) continues to stall meaningful peace talks.
11	the stalled negotiations
12	no sign to the end of the stalemate between the PLO and the Israelis
13	fuelling fears that a lasting peace may not be possible
14	Peace does not come easily to the Middle East.
15	cast doubts on the latest peace talks
16	the hold up in the talks
17	The road to peace will be very long.
18	peace talks
19	a peaceful solution to the crisis
20	the proposed peace plan
21	peace negotiations
22	peace and reconciliation
23	lay down their arms
24	a pull-out by British troups
25	agreeing to resume talks
26	We reach for the olive branch ... so that together we can forge peace.

Table 6.4: Conflict resolution

A comparison of the vocabulary of Tables 6.2 and 6.3 provides a basis for the exploration of the kind of semantic relationships looked at briefly above. Synonymy and homonymy have already been touched upon. The comparison of Tables 6.2 and 6.3 throws up another semantic relationship, that of antonymy, though this usual term is too rigorous for the much looser relation looked at here. Such 'looseness' is unavoidable at the collocational level where what we have are paraphrases of varying semantic 'oppositeness'.

The most noteworthy features of Tables 6.2 and 6.3 thrown up by a comparison are discussed below.

The topic-related collocations of Tables 6.2 and 6.3 clarify the overall discoursal meanings being conveyed by conflict and conflict resolution, especially when contrasted. Contrasting idioms and *ad hoc* collocations foregrounding what these two notional domains are about are: *a large array of weapons* (9), *tit for tat killings* (19), *a serious escalation of the conflict* (20), *a horrific massacre* (36), etc. in Table 6.2, and *lay down their arms* (23), *olive branch* (26), *peace and reconciliation* (22), *defusing the situation* (9), *will not accept violent solutions* (4), etc. in Table 6.4. The oppositions realized in the collocations of these two figures are far less rigorous than those in single words like *fat/thin, dead/alive, mother/father,* etc. The only clear-cut antonymous pair in Figure 6.3 is *violent/peaceful solution(s)* (4 and 19). The collocational clusters comprising these figures signal contrasting textual meanings: whereas conflict is destructive, conflict resolution is constructive. But, of course, conflict resolution is not peace, but working towards peace. Accordingly, while items like *A mortar shell/A bomb (has) exploded* (31 and 18), *A sniper opened fire* (17), *Gunmen sprayed the bar ...* (16), *A mortar round slammed into a line of people* (1), etc. abound in Table 6.2, references to the obstacles bedevilling conflict resolution abound in Table 6.4: *deadlock* (8), *stalled negotiations* (11), *stalemate* (12), *hold-up ... talks* (16), *stumbling blocks* (2). etc.

Only Table 6.4 yields clear examples of synonymy: *stalemate, deadlock,* and *hold up* are recognizable as synonyms even outside this context. Similarities in terms of a paraphrasal likeness specific to this context are:

Peace does not come easily to the Middle East. (14)
The road to peace will be very long. (17)
... a lasting peace may not be possible. (13)

A good example of a superordinate item, more rigorously hyponymy, is *campaign of violence* (Table 6.2, 28) subsuming specific violent acts: *A bomb has exploded* (18), *a mortar attack* (33), *a horrific massacre* (36), etc. A similar example (Table 6.4) is *Peace does not come easily to the Middle East* (14), a general statement subsuming (6) and (12), both pertaining to the same region.

Contrasting Tables 6.2 and 6.3 also reveals that conflict appears to elicit more concrete descriptive details than conflict resolution does. Not only do specific words enter into more varied relationships with other words in the phrases and clauses cited, but the vocabulary used is also more varied: *a row erupts* (3), *strongholds* (14), *Gunmen sprayed the bar* (16), *violent backlash* (27), *heinous act* (29), *horrific massacre* (36), *carnage* (38), *a game of brinksmanship* (39), etc.

In the collection (Table 6.4) comprising conflict resolution, the vocabulary is relatively more abstract. Peace (10, 13, 14, 15, 17, 18, 20, 21, 22, 26) preponderates here, collocating most frequently with *talks* (10, 15, 16, 18, 25). Other collocates of *peace* or one of its forms are: *plan* (20), *negotiations* (21), *solution* (19), and *reconciliation* (22). Other repeated items are *talks* (10, 15, 16, 18, 25) and *negotiations/negotiator* (6, 7, 11, 21).

News reports cover a recurrent set of topics of which the most common are conflict, conflict resolution, natural and other disasters, trade and finance, with each main topic having its sub-topics. Recurrent topics means repeated vocabulary items in repeated contexts. This is another way of saying that predictable collocations are plentiful in topic-related vocabulary, making it specially relevant in language acquisition. Why this should be so will be looked at in section 6.6.

6.5 Idioms, topic, theme: the role of vocabulary in getting the message across

I have already quoted Sinclair (1991) on the difficulty of finding recurrent patterns among the huge amounts of casual collocations in any corpus. This difficulty suggests that most vocabulary items, whether single or multiword, have a low frequency in relation to the total language output of an individual or a group even in a single day, let alone a longer period. However, elsewhere in the same work (ibid.: 116), Sinclair observes:

> Because of the low frequency of the vast majority of words, almost any repeated collocation is the most unlikely event, but because the set of texts is so large, unlikely events of this kind may still be the result of chance factors.

One such chance factor is the decision of language-users to fore-ground topics or aspects of given topics which strike them as important through the repetition of certain expressions. In Table 6.2 (conflict) *violent campaign* (21, 25) is repeated. *Campaign of violence* (twice) and *A total fire ban has been declared indefinitely* (four times) were also repeated in different news reports, but these repetitions were not included in the relevant figures. Far more common than repeated collocations are repeated idioms and single words. It is this latter kind of repetition that will be the subject of this section.

Certain vocabulary items underpin the topic of discourse, not simply at the level of what it is about but, if academic, also on the level of the thesis that is being argued over and above subject matter. If literary, such items underpin the theme in contradistinction to content, especially story content. These repeated items function as 'text-forming' repetitions, to use a term borrowed from Hoey (1991: 57) by virtue of forming a chain of connections in the discourse containing them. Any discourse, unless it serves a phatic function, seeks to make a point which the addressee has to deduce from what is written or spoken. The difference between the point of the discourse as a whole and its content is the difference between high- and low-level information. How high- and low-level information is conveyed in two types of discourse (examples (3) and (4)) through the repetition of relevant vocabulary is the concern of the rest of this section. Additionally, (3) and (4) indicate the factors that may lead to lexical repetition.

In (3), *whistleblowers*, a variation of *blow the whistle on sth*, *dissent*, and *suppression* gain prominence because the longer discourse they are taken from warrants their repetition in terms of both high- and low-level information.

Examples (3a. to e.) are excerpts from this longer discourse taken from *Australian Campas Review Weekly* (7 April 1993: 4).

(3) a. Eric Aubert reports from last weekend's conference on intellectual suppression in Canberra:
Whistleblowers in chorus on dissent (headline)
… The diversity of cases presented by the whistleblowers themselves (none of the claimed suppressors were there) to a conference on intellectual dissent and whistleblowing in Canberra last weekend left little doubt that suppression is endemic in Australian society.

Blow the whistle on sth in various forms appears twenty times in the feature article of 1,090 words that (3a. to e.) are taken from. Various forms of *suppress* appear twenty-two times and various forms of *dissent* appear eight times. The article depends on the reader knowing the meaning of the key lexical item, *blow the whistle on sth*, 'stop sth one disapproves of on social, ethical, etc. grounds', to make its point.

The subject of the article (low-level information) is the retaliatory penalties meted out to many whistleblowing academics in order to silence them by different vested interests. The point of the article (high-level information) is the political implication of whistleblowing for both the academic and wider community:

(3)   b.   ... the clearest message from the conference was that traditional methods of rectifying suppression—ombudsmen, trade unions, tribunals and using members of parliament in most cases do not work.

The three items repeated throughout the article, as well as the issue their association in the one discourse signifies, appear in (3a.). Both *whistleblowers* and *suppressors/suppression* generate *ad hoc* related expressions, many of them paraphrases of each other specific to this text; additionally, as with the earlier collocational clusters generated by conflict and conflict resolution, this text also yields several collocations in antonymous oppositions specific to it. Table 6.2 shows these paraphrasal similarities and oppositions.

Whistleblowing is a form of dissent; consequently, the two are semantically and collocationally related in this discoursal context, though not necessarily outside it:

(3)   c.   *Whistleblowers* in chorus on *dissent*

      d.   a conference on intellectual *dissent* and *whistleblowing*

      e.   The conference was organised jointly by the Intellectual *Dissent* in Australia network and *Whistleblowers* Anonymous.

The means used by society's vested interests to control whistleblowing and dissent is suppression. The last term is used nineteen times: *cases of suppression, tactics against suppression*, etc. All these repetitions connect up directly or indirectly with references to

Whistleblowers	Suppressors
1 people who resist what they see as suppression	A alleged suppressors
2 academics who speak out	B employers
3 Whistleblowers Anonymous (which decide to rename itself Whistleblowers Australia) a support group for people who have blown the whistle on corruption ...	C very rich and powerful organizations
4 dissenters/dissident	D a warning to vested interests that attacks will not be tolerated
5 Intellectual Dissent in Australia network	E a common tactic used by employers was to refer whistleblowers to psychiatrists.
6 One whistleblower was sent to a total of eight psychiatrists. This practice fits in with the most common form of action used against dissenters ...	
7 nut case radicals or part of a 'crazy fringe'	

Table 6.5

whistleblowers or their activities and so are genuinely text-forming, elaborating as they do on the main point of the discourse. Discourses such as (3) are, therefore, ideal for demonstrating the way lexical repetition and collocational patterns establish connections between facts, maximizing the coherence of the 'message' conveyed.

Example (4), a literary discourse, exemplifies a more sophisticated use of repetition than (3) does:

(4)   Then Henry let her down: for two reasons. He couldn't stand her mother. Her mother *couldn't stand him*. And anyone Mrs Bodoin *could not stand* she managed to *sit on*, disastrously. So Henry had writhed horribly feeling his mother-in-law *sitting on* him tight, and Virginia after all, in a helpless sort of family loyalty, *sitting* alongside with her mother. Virginia didn't really want to *sit on* Henry. But when her mother egged her on, she couldn't help it.
    (D. H. Lawrence, *Mother and Daughter* 1967: 9)

Example (4) has a total of twelve verbs excluding *managed* used here as a catenative. *Cannot stand* occurs three times and forms of *sit on/sit* four times in this total. This repetition has both thematic and rhetorical point. The two verbs contrast in their literal senses: an upright position *stand* with a non-upright one, *sit*. The idioms differ in form and meaning: *stand* must co-occur with a negative form when it is part of the idiom meaning 'have a strong dislike for sb/sth' and *sit* needs *on* when part of the idiom meaning 'handle sb firmly', 'put sb in their place'. In the power game presented in (4), figuratively speaking, Mrs Bodoin can't stand Henry so she sits on him, while Henry can't stand Mrs Bodoin, but since he lacks her forceful energy he can't sit on her, leaving her, as a result, the victor. Lawrence plays on both the literal and the non-literal senses of *can't stand* and *sit on* giving the reader by this kind of play an ironic assessment of the battle of the sexes at the higher thematic level.

Two classes of metaphorical idioms were identified in Chapter 3. English has isolated idiom metaphors exemplifying different facets of a concept like strategy (see sections 3.2 to 3.2.3). *Blow the whistle on sb* belongs to this class. Idioms like *sit on sb*, on the other hand, belong with idioms constituting families such as those with *up* (joy) and *down* (grief) (see sections 3.3.3 and 3.3.4). This second class consists of idioms contrasting with each other. Thus, *Sit on sb* contrasts with *stand up to sb* 'resist strongly'. Some other phrasal verbs showing similar contrasts are: *turn up sth* (like a radio) 'increase the volume of', *turn down* 'decrease the volume of', *build up* 'nourish in order to strengthen', *pull down* 'cause to diminish in strength', etc. Lawrence's wit created by the way he uses his verbs makes (4) more suitable for advanced stylistic analysis than (3).

I began this section by referring to the factors that could lead to lexical repetition. One such factor is subject matter. Where synonyms may not be available as in scientific, medical, or legal terminology, a word has to be repeated. Example (3) does not belong to any of these registers. *Whistleblowers* is repeated for different reasons: its conciseness, its function as the part of an organization's title (see Table 6.5), and the fact that the article is about whistle-blowers. In (4) repetition not only reinforces the theme of this text, it is also a stylistic technique enhancing the complementarity of *not stand* and *sit on*, both literally and idiomatically. In summary, subject matter, register, and stylistic skills leading to cohesive lexical links across a discourse are three factors determining lexical repetition.

6.6 Practicalities

6.6.1 Introduction

The foregoing chapters, as well as the preceding sections of this chapter, focus on the description, categorization, and analysis of idiomatic expressions, an exercise intended to demonstrate and account for the ubiquity of idioms I referred to at the beginning of this book. The 'practicalities' of both chapter and section titles point to the utilitarian value of such an exercise. Apart from the intrinsic value of a description of multiword expressions, what other purpose can such an account serve? The rest of this section attempts to answer this question.

6.6.2 The role of idioms in language learning

Prefabricated language

It is only relatively recently that books devoted to multiword expressions have appeared. I have discussed three such works (Smith 1925; Makkai 1972; Strassler 1982) in Chapter 1. The works I look at here, with one exception, are very different, having as they do, a primarily utilitarian purpose. Even the exception (Nattinger and DeCarrico 1992), though theoretically oriented, contains many insights relevant to language teaching and learning. From a theoretical point of view, it is Nattinger and DeCarrico who cast the most light on the role of prefabricated multiword expressions in language acquisition. Many of these expressions correspond to what I am calling idioms, though Nattinger and DeCarrico term them *lexical phrases*, reserving *idiom* for expressions like *hell for leather, by the way*, etc. which admit no variation whatsoever.

Nattinger and DeCarrico observe (ibid.: xv) that recent research into language learning pays more attention to how rules are learnt, rather than to the goals of such learning. Picking up prefabricated expressions constitutes one of the means of acquiring language whether this is a first (L1) or second (L2) language. Nattinger and DeCarrico focus on an advanced stage of L2 acquisition, namely the mastery of academic English, spoken (lectures) and written (the formal essay and the scripted lecture). The academic register is a highly complex one requiring a distinctive organization and signposting devices functioning as creators of coherence and intelligibility in such discourse.

Nattinger and DeCarrico pick out two major classes of lexical phrases: those which organize discourse at the global level (e.g. *let me start with X, the first thing is, by the way, in a nutshell*) and at the local one (e.g. *in other words; not only X, but (also) Y; where was I?*). These categorizations of lexical phrases are accompanied by accounts of their functions: the *first thing is* introduces a topic, *by the way* indicates a topic shift, and *in a nutshell* summarizes the discourse (ibid.: 94–6). Nattinger and DeCarrico observe that academic lectures are full of such multiword expressions. Teaching language-learners these expressions sharpens their skill in recognizing the overall structure of a lecture, in other words, they are trained in a top-down mode of information processing. Such training also helps them produce lecture-style discourse, if necessary.

Idioms employable in a range of discourse types, besides the academic, have the same general function: they save language-users composing texts entirely from scratch by enabling the interweaving of the *ad hoc* and the conventional. I now turn to two workbooks presenting language-users with collections of idioms as aids to understanding and using this most opaque component of the vocabulary.

Peaty's *Working with English Idioms* (1983) and McLay's *Idioms at Work* (1987) introduce learners to sets of idioms classified under various headings. Peaty classifies idioms according to their grammar in sentence context: phrasal verbs without an object (e.g. *wake up*), separable phrasal verbs (e.g. *put (it) on*), inseparable ones (e.g. *call on sb*), and so on. Each idiom is defined and appears in an invented sentence. Peaty foregrounds the grammar of idioms, McLay foregrounds their functions. The latter's classification of idioms into those signifying knowing, agreeing, contradicting, disagreeing, and so on make clear her pragmalinguistic concerns. The idioms in McLay's book are contextualized in short invented dialogues.

A feature of McLay's workbook, one which links up with the sections on interlingual lexical phrases in Nattinger and Decarrico (1992), are the translation equivalents she provides from French, German, Spanish, and Italian for the English idioms listed in each lesson unit. These equivalents illuminate some similarities, but much more so the dissimilarities in the five languages drawn upon. The examples that follow are restricted to English, French, and German. While *Je l'ai sur le bout de la langue* and *es liegt mir auf der Zunge* are very close to *It's on the tip of my tongue* (p.15), the body-part image of *know sth like the back of one's hand* changes to one of apparel in *le connaît comme le fond de sa poche and kenne es wie meine Westentasche* (p.19). The special genius of the source and target languages, in terms of their idioms and their idiomatic design, is foregrounded by translation. The target language could impose a spareness of expression in translation brought on, for example, by greater possibilities of deletion than the source language permits. No translator or language-teacher can afford to ignore idioms or idiomaticity if a natural use of the target language is an aim. Such a consideration obviously underlies McLay's presentation of parallel idioms in the languages named above.

McCarthy's *Vocabulary* (1990) is a teacher's handbook and so very different from the workbooks of Peaty and McLay. Unlike Peaty and McLay, McCarthy draws extensively on current semantic and psycholinguistic theory to foreground two major concerns in vocabulary teaching:

1 The role of gestalts in mental lexicons: words are stored as single and multiword units as well as in associative gestalts

2 The role of knowledge of the world in understanding and using the vocabulary

Pragmalinguistic concerns such as these lead McCarthy to the following:

1 Attention to word frequency and range based on corpus data

2 Learnability and the learner's needs

3 Discourse and register

4 Student autonomy and student input, e.g. the student compiled vocabulary notebook consisting of both single and multiword expressions

5 Learning strategies, e.g. inference, a form of meaning construction

6 The use of naturally-occurring data in exercises

A concept reflecting both the gestalt notion and the centrality of knowledge of the world in learning vocabulary is that of topic

(McCarthy 1990). Topic offers a basis for organizing vocabulary in a notional-centred way for teaching purposes, as well as for devising topic-based exercises, and as such links up with 3 listed above. I have already shown how common collocations can be collected and high-lighted in terms of a specific topic (see conflict and confict resolution, Figures 6.2 and 6.3) and how these also show up lexical relations such as homonymy, antonymy, and loose forms of synonymy. What follows is intended to illustrate stated student needs and student input (see 2 and 4 listed above). Example (5) to (8) below were composed by the students at the Institute of Languages of New South Wales as a response to tasks designed to teach them the use of idioms selected from their notebooks. Additionally, these tasks reflect the results of a needs analysis in which vocabulary learning was given high priority due to its perceived importance in under-standing the print and broadcast media and in conversation.

Perfect machinery

(5) If your company need any heavy machinery or mechanical equipment for construction works, do not hesitate—*call now*!!! We can offer you one of the best equipment in Australia. Our machinery always *sell like hot cakes*!
Do not miss your chance!
Ph. (043) 223322
   (043) 223326 [A]

(6) *Racking your brain* about choosing car's alarm! Just call us, we are *on the ball* and we will *put our finger on* it
Call now, it will not *cost* you *an arm or a leg*
Ph. 777000 [A]

(7) A: Bill, could I ask you? I have a problem …
B: Yes, sure. I'm listening.
A: You know, yesterday we bought a new software, and I spent a whole day trying to run it, but …
B: Oh, *I'm sorry. Don't ask me. I haven't a clue*! Really you know, I'm absolutely hopeless in personal computers … [A]

(8) Tom, how we prepare alcoholic drink from grape?
Don't ask me. I haven't a clue. You know, I'm hopeless at chemistry. [A]

The rationale underlying these two types of tasks, the composition of advertisements and conversations, derives from the stated needs of the Institute students.

Understanding advertisements in the broadcast and print media is important for survival in a consumer society. The usefulness of a copywriting task is twofold. It gives the learner practice in using multiword expressions with a wide range of interpersonal functions and frequencies (*call now, don't miss the chance of sth*, etc.), as well as ideational idioms of varying frequencies (*rack one's brains, in the red, sell like hot cakes, on the ball*, etc.). Active use ensures an item a place in the learner's mental lexicon in terms of production and reception. Additionally, the copywriting task familarizes the learner with the advertising register: advertisements show a concentration of idiomatic expressions, figurative ones being frequent. An advertisement which uses only literal language is unusual (see also Cook 1992 and Carter and McCarthy 1995, both of which contain numerous suggestions for related teaching procedures).

Composing dialogues relates to the need of these L2 students to communicate with the locals in face-to-face and telephone conversations. Interpersonal idioms dominate here (*you know, I'm sorry, I'm listening, How are you?*, etc.), though ideational ones also occur. Noteworthy is the way these learners are directed to clusters of idioms, the interpersonal and the ideational complementing each other in a coherent way.

Idioms, knowledge of the world, and inference

Inference is a form of meaning construction, essentially the same for single and multiword expressions: knowledge of the world plays a part in the semantics of both types, but the following discussion focuses on inferring idiomatic meaning. We draw inferences almost all the time in our daily lives, especially in responding to language, chief among sign systems. In so doing we draw conclusions, though not always consciously, based on whatever information is available. (For further related discussion see Low 1988 and, with particular reference to language teaching, Nesi 1995.)

For example, that *beech* is a noun and a kind of tree can be inferred from its co-occurrence with *a* and *branches*, given that the function of the indefinite article and *branches* as a word is known in:

(9)   Jack sat down beneath the branches of a beech.

236

Sublunary is a different case as its meaning can be deduced even out of context, if its parts can be decoded:

Sub–	lunar–	y
beneath	the moon	adjective marker

However, a further inference is necessary in order to arrive at the meaning 'earthly', 'terrestrial': the earth lies beneath the moon in our view of the heavens.

What happens when the available information for decoding an expression yields several possibilities? *Bottom line* is a relatively recent idiom used in a wide range of contexts. Its source is accountancy where what the figures add up to appears on the bottom line of the accounts ledger: the total indicates the exact financial position. Figuratively, *bottom line* signifies 'what an issue/situation, etc. is about', 'the essentials'. The book-keeping origin of *bottom line* is clearest in (10):

(10) a. [radio news bulletin]
        The Treasurer felt obliged to reduce the *bottom line* Budget deficit of $16 billion. [A]

      b. [radio news bulletin]
        That's the *bottom line*—that it costs $50,000 a day. [A]

Even in (10a.), the idiom's meaning will be clear only to those who already know its origin or its figurative sense. If *bottom line* was taken to refer to the last line of a ruled page, then (10b.) could be interpreted as 'the limits of sth'. Both this interpretation and even 'ultimatum' are possibilities in (10c.) in the context of North Korea's refusal to allow a UN inspection of its nuclear arsenal:

(10) c. [radio news bulletin]
        The US has now given North Korea its *bottom line* position. [A]

Inferring the meaning of an expression like *bottom line* can result in misfires arising from choosing incorrect information as a cue to interpretation. Particularly relevant to the role of knowledge of the world in inferential strategies is the availability of specific information. Empirical regularities are discernible in generalities such as *Reindeer have antlers*, not in specificities: *Rudolph has a red nose* (Garnham 1985: 111). *Bottom line*, like most other idioms, conveys a very specific package of information, ignorance of which could cause the language-user problems. Additionally, an expression, whether an idiom or not, has to be first identified as literal or non-literal:

(11)   Create jobs: let *fat cats* quit at 55
       (*The Australian* 1 April 1976: 6)

shows a mismatch between empirical regularities and what is asserted, if the latter is interpreted literally. Cats are not employed nor is fifty-five their normal life span. This kind of anomaly is likely to trigger a non-literal interpretation as a survey showed (Fernando and Flavell 1981: 53). A further cue to figurative interpretation is discoursal incoherence: if interpreted literally, non-literal expressions may not make sense in relation to their co-text.

The inferential strategies used to interpret vocabulary, in this case idioms, appear in the responses to a task set thirty-two native speakers (Fernando 1981), which is discussed below. The non-literalness of the task-based idioms is clear from their contextualization and the wording of the task:

A metaphor makes an implicit comparison. Which of these two phrases seems to you to be establishing a recognizable comparison? If you recognize a comparison state the points of similarity between X and Y which lead to the comparison.

(12)   a.   Arctic[X] University is a white[Y]elephant.
       b.   Public servants are fat cats.

There were three types of responses to *white elephant* 'an useless though expensive object' originating in the practice of Siamese kings who gifted costly-to-maintain white elephants to retainers they wished to ruin.

1   Group 1 consisted of subjects who knew the idiom and responded accordingly.
2   Group 2 attempted to infer its likeliest meaning by drawing on their knowledge of the world in so far as it seemed relevant to (12a.): X Y has not proved useful as a University. White elephants are sacred and therefore not used as workers.

White elephants though attractive do not last long, therefore Arctic University is unusual and attractive but not much use.

3 Group 3 identified the idiom with an extended use, a white elephant stall: *Arctic University is a white elephant* makes a comparison between an institution (i.e. education) and a second-hand opportunity shop. A white elephant stall is made of unwanted odds and ends. This too could apply to Arctic University.

Group 2 came closer to the sense of *white elephant* than Group 3, but Group 3 was being equally deductive. It just happens that the information used as evidence for their conclusion was inappropriate.

The moral to be drawn from these different conclusions is that correct inferences, especially in the case of non-literal expressions, are most likely to be drawn if language-users can access the right piece of information. Thus, knowing that cows are sacred in some cultures led to a similar conclusion for white elephants: in terms of work, they are useless.

My assumption regarding the role of knowledge of the world in assisting interpretation of vocabulary was borne out by the responses to *fat cat* (12b.), 'a paid official who does little or no work'. The following are typical of the majority:

> The metaphor is suggesting that public servants get paid for doing nothing. Here an undesirable connotation is being given to fat cats. An alternate view could be to see fat cats as cuddly and content—even this would suggest that public servants are pleasurably idle and loving it.

> X are assumed to be lazy and overpaid. Y are fat (overpaid/well fed) and do not earn their living (i.e. by chasing rats and mice).

> Fat cats are lazy according to the stereotype, so are public servants.

A stereotype plays an equivalent role to an empirical regularity in inference, which is what it does in the case of public servants and fat cats, a function recognized by the third respondent above. Overall, the responses to *fat cats* 12b.) were accurate. Those which were off the mark attributed irrelevant features carried over from fat cats to public servants: sleepy, slow, immobile, awful, mean, etc. Both public servants and fat cats (pets) are experientially familiar, unlike white elephants (rarities), making a correct interpretation of the idiom likelier. The metaphor here is not yet fossilized.

Though having the same grammatical form as a definition, neither 12a. nor 12b. are like *philatelists are stamp collectors*. They function as evaluations, a function all my subjects were aware of. It is worth underlining that some metaphoric expressions involve very simple vocabulary and structure and that habits of inference can be developed at the very earliest stage of language learning. For example:

David is a lion
Jill is a real mouse
Manolo is an open book

In summary, inferring the meaning of vocabulary requires grammatical and situational knowledge, as well as an ability to see the relationship between a lexical item and its co-text. In other words, inference depends on access to different kinds of information. How can teachers help learners in this regard? The more samples of language of a topic-related sort learners are exposed to, the more focused and systematic practice they get in deduction. Such samples collected over time (Tables 6.1, 6.2, and 6.3, for example) provide useful teaching and learning resources. The ten instances of *put/turn back the clock* (see section 2.4) is another such set. Study of the accompanying co-text and the different situations in which this idiom is used give learners the information for inferring what it means. Asking learners to define *put/turn back the clock*, or any other lexical item, using a collection of texts in which that item appears, gives them practice in using collocational and situational information as a basis for conclusions regarding the meaning of that item. Definition arrived at in this way is inference in action. Carter (1993) and McCarthy and Carter (1994, Chapter 4) discuss the importance of the development of inferential procedures in the development of language awareness in relation to language learning. See also James and Garrett (1991) for more general discussion relevant to this section.

6.7 Interlocutor, thinker, and experiencer/reporter

This section deals with the three interrelated roles assumed by the language-user in any act of communication as presented in Chapters

2 to 5 in this book. Additionally, it points to areas for further research in the relatively early stages of language development. When do ideational idioms, for example, appear in child language? What use can idioms be put to, especially in variations of ideational ones in forms of guided creative composition? Each functional role signals an interpersonal, a ratiocinative, and an informing/representational aptitude. One of the major concerns of this book has been to show the workings of all three through an examination of idiomaticity and idioms, which, while exemplifying specific features and parts of the vocabulary, also exemplify these general aptitudes.

Interpersonal relations, verbal and non-verbal, are at the heart of social life. Such relations appear early as the interchange of smiles, cooings, and babblings between mother and infant shows. Baby talk constitutes a proto-language, often with discernible beginnings of interpersonal expressions such as *Tata*. Many parents teach children politeness routines in the early stage of their upbringing, for example, *Thank you, Excuse me*, etc. Apart from my own informal observations, some evidence for the early mastery of interpersonal expressions appears in Carter (1987: 150). Further evidence of the early mastery of interpersonal expressions is provided by the tendency children show of relying on dialogue in reporting their experiences (personal observations). The following comes from a primary school child:

(13)   [child's essay]
A bad day at the Museum
One day me and my mum went to the Royal Dinosaur Museum. When I got there I nearly tripped over a model. The lady who worked there said 'you will have to pay for it if you knock it over.'
'*Bossyboots*' I said quietly. She heard me and said 'you are a very cheeky young girl.'
'Is she a *mind reader or what*?'
After, my shoe lace came undone. Just my luck, the lady who worked there said 'your lace is undone.'
Me thinking she was a *mind reader* said in my mind 'I'll do it when I get to a model of a dinosaur.' Then she said '*are you deaf*?' I said NO then me and my mum went home. [A]

At the more sophisticated adult level what we get, if the discourse is

241

written, is not so much the use of interpersonal expressions, for example, *Is she a mind reader or what? Are you deaf?*, functionally similar to *Has the cat got your tongue?*, *'Bossyboots', I said*, and *Just my luck*, etc. as in (13), but a colloquial vocabulary and syntax to create a 'chatty' style signalling shared knowledge and attitudes as in (14), a supposed monologue of a former Australian Prime Minister, serving as a send up of his public stance of righteous indignation:

(14)   This is just typical of course. Things start going wrong and people immediately go *pointing the finger* at those who are to blame. *If that wasn't enough*, the trade unions decided they might want to ditch the Accord. Well, now is really *the winter of our discontent* if the leader of our Labour Party can't *count* on unswerving loyalty from the trade union movement. *Anyone would think* this is England.
(*The Australian* 29 June 1991: Review Section 3)

The child relies mostly on dialogue, the adult on a blend of colloquialisms (*ditch, if that wasn't enough, anyone would think*, etc.) and formalities (*the winter of our discontent* (Shakespeare's *Richard III*, I.i), *unswerving loyalty*, etc.) to create an interactive style. While *unswerving loyalty* is an *ad hoc* collocation, *the winter of our discontent* is a saying. There were three instances of this saying in my corpus.

Connecting sentences by juxtaposition is the main means of establishing textual unity in both (13) and (14). Few conjunctions are used (*and, if*), but other types of connectives are present in both discourses: *when, who*, etc.

And, probably the most widely used connective, is one of the first to appear in child language (personal observation). However, depending on what they hear from adults around them, children are able to use relatively sophisticated connectives:

(15)   [child's essay]
Sophia and Christine are leaving. They are going to Ireland. *Speaking of* Sophia and Christina, Sophia made her first holy communion. [A]

If that wasn't enough (14) is similar to *speaking* of but conveys, in addition, the evaluation *bad*. What signals the maturity of (14) is the range of its vocabulary (common collocations and idioms, formal and colloquial) as well as its much greater syntactic and semantic complexity in comparison with (13) and (15).

Ideational idioms are packages of information of varying degrees of complexity functioning as mini-commentaries on the world and its phenomena. The constructional homonymity of idioms such as *tighten one's belt, kick the bucket*, etc. (see section 2.3) could present special difficulties of interpretation and use to children and L2 learners. There were no idioms of this type from children below the age of twelve in my corpus, though this could be due to the smallness of my sample of child language in that age group in relation to the adult one. It is my impression, however, that ideational idioms come into their own only at a later stage of language development.

Ideational idioms are conventionally used as so many texts cited in this book show, but they also bring out homo ludens in the language-user, the urge to play on words in novel ways much more often than other types do, revitalizing both language and the passing moment. Journalists capitalize on novel combinations and variations of ideational idioms, but other sorts of language-users are also capable of such play:

(16)   *Green light for blue-collar* reform
       (*The Australian* 23 March 1993: 2)

(17)   We got married and *before we knew where we were we were knee-deep in babies*. [A]

Whereas language-users can get by without ideational idioms, they would find it much more difficult to do without interpersonal and relational ones. It is for this reason that ideational idioms are prominent among particular groups, those whose bread and butter depends largely on their language skills, especially a ludic skill: journalists, writers, and entertainers. The other types are widely used by language-users of all ages and backgrounds beyond the proto-language stage. (For an extensive discussion of verbal play and creativity, see Chiaro 1992.)

6.8   Conclusions

Though hardly the whole truth, words appear to hold the key to talking about the world, to creating new worlds and to influencing our fellows by this means.

Grammar reflects the ratiocinative processes associated with the intellect; while also reflecting similar mental processes in that the content vocabulary of a language symbolizes the typical with the unique particularities of real-life concretissima filtered out, such vocabulary conveys, none the less, various kinds of information of varying degrees of specificity as I have tried to show in the foregoing chapters, as well as in this one. Arguably, vocabulary mirrors the many-sided human personality more obviously than do other language components. The descriptive, representational role of lexis in relation to experiential phenomena is greater and more apparent than that of grammar in the functioning of lexicogrammar. The lexis also carries the greatest informational load in the interpersonal working of language, especially in informal speech where it is possible to use the grammar of utterances in which contracted forms and truncated syntactic units are the most natural, thereby highlighting content vocabulary. Evidence for humans as thinkers appears in its most obvious form in their production of coherent discourse. Such discourse, typically directed at others, ranges from service encounters, small talk and other routines, to the familiar but non-routine, such as the once-explosive *Liberty, Equality, Fraternity* and the lexically more novel *Skater on thin ice of truth* (headline). Both texts illustrate what the vocabulary can do even without drawing on the full resources of the grammar of a language, as well as the interweaving of the familiar and the new, so common in discourse.

In a very real sense the perception of the physical world and the creation of the non-physical one originates in the vocabulary though it does not stop there. Multiword expressions, whether conventional or *ad hoc*, provide an interface between the lexis and the grammar, and while they foreground vocabulary, they also illustrate powerfully the complementarity of the two evident in the term *lexicogrammar*. Lexis and grammar working together enable the use of the habitual and the creation of the new in order to communicate with others in ways that are familiar, but at the same time interesting and newsworthy.

Appendix

The following questionnaire was given to a group of twenty-six tertiary students, all of whom had native or near-native control of English.

Viewpoint through idioms

Below are 15 different idioms, each accompanied by a definition and an illustrative sentence(s). Please read through them. Then on a separate sheet, to be attached to and returned with the questionnaire, state the viewpoint/attitudes/evaluation(s) you think the idiom *in each example* conveys:

Good is *praiseworthy* because:	*Bad* is *unpraiseworthy* because:	*Ambivalent* is a *mixture* of *good–bad*, e.g.
honest	dishonest	X can be exciting and
accurate	inaccurate/ misleading	suspenseful despite being misleading; or
frank/direct	indirect/devious; blunt	bluntness can be good sometimes and bad at
pleasantly suspenseful	dull/unexciting	other times.
genuine	false	
challengingly intriguing	dull/unchallenging	
not quibbling	quibbling	
unhurtful	hurtful	
unpretentious/humble	pretentious/arrogant	
conciliatory/peaceful	aggressive	
tolerant	intolerant	
significant	trivial	
strong/firm	weak	
famous	obscure/unknown	
versatile	Jack of all trades, master of none	
fundamental/basic	marginal/superficial	
not domineering	domineering/bossy	
uncomplaining	complaining/whingeing	
calm/controlled	excitable/uncontrolled	
speaks sensibly	speak foolishly/nonsense	
constructive talk/acts	destructive talk/acts	

You may go outside my lists (above) if necessary, and give your own interpretation or the viewpoint in the idioms below.

Specific questions:

a. Give reasons for your choice of viewpoint in each example, i.e. Do any words in the idiom itself or in the sentence help you identify the viewpoint conveyed by the idiom? If so, list them.

b. Is there anything in the implied situational context, which identifies viewpoint?

c. Is your identified viewpoint a matter of learned convention or personal experience?

Example provided by author: *Skate on thin ice* (go into a situation where there are risks and where, therefore, one has to act carefully).

'If I were you, I shouldn't come in here telling experienced staff their business. You're *skating on thin ice*.'

1 Bad because *skate on thin ice* in this context indicates that the addressee shows poor judgement and is foolish.

2 Textual cues: *telling experienced staff their business.*

3 Partly learned convention: 'as a child I knew I wasn't expected to advise adults and later on I realized that continual inward social assessment of people and situations was necessary to get on in society.'

red herring (a suggestion or piece of information, etc. which draws sb's attention away from the truth or more important part of the situation).

1 *Herrings* supreme: There are enough *red herrings*, plots, twists and anticlimaxes in the first two hours of this drama to keep the keenest mind guessing. (*TV Guide*)

2 It is this simple fact but disruptive implication that English critics of Getzels and Jackson have overlooked. They land claws extended on a technical *red herring*. (From *Creativity*).

3 ... it was Mr Whitlam's campaign strategy that led the party baying after the constitutional *red herring*, instead of concentrating on the real issue on which people finally voted. (*The Australian*).

4   There will be many *red herrings*, personal attacks and low blows by men at the end of their patience. (*The Australian*).

nit picking (petty fault finding; quibbling)

5   He accused the Opposition of *nit picking* and said that despite months of questioning the Opposition had been unable to find anything against the Government. (*The Australian*).

olive branch/twig (peace offering)

6   Packer waves *olive twig* towards ABC.

Mr Kerry Packer's World Services Cricket Organization offered a faint glimmer of hope yesterday of a compromise with establishment cricket. Mr Andrew Caro said, 'The situation is more conducive to conciliation than six months ago. (*The Sydney Morning Herald*)

tear sth to pieces (savage criticism or attack)

7   I don't buy the Herald myself except to mark those macabre occasions when your drama critic *tears* yet *another of my plays* before my astonished eyes. (P. Kenna)

backroom boy (expert engaged in work of a confidential nature)

8   At that time your servant was far too obscure to hobnob with the hero of the hour. His role in the performance was merely that of *backroom boy* ... to draft the panel's judgement of Mr White's book. (Roderrick on White in the *Herald*)

to call a spade a spade (to be direct, straightforward; blunt)

9   This wedding became a fertility rite, a mating with the earth itself, wonderfully poetic at its most lyrical but stark and uncompromising in *calling a spade a spade* and not an implement for digging. (*The Australian*)

calling a spade a spade

10 Wole Soyinka has a rather stunning technique of facing his audience like some young black god and declaring: I feel I'm just ministering to your desire for self-flagellation. (*The Australian*)

(not be able to) *stand sb* (feel extreme dislike) sit on sb

11 Then Henry let her down: for two reasons. He *couldn't stand her mother*. Her mother *couldn't stand him*. And anybody Mrs Bodoin *couldn't stand*, she managed *to sit on*, disastrously ... Vinny didn't really want *to sit on* Henry but when her mother egged her on she couldn't help it. (D. H. Lawrence)

to break the ice (to deformalize a social situation)

12 DB: Those people are hoping they don't have Arthur as chairman.
    YM: Oh I don't, it served *to break the ice*.
    CF: I hope the new chairman has something *to break the ice* with Peter—he's feeling a bit nervous. (From a conversation)

to turn up one's nose at sth (to show contempt for)

13 Some people *turn up their noses* if you say your father is a docker or miner.

14 There's no reason for him to follow Chomsky and *turn up his nose* at both the feast and the crumbs. (Robinson)

to wear x hats (to play x number of roles)

15 Mr Johnson said Mr Hawke was having problems *wearing 3 different hats* ... Mr Hawke *was wearing the hats* of President of ACTU, President of the ALP and yet *another hat*, 'that of getting off the hook'. (*The Australian*)

16 Bob Hawke ... *is wearing the ACTU President's 'hat'* while in the boardroom of his headquarters in Melbourne. Not that he thinks as much of his famous hats as his critics do. While his left-wing brothers are persistently preoccupied with their leader's millinery, Mr Hawke claims to give the matter no thought. *A hat* he says, is something which *his critics talk through*. (*The Australian*)

to cry over spilt milk (to complain over minor mishaps)

17 Well, it's no use *crying over spilt uranium*, said Professor Hippo (O'Connor).

grass roots (basic, bottom; one's origins)

18 Sydney Poitier, while working on the set of his latest film was asked what it felt like to stand on his *grass-roots* again. 'I can't feel them, not through my Gucci shoes', he replied. (*The Australian*)

19 He looked to the *grassroots* for support, to the people of his state and the people of the Labour branches. (*The Australian*)

to fly off the handle (lose one's temper/control)

20 When I came back and read the minutes, *I flew off the handle* ... it's the old thing of we don't want to fight but by jingo if we do, then I'll go in boots and all. (From a conversation)

General questions:

a. Is any piece of language ever negative in terms of attitudes/evaluations, i.e. point of view? If such texts exist, would you impose your own point of view on them?

b. Why, if you do, would you consider point of view important in discourse? Are attitudes and judgements necessary in social interactions? i.e. is your preference for positive or negative interactions?

Glossary

ad hoc
ad hoc pieces of language are 'one-offs' appropriate to the varying language requirements of different participants and situations. They exemplify the working of the open-choice principle.

collocation
Collocation is used in the sense J. R. Firth used it: 'the company words keep'. Put differently, words generally co-occur in groups that conform to grammatical and semantic usage, e.g. *strong/weak/ black/Ceylon, etc. tea* (Adj + N). While the majority of collocations in a language are ad hoc, some are habitual in that they recur. These latter, along with idioms, exemplify the idiom principle. See section 2.1.2, especially Table 2.1.

conjunctive
The term conjunctive as adjective or noun is related to conjunction. In this book, conjunctive denotes expressions such as *as a result, no matter what, in case*, etc. which do not qualify as *par excellence* conjunctions, for example, *and, but, because either ... or*, but which nevertheless connect parts of the same sentence or establish connections between different sentences in the same discourse.

context
Context is used in this book as a general term which can refer to the co-text of an expression or to any situation in which the expression occurs.

context of situation
This term signifies an institutionalized situation characterized by specific participants and settings and either a spoken or written mode or a combination of both. Some examples are: a lecture, dining out at a restaurant, Christmas festivities, etc. These are all institutionalized contexts, more precisely contexts of situation, as opposed to seeing a ghost, a random context.

context-specific language use/discourse
These terms refer to the *ad hoc* use of language elicited by a given situation but not likely to occur again. In other words, such pieces of language are 'one-offs' elicited by a specific contextual variable such as the emotions or attitudes of the language-user.

conventional, conventionalized
These terms are used of expressions that conform to usage and which, therefore, do not attract attention. Such expressions contrast with novel ones, e.g. *a year ago* vs. *a grief ago* or the *cat swallows the canary* vs. the *canary swallows the cat*.

co-text
This term signifies those words and phrases that are semantically and collocationally connected to the expression under consideration and help define its meaning and function. Typically, the co-text of an expression occurs within the same utterance or sentence, but co-text may also occur outside them as in preceding and following utterances or sentences.

discourse
In this book, discourse is used to signify an organized piece of language, spoken or written, functioning at a level above the units of grammar, though composed of these units at the micro-level. An extract from a complete discourse, the macro-level, can also be referred to as a discourse as it comes from the same continuous piece of language.

an exchange
An exchange, for example, a sale-purchase encounter or a discussion, exemplifies an interaction through language between at least two persons with some goal in view. Exchange and interaction are used interchangeably in this book.

experiential gestalts
This term, borrowed from Lakoff and Johnson's *Metaphors We Live By* (1980), signifies 'ways of organizing experiences into structured wholes' (p. 81).

formulaic discourse
This phrase refers to a prescribed expression or expressions such as a spell, marriage vows, or parts of the preamble to a will couched in the unvarying form necessary for such speech acts to be valid. The invariant form of formulaic discourse also makes the phrase synonymous with another, namely *language routines*, both having connotations of predicability.

idiom
This term exemplifies the form of the headword of this item in dictionaries. It is used in this book in two senses:

1 a conventionalized multiword expression, often, but not always, literal. *Idiom* in this sense is very close to the *OED* definition cited at the conclusion to Chapter 2 (section 2.10). See also sections 2.1.2 and 2.1.3.

2 *Idiom* is also used to refer to the structural design of a language, for example, the extent to which deletions are acceptable in locutions, spoken or written, as well as conventionalized, but non-canonical, idiosyncrasies peculiar to a given language. This second sense of *idiom* is the same as that given by the *OED* definition cited in Chapter 1, section 1.3 and 1.3ff. There are, of course, idioms such as *nothing loath* or *for better or worse* to which both of the *OED* definitions apply, as they are expressions which, though idiosyncratic, are conventionalized.

idiomatic
This term signifies conformity with the usage of a language.

ideational idioms
This type of idiom conveys impressionistic representations of aspects of the physical, social, and emotional worlds of a language community. The type is a functional one. See Chapter 3.

interpersonal idioms
This type of idiom occurs in discourse in a pragmatic function: greetings, farewells, warnings, disclaimers, etc. See Chapter 4.

lexical item
In this book, lexical item is used in a relatively loose way as a general term to refer to single words, compounds, and multiword expressions. In the case of the last, only those items which are fixed expressions, that is, idioms, semi-idioms, literal idioms, and restricted collocations qualify as lexical items.

lexicogrammar
This term is borrowed from the terminology of the Hallidayan model of language. In this model, vocabulary is not hived off from grammar, but rather vocabulary and grammar are presented as being interdependent and interrelated. The term lexicogrammar points to the arrangement of vocabulary in accordance with the rules of grammar so as to communicate coherent messages at the micro-level of discourse.

novel
This term, like *ad hoc*, refers to an attribute of pieces of language composed by the language-user on the open-choice principle and is used synonymously with *ad hoc* in many places in this book. In such places, both terms signify novelty only in the sense of an expression not being ready-made as idioms, semi-idioms, and literal idioms are. However, there are instances when the use of the term novel, but not *ad hoc*, signifies an original use of language.

pure idioms, semi-idioms, and literal idioms
These are categories referring to the semantics of idioms. While pure idioms are completely non-literal, semi-idioms are only partly so. See Chapter 2, sections 2.1.2 and 2.1.3, especially Table 2.1.

register
Register is used in the Hallidayan sense: a specific register is created when a choice of forms, lexical, grammatical, and discoursal, dictated by field, or subject matter, tenor, or participant relations and mode, or channel of communication, is made. Legalese is a strong example of a register, journalese a less strong one, not being governed as legalese is by the rigorous language conventions of an institution such as the law.

253

relational
Relational is a general term for an attribute characterizing a diverse number of language forms (conjunctions, adverbial, and prepositional phrases, etc.) all of which have a cohesive function in a discourse. See Chapter 5.

restricted collocation
This term refers to a group of words which co-occur with each other only in limited ways, e.g. *shrug one's shoulders, addled eggs/brains*.

text
In this book, text is used interchangeably with discourse as they both share the definitive feature of coherent organization. Text is the preferred term for short pieces of language, extracts from a larger whole.

transformation
This term denotes those operations (permutation, deletion, addition, substitution, etc.) which change the form of a syntactic unit like a sentence.

truth value
In this book, truth value signifies that something is true for the speaker, regardless of whether it has been proven or not.

utterance
Utterance is a speech unit identified by intonation, not by grammar and punctuation, as the written sentence is. An utterance can be incomplete in terms of sentence grammar. Incomplete written sentences, such as headlines, have a different structure from that of utterances. Headlines are not speech forms.

Bibliography

Alexander, R. J. 1984. 'Fixed expressions in English: reference books and the teacher'. *English Language Teaching Journal* 38/2: 127–34.

Appadurai, A. 1990. 'Topographies of the self: praise and emotion in Hindu India' in Abu-Lughod, L. and Lutz, C. A. (eds.) *Language and the Politics of Emotion*, 92–112. Cambridge: Cambridge University Press.

Bird, G. H. 1969. *A Student's Guide to Intellectual Methods*. Edinburgh: Edinburgh University Press.

Bolinger, D. 1976. 'Meaning and memory'. *Forum Linguisticum* 1/1: 1–14.

Brown, R. 1968. 'How shall a thing be called?' in Oldfield, R. C. and Marshall, J. C. (eds.) 1968, *Language*, 82–91. Harmondsworth: Penguin.

Bull, W. E. 1968. *Time, Tense and the English Verb*. Berkeley, L.A.: University of California Press.

Burchfield R. W. (ed.) 1989. *Oxford English Dictionary*. Oxford: Clarendon Press.

Carpenter, H. 1989. *Geniuses Together*. London: Unwin Hyman Ltd.

Carter, R. A. 1987. *Vocabulary: Applied Linguistic Perspectives*. London: Routledge.

Carter, R. A. 1993. 'Language awareness and language teachers' in Hoey, M. (ed.) *Data, Discourse and Description: Essays in Honour of Professor John Sinclair*. London: Collins.

Carter, R. A. and M. J. McCarthy. (eds.) 1988. *Vocabulary and Language Teaching*. London: Longman.

Carter, R. A. and M. J. McCarthy. 1995. 'Discourse and creativity: bridging the gap between language and literature' in Cook, G. and Seidlhofer, B. (eds.) *Principle and Practice in Applied Linguistics: Studies in Honour of H. G. Widdowson*, 303–23. Oxford: Oxford University Press.

Channell, J. 1994. *Vague Language*. Oxford: Oxford University Press.

Chiaro, D. 1992. *The Language of Jokes: Analysing Verbal Play*. London: Routledge.

Chomsky, N. 1965. *Aspects of the Theory of Syntax*. Cambridge, Mass.: MIT Press.

Clark, M. 1981. 'Introduction' in *The Macquarie Dictionary*, p.1. Sydney: The Macquarie Library Pty Ltd.

Collier, G. 1985. *Emotional Expression*. Hillsdale, N.J.:/London: Lawrence Erlbaum.

Cook, G. 1992. *The Discourse of Advertising*. London: Routledge.

Coulmas, F. 1979. 'On the sociolinguistic relevance of routine formulae'. *Journal of Pragmatics* 3: 238–66.

Cowie, A. P. 1981. 'The treatment of collocations and idioms in learner dictionaries'. *Applied Linguistics* 2/3: 223–35.

Cowie, A. P. 1988. 'Stable and creative aspects of vocabulary use' in Carter, R. A. and McCarthy, M. (eds.) 1988. *Vocabulary and Language Teaching*, 127–39. London: Longman.

Cowie, A. P. and R. Mackin. (eds.) 1975. *Oxford Dictionary of Current Idiomatic English*, Vol. 1. London: Oxford University Press.

Cowie, A. P., R. Mackin, and I. R. McCaig (eds.) 1983. *Oxford Dictionary of Current Idiomatic English*, Vol. 2. Oxford: Oxford University Press.

255

Cranny-Francis, A. 1992. *Engendered Fictions*. Sydney: University of New South Wales Press.

Crismore, A. and R. Farnsworth. 1990. 'Metadiscourse in popular and professional science discourse' in Nash, W. (ed.) *The Writing Scholar*, 118–36. New York: Sage Publications.

Crombie, W. 1985. *Process and Relation in Discourse and Language Learning*. Oxford: Oxford University Press.

Cruse, D. A. 1977. 'The pragmatics of lexical specificity'. *Journal of Linguistics* 13: 153–64.

Curry, W. C. 1960. *Chaucer and the Medieval Sciences*. New York: Barnes and Noble.

Davitz, J. 1969. *The Language of Emotion*. New York: Academic Press.

Delbridge, A. et al. (eds.) 1981. *The Macquarie Dictionary*. Sydney: The Macquarie Pty Ltd.

Downes, W. 1984. *Language and Society*. London: Fontana.

Downing, P. 1980. 'Factors influencing lexical choice in narrative' in Chafe, W. (ed.) *The Pear Stories: Cognitive, Cultural and Linguistic Aspects of Narrative Production*, 89–126. Norwood, N.J.: Ablex.

Fernando, C. 1981. *The Nature and Function of Idiom with Special Reference to English*. PhD. thesis, Macquarie University.

Fernando, C. 1985. 'Australian idiom' in Clark, J. (ed.) *The Cultivated Australian: Festschrift in Honour of Arthur Delbridge*, 349–59. Hamburg: Verlag.

Fernando, C. 1989. 'The emotions and their linguistic expression: joy and grief' in Mannell, R. H. (ed.). *Working Papers of the Speech, Hearing, and Language Research Centre*. Sydney: Macquarie University

Fernando, C. and R. Flavell. 1981. *On Idiom*. (Exeter Linguistic Studies, 5). Exeter: University of Exeter.

Fillmore, C. J., P. Kay, and K. C. O'Connor. 1988. 'Regularity and idiomaticity in grammatical constructions: the case of let alone'. *Language* 64/3: 501–38.

Firth, J. R. 1957. 'Modes of meaning' in *Papers in Linguistics* 1934–1951. London: Oxford University Press.

Fishman, J. A. 1968. 'The relationship between micro- and macro-sociolinguistics in the study of who speaks what language to whom and when' in Dil, A. S. (ed.) 1972, *Language in Sociocultural Change: Essays by Joshua A. Fishman*, 244–67. California: Stanford University Press.

Fogelin, R. J. 1978. *Understanding Arguments: An Introduction to Informal Logic*. New York: Harcourt Brace and Jovanovich.

Fraser, B. 1970. 'Idioms within a transformational grammar'. *Foundations of Language* 6: 22–42.

Fridja, N. H. 1986. *The Emotions*. Cambridge/Paris: Cambridge University Press/Maison des Sciences de l'Homme.

Garmonsway, G. N. and J. Simpson. (eds.) 1979. *The Penguin English Dictionary*. Harmondsworth: Penguin.

Garnham, A. 1985. *Psycholinguistics: Central Topics*. London/New York: Methuen.

Gibbs, R. W.Jr. 1980. 'Spilling the beans on understanding and memory for idioms in conversation'. *Memory and Cognition* 8/2: 149–56.

Gibbs, R. W. Jr., and G. P. Gonzales. 1985. 'Syntactic frozenness in processing and remembering idioms'. *Cognition* 20: 243–59.

Gilbert, G. N. and M. Mulkay. 1984. *Opening Pandora's Box: a sociological analysis of scientists' discourse.* Cambridge: Cambridge University Press.

Gove, P. B. *et al.* (eds.) 1975 *Webster's Third New International Dictionary.* Massachusetts: Merriman Company.

Grice, H. P. 1975. 'Logic and conversation' in Cole, P. and Morgan, J. L. (eds.) *Syntax and Semantics*, Vol. 3, 41–58. New York: Academic Press.

Gunn, J. S. 1989. 'The shearing shed society' in Collins, P. C. and Blair, D. (eds.) *Australian English: The Language of a New Society*, 78–88. St. Lucia: University of Queensland Press.

Halliday, M. A. K. 1961. 'Categories of the Theory of Grammar'. *Word* 17/3: 241–92.

Halliday, M. A. K. 1966. 'Lexis as a linguistic level' in Bazell, C. E. *et al.* (eds.) In *Memory of J. R. Firth*, 148–62. London: Longman.

Halliday, M. A. K. 1973. *Explorations in the Functions of Language.* London: Edward Arnold.

Halliday, M. A. K. 1978. *Language as a Social Semiotic.* London: Edward Arnold.

Halliday, M. A. K. 1985. *An Introduction to Functional Grammar.* London: Edward Arnold.

Halliday, M. A. K. and R. Hasan. 1976. *Cohesion in English.* London: Longman.

Halliday M. A. K. and R. Hasan. 1985. *Language, Context and Text: a social-semiotic perspective.* Geelong: Deakin University Press.

Hawking, S. 1988. *A Brief History of Time.* New York: Bantam.

Healey, A. 1968. 'English idioms'. *Kivung* (Journal of the Linguistic Society of the University of Papua New Guinea) 1/2: 71–108.

Hintikka, K. J. J. 1973. *Logic, Language Games and Information.* Oxford: Clarendon Press.

Hite, S. 1987. *Women and Love: A Cultural Revolution in Progress.* New York: Alfred A. Knopf.

Hockett, C. F. 1958. *A Course in Modern Linguistics.* New York: The Macmillan Company.

Hoey, M. 1991. *Patterns of Lexis in Text.* Oxford: Oxford University Press.

Huddleston, R. 1984. *Introduction to the Grammar of English.* Cambridge: Cambridge University Press.

Hymes, D. 1971. 'On communicative competence' in Pride, J. B. and Holmes, J. (eds.) 1972, *Sociolinguistics*, 269–93. Harmondsworth: Penguin.

James, C. and P. Garrett. (eds.) 1991. *Language Awareness and the Classroom.* Harlow: Longman.

Jespersen, O. 1975. *The Philosophy of Grammar.* London: Allen and Unwin.

Joos, M. 1964. *The English Verb: Form and Meanings.* Madison: University of Wisconsin Press.

Kachru, B.B. 1986. *The Alchemy of English: The spread, functions and models of non-native Englishes.* Oxford/New York: Pergamon.

Kandiah, T. 1985. 'Disinherited Englishes: the case of Lankan English, Part 2'. *Navasilu* (Journal of the English Association of Sri Lanka) 4: 92–113.

Katz, J. J. 1964. 'Semantic theory and the meaning of good'. *Journal of Philosophy* LXI/23: 736–66.

Katz, J. J. and P. Postal. 1963. 'The semantic interpretation of idioms and sentences containing them' in *MIT Research Laboratory of Electronics Quarterly Progress Report.* 70: 275–82.

Keller, E. 1979. 'Gambits: conversational strategy signals'. *Journal of Pragmatics* 3, 3/4: 219–38.

Lakoff, G. and M. Johnson. 1980. *Metaphors We Live By.* Chicago: University of Chicago Press.

Law, M. H. 1964. *How To Read German.* London: Hutchinson Educational Ltd.

Leech, G. N. 1983. *Principles of Pragmatics.* London/New York: Longman.

LeVine, R. A. 1984. 'Properties of culture: an ethnographic view' in Schweder, R. and LeVine, R. A. (eds.) *Culture Theory: Essays on Mind, Self and Emotion,* 67–87. Cambridge: Cambridge University Press.

Long, T. H. *et al.* (eds.) 1979. *Longman Dictionary of English Idioms.* London: Longman.

Low, G. 1988. 'On teaching metaphor' in *Applied Linguistics* 9/2: 125–47.

McCarthy, M. J. 1990. *Vocabulary.* Oxford: Oxford University Press.

McCarthy, M. J. and R. A. Carter. 1994. *Language as Discourse: Perspectives for Language Teaching.* Harlow: Longman.

MacDougal, B. G. and K. de Abrew. 1979. *Sinhala,* Module 3. New York: Foreign Service Institute.

McIntosh, A. 1966. 'Patterns and ranges' in McIntosh, A. *et al.* (eds.) *Patterns of Language: Papers in General, Descriptive and Applied Linguistics,* 182–99. London: Longman.

Mackin, R. 1978. 'On collocations: "words shall be known by the company they keep"' in P. Strevens (ed.) *In Memory of A. S. Hornby.* Oxford: Oxford University Press.

McLay, V. 1987. *Idioms at Work.* Sussex: Language Teaching Publications.

McMordie, W. (revised by Goffin, R.) 1972. *English Idioms.* London: Oxford University Press.

Makkai, A. 1972. *Idiom Structure in English.* The Hague: Mouton.

Malkiel, Y. 1959. 'Studies in irreversible binomials'. *Lingua* 8: 113–60.

Martin, J. R. 1985. *Factual Writing.* Deakin: Deakin University Press.

Mitchell, T. F. 1975. 'Linguistic "goings-on": collocations and other lexical matters arising on the syntagmatic record' in Mitchell, T. F. (ed.) *Principles of Firthian Linguistics,* 99–136. London: Longman.

Moon, R. 1986. 'Time and idioms' in Snell-Hornby, M. (ed.) *Zurilex '86 Proceedings: Papers Read at the Euralex International Congress,* 107–15. Franke: Verlag.

Moon, R. 1990. ' "There is reason in the roasting of eggs": a consideration of fixed expressions in native-speaker dictionaries' in Tommola, H. *et al.* (eds.) *Euralex '92 Proceedings,* 493–502. Department of Translations: University of Tampere.

Nattinger, J. R. and J. S. DeCarrico. 1992. *Lexical Phrases and Language Teaching.* Oxford: Oxford University Press.

Nesi, H. 1995. 'A modern bestiary: a contrastive study of the figurative meanings of animal terms' in *ELT Journal* 49/3: 272–78.

Orwell, G. 1946. '*Politics and the English language*' in G. Orwell. 1968. *Collected Essays*. London: Secker and Warburg.

Partridge, E. 1935. *Slang Today and Yesterday*. London: Routledge and Kegan Paul.
Pawley, A. 1986. 'Lexicalization' in Tannen, D. and Alatis, J. E. (eds.) *Languages and Linguistics: The Interdependence of Theory, Data and Application. Georgetown University Round Table on Languages and Linguistics 1985*, 98–120. Washington D.C.: Georgetown University Press.
Pawley, A. and F. H. Syder. 1983. 'Two puzzles for linguistic theory: nativelike selection and nativelike fluency' in Richards, J. C. and Schmidt, R. W. (eds.) *Language and Communication*, 191–227. London/New York: Longman.
Peaty, D. 1983. *Working With English Idioms*. Walton-on-Thames: Thomas Nelson and Sons Ltd.

Ramson, W. S. 1988. *The Australian National Dictionary*. Oxford/Melbourne: Oxford University Press.
Rapoport, A. 1960. *Fights, Games and Debates*. Ann Arbor: Michigan University Press.
Redfern, W. 1989. *Clichés and Coinages*. Oxford: Blackwell.
Roberts, M. H. 1944. *The Science of Idiom: A Method of Inquiry into the Cognitive Design of Language*. Publication of the Modern Language Association of America 69: 291–306.

Sapir, E. 1921. *Language*. New York: Harcourt Brace and Jovanovich.
Scherer, K. R. 1988. 'Cognitive dimensions of emotional appraisal' in Scherer, K. R. (ed.) *Facets of Emotion*, 57–79. Hillsdale, N.J.:/London: Lawrence Erlbaum.
Searle, J. 1975. 'Indirect Speech Acts' in Cole, P. and Morgan J. L. (eds.) *Syntax and Semantics*, Vol. 3. New York: Academic Press.
Simpson, L. and C. Lumby. 1989. 'Feral, desperate, deluded' in *The Sydney Morning Herald*, 25 February, p.81.
Sinclair, J. M. 1966. 'Beginning the study of lexis' in Bazell, C. *et al.* (eds.) *In Memory of J. R. Firth*, 410–30. London: Longman.
Sinclair, J. M. 1987. 'Collocation: a progress report' in Steele, R. and Threadgold, T. (eds.) *Language Topics: an international collection of papers by colleagues, students and admirers of Professor Michael Halliday to honour him on his retirement*, Vol. 2, 319–31. Amsterdam: John Benjamins.
Sinclair, J. M. 1991. *Corpus, Concordance, Collocation*. Oxford: Oxford University Press.
Smith, L. P. 1925. *Words and Idioms*. London: Constable.
Solomon, R. C. 1984. 'Getting angry: the Jamesian theory of emotion in anthropology' in Schweder, R. and LeVine, R. A. (eds.) *Culture Theory: Essays on Mind, Self and Emotion*, 238–54. Cambridge: Cambridge University Press.
Strässler, J. 1982. *Idioms in English: A Pragmatic Analysis*. Tubingen: Verlag.
Stubbs, M. 1983. *Discourse Analysis: A Sociolinguistic Analysis of Natural Language*. Oxford: Blackwell.

Tannen, D. 1989. *Talking Voices: Repetition, dialogue and imagery in conversational discourse*. Cambridge/New York: Cambridge University Press.
Thackeray, W. M. 1969. *The Rose and the Ring*. London: Edward Arnold.

Thapar, R. 1979. *A History of India*. Harmondsworth: Penguin.
Twain, M. 1912. 'The Awful German Language', Appendix D, in Twain, M. *A Tramp Abroad*, 353–71. London: Everett.

van der Helder, E. and L. McGlashan. 1970. *Modern German*, Vols. 4 and 5. Sydney: McGraw-Hill.

Weinreich, U. 1969. 'Problems in the analysis of idioms' in Puhvel, J. (ed.) The *Substance and Structure of Language*, 23–81. Berkeley: University of California Press.
Wells, H. G. 1987. *A Short History of the World*. London: Pelican.
Whitrow, G. J. 1972. *What is Time?* London: Thames and Hudson.
Windisch, U. 1990. *Speech and Reasoning in Everyday Life*. Cambridge/Paris: Cambridge University Press/Maison des Sciences de l'Homme.
Wittgenstein, L. 1953. *Philosophical Investigations*. Oxford: Blackwell.
Witton, N. D. 1979. 'The classification of English phrasal and prepositional verbs' in Clark, J. (ed.) *Working Papers of the Speech, Hearing and Language Centre*, 1–38. Sydney: Macquarie University.
Wolfson, N. 1981. 'Invitations, compliments and the competence of native speakers.' *The International Journal of Psycholinguistics* 24/4: 7–22.
Wood, F. T. 1966. *English Verbal Idioms*. London: Macmillan.
Wood, F. T. 1969a. *English Prepositional Idioms*. London: Macmillan.
Wood, F. T. 1969b. *English Colloquial Idioms*. London: Macmillan.

Yorio, C. A. 1980. 'Conventionalized language forms and the development of communicative competence'. *TESOL Quarterly* 14/4: 433–42.

Zipf, G. K. 1972. *Human Behaviour and the Principle of Least Effort*. New York: Hafner.

Index

The index refers to Chapters 1 to 6, the appendix and the glossary. Entries are in letter-by-letter alphabetical order, which ignores spaces and hyphens between words; 'semantics' therefore comes before 'semantic unity'. Terms in italic refer to usage of individual words or phrases. Glossary references are indicated by 'g' after the page number. Where more than one location reference is listed against a heading, bold type indicates any principal reference(s).